The Connecting Leader

Serving Concurrently as a Leader and a Follower

A Volume in Leadership Horizons

Series Editors:
Michelle C. Bligh, *University of Sussex Business School*
Melissa K. Carsten, *Claremont Graduate University*

Leadership Horizons

Michelle C. Bligh and Melissa K. Carsten, Series Editors

The Connecting Leader:
Serving Concurrently as a Leader and a Follower (2020)
Zahira Jaser

Advancing Relational Leadership Research:
A Dialogue Among Perspectives (2012)
Mary Uhl-Bien and Sonia M. Ospina

Follower-Centered Perspectives on Leadership:
A Tribute to the Memory of James R. Meindl (2009)
Raj Pillai, Michelle C. Bligh, and Mary Uhl-Bien

Complexity Leadership: Part 1: Conceptual Foundations (2007)
Mary Uhl-Bien and Russ Marion

Implicit Leadership Theories: Essays and Explorations (2005)
Birgit Schyns and James R. Meindl

Teaching Leadership: Innovative Approaches for the 21st Century (2003)
Raj Pillai and Susan Stites-Doe

Grounding Leadership Theory and Research:
Issues, Perspectives, and Methods (2002)
Ken Parry and James R. Meindl

The Connecting Leader

Serving Concurrently as a Leader and a Follower

Edited by

Zahira Jaser
University of Sussex Business School

IAP
Information Age Publishing, Inc.
Charlotte, North Carolina • www.infoagepub.com

Library of Congress Cataloging-in-Publication Data

CIP data for this book can be found on the Library of Congress website:
http://www.loc.gov/index.html

Paperback: 978-1-64802-204-3
Hardcover: 978-1-64802-205-0
E-Book: 978-1-64802-206-7

Printed and bound by CPI Group (UK) Ltd, Croydon, CR0 4YY

CONTENTS

Foreword
Mary Uhl-Bien and Sonia M. Ospina ... vii

1. Introduction: The Connecting Leader
Zahira Jaser ... 1

PART 1: INTERCONNECTED LEADER-FOLLOWER IDENTITIES

2. From a Leader and a Follower to Shared Leadership: An Identity-Based Structural Model for Shared Leadership Emergence
Elisa Adriasola and Robert G. Lord ... 31

3. Bridging Gaps in Organizations: Leaders as Entrepreneurs of Identity
Martin P. Fladerer, Niklas K. Steffens, and S. Alexander Haslam ... 67

PART 2: JANUSIAN TENSIONS

4. Paradox, Leadership, and the Connecting Leader
Camille Pradies, Marieke Delanghe, and Marianne W. Lewis ... 99

5. Meddling in the Middle: The Middle Manager Yo-Yo on a Constant Move
Mats Alvesson and Susann Gjerde ... 131

PART 3: THE CONNECTING LEADER IN PRACTICE

6. From Connecting Leaders to Connecting Leadership: A Study of Interaction
Christian Dyrlund Wåhlin-Jacobsen and Magnus Larsson ... 155

7. The Connecting Leader and Managerial Stances at Work: A Practice Perspective
Roddy Walker ... 191

PART 4: LEADER AND FOLLOWER AS ONE

8. Leadership and Followership as One: Connecting Leaders in the Military
   Melanie A. Robinson, Nicole Bérubé, and Ann Langley 221

9. Everyday Leadership and Engaged Followership: Two Sides of the Same Construct
   Ronald E. Riggio, Zhengguang Liu, Rebecca J. Reichard, and Dayna O. H. Walker 245

FOREWORD

Mary Uhl-Bien and Sonia M. Ospina

Mary Uhl-Bien

The Connecting Leader is an ambitious and timely book. It provides both theoretical and empirical contributions from top scholars in our field. The chapters present a range of perspectives that cross ontologies and epistemologies, providing for good "paradigm interplay" as described by Sonia Ospina and myself in our *Advancing Relational Leadership Research: A Dialogue Among Perspectives* (Uhl-Bien & Ospina, 2012), also published in this *Leadership Horizons* series. As a next iteration in this series, *The Connecting Leader* continues the work begun long ago by Jim Meindl, who originated this series, by offering a framework that pushes at the forefront our horizons in leadership.

It is an exciting time to be a leadership scholar. The days of a few theories/measures dominating the field are giving way to an openness to new approaches that start with interesting research questions. *The Connecting Leader* is one of these approaches. It asks the question, what if we thought of leadership not as a leader always leading downward, but as a role that goes both up and down? In these roles, individuals must simultaneously shift between reporting up to a boss and being a boss themselves to those who report to them. How does that change the way we think about leadership and followership?

These questions get at the heart of what most leaders in organizations experience—being a manager in the middle. These challenges have long been known in the management field. *Harvard Business Review* wrote

The Connecting Leader: Serving Concurrently as a Leader and a Follower
pp. vii–xii

about them at length in the 1970s and 1980s, and most of us who teach leadership have long addressed them in our classroom. Like many other aspects of leadership, however, there is a huge gap between what we teach in our classrooms and what we investigate in our research. It's time we close that gap.

The Connecting Leader helps us to do this by laying out a platform for research that marries leadership and followership as something that cannot be separated and must be studied together. It offers a particular context for advancing the notions of *leading* and *following* introduced by followership theory (Uhl-Bien et al., 2014) into the connecting leader role: connecting leaders are those who switch between leading and following on a regular basis. In taking this stance it reinforces a truism that has long been overshadowed by predominant leader-centric thinking—that leadership and followership are two halves of a whole. One does not exist without the other.

The approach described in this book goes even further by suggesting that those who are the most effective followers are the most effective leaders. This is because the characteristics that constitute effective followership are also those that make for good leadership: consideration, collaboration and competence. Ask any leader or follower what makes for good leadership and they will tell you: the most effective leadership is that in which leaders and followers partner together—through mutually reinforcing role behaviors—to get things done. Connecting leaders recognize this by seamlessly transitioning between leading and following to most effectively construct their own leader and follower roles.

Like many relational approaches, the connecting leader concept creates challenges in terms of language. This is recognized in Robinson, Bérubé and Langley's chapter, who question "leader" and "follower" as analytical labels for more pluralistic approaches to leadership like connecting leaders. While some call for movement away from leadership language (leaders, followers), I disagree. I think the terms exactly describe what is going on and fully constitute the leadership construct—*as long as you understand what the words signify and how they are being used*. The words leader and follower denote a position (e.g., manager), role, or identity, and the words leading and following represent a type of behavior (Uhl-Bien & Carsten, 2018). The two are not parallel, meaning that just because you are a leader it does not mean you are always leading, and vice versa for followers. This raises yet another truism still largely unacknowledged by leadership scholars: leaders do not always lead, and followers do not always follow. The most effective leadership/followership occurs when individuals know how to seamlessly interchange leading and following behaviors in ways that best support their relational partner (either a leader or a follower).

The connecting leader perspective brings this to the fore by acknowledging that individuals do interchange these behaviors regularly, on a daily basis, as they enact manager/subordinate roles. I suggest that connecting leader research takes this one step further to fully embed the notion of leading and following "switching" not only between roles, but also within roles. To most accurately reflect how leadership gets done in organizations, we need to view connecting leaders as occupying a multitude of relationships in which they coconstruct leadership and followership by engaging in leading and following "switching" behaviors within each of their leader and follower roles.

Sonia M. Ospina

It is gratifying to write this foreword for *The Connecting Leader,* a fitting successor in the *Leadership Horizons* series of our coedited book *Advancing Relational Leadership Research: A Dialogue Among Perspectives* (Uhl-Bien & Ospina, 2012). The volume not only deepens our understanding of relational leadership theory, it also encourages productive cross-pollination among diverse perspectives, this time around the leader-follower relationship.

The ideas are introduced through the figure of the connecting leader, defined by the book editor as someone "who embodies concurrently the roles, identities and positions of *both* leader and follower," thus coenacting these within a single individual. In the book introduction Jaser sets the tone for dialogue by anchoring her arguments about coenactment on both entity and constructionist leadership insights and drawing from leadership and management empirical research. The chapter contributions reveal the promise of deconstructing the traditional ways in which the notions of *role, identity* and *the leader-follower relationship* have been conceptually associated.

I must confess I was ambivalent about the connecting leader figure. The label seemed to invoke the individual leader at a time when leader-centered perspectives are being challenged. I probed deeper by placing the proposed ideas in relation to some of the generative tensions of today's leadership studies conversation. Would the underlying assumptions align with an entity leadership perspective or would they reflect a "turn" toward the collective? If the label suggested the former, ideas like role coenactment and the emphasis on identity suggested the latter.

A recent map of the collective leadership landscape (Ospina et al. 2020) was helpful to go deeper. Book contributions resonated with fundamental ideas of collective leadership scholarship, viewed as a broad theoretical umbrella; yet differentiated collective leadership perspectives were also apparent.

Whether the authors viewed leadership as residing in the group or in the system, they all ascertained the fluidity, interconnectedness and simultaneous enactment of leader and follower roles (and thus identities), and questioned their ontological status as separate phenomena that distinguish leader from follower. Problematizing the traditional leader-follower relation, these ideas challenge the ingrained assumption of the dyad as the core building block of leadership. This, in turn, highlights the promise of shifting attention to triads (collectives) for understanding the microdynamics of relational leadership, just as Jaser proposes.

This common collective ground, however, hides fundamental differences among book contributors. Some seemed better aligned with scholars who interpret "collectivity" as a "type" of leadership in the world (distinguishing unitary from plural forms); others appeared to define "collectivity" as a "lens" to study any type of leadership. The former drew from theories like "dual leadership" and "shared leadership" to study roles and identities coenacting in contexts demanding plural leadership types; the latter used broader theoretical lenses—symbolic interactionism, social constructionism, critical theory—that problematize the very nature of fixed leadership of fixed leadership roles (Ospina et al., 2020). I saw great potential for fruitful interplay among these perspectives.

I was still left with some unanswered concerns. For example, is the connecting leader simply a particular enactment of leadership in unique (e.g. middle management) or plural contexts (e.g., self-directed teams, goal directed networks)? Or are *all* leaders connecting leaders? I also continue to wonder whether the connecting leader figure fosters a narrow view that traces the source of leadership exclusively to individuals. These, I suggest, become important queries for future conversations.

Be that as it may, the book opens exciting paths to explore the collective dimensions of leadership. For example, the idea of identity coenactment spoke to my research team's constructionist study about the process of leadership identity construction in the case of Indigenous women leaders. Our field observations did not fit the sequential nature of the claiming and granting processes proposed in leadership identity construction relational leadership models. Our analysis gained traction and nuance when we relaxed the idea of separate leader and follower roles, which seemed consistent with our use of intersectionality as a power lens to understand the leader's lived experience of leadership identity construction. We stopped asking *who* claims, grants, and is granted *what* and *when*?; and started exploring instead *how* Indigenous women leaders navigate the situated spheres of action where leadership identity construction unravels within multiple and often contradictory claims and grants embedded in variegated power relations.

In sum, this volume explores various ways of thinking about the leader-follower relationship that expand our horizons. I find especially stirring the idea of role and identity coenactment (and its implications for those engaged in leadership). As often happens with a brilliant idea, once it is successfully enunciated, we have a sense that we knew this, and can now articulate it in a coherent whole–in this case, to sharpen our view of leadership.

REFERENCES

Ospina, S. M., Foldy, E. G., Fairhurst, G. T., & Jackson, B. (2020) Collective dimensions of leadership: Connecting theory and method. *Human Relations*. http://doi.org/10.1177/0018726719899714

Uhl-Bien, M., & Ospina, S. M. (Eds.). (2012). *Advancing relational leadership research: A dialogue among perspectives*. Information Age.

Uhl-Bien, M., & Carsten, M. (2018). Reversing the lens in leadership: Positioning followership in the leadership construct. In Y. Berson, I. Katz, G. Eilam-Shamir, & R. Kark (Eds.), *Leadership now: Reflections on the legacy of Boas Shamir* (pp. 195–222). Emerald.

Uhl-Bien, M., Riggio, R., Lowe, K., & Carsten, M. (2014). Followership theory: A review and research agenda. *The Leadership Quarterly, 25*(1), 83–104.

CHAPTER 1

INTRODUCTION

The Connecting Leader

Zahira Jaser
University of Sussex Business School

ABSTRACT

This introductory chapter presents the emergent concept of a connecting leader, who coenacts both roles, behaviors, and identities of a leader and a follower. This concept is at best under theorized by the literature, which mostly presents the roles as enacted by separate individuals facing each other. To advance our understanding of connecting leaders we might consider to shift our focus on leadership in 3 ways: unpack the leader and follower role interconnectedness and interplay of identities; investigate the tensions arising from the coenactment and how these can be overcome; widen the way in which we study leadership, through new configurations (e.g., leadership triads), ontologies, and by considering the similarities between leading and following. The book chapters, summarized in this section, are organized to mirror these areas of exploration. Understanding leadership from a perspective that acknowledges that many individuals in organizations are not just leaders or followers, but both, democratizes the way we theorize leadership, and moves us further away from the temptation to romanticize it.

The Connecting Leader: Serving Concurrently as a Leader and a Follower
pp. 1–28

> In the deepest sense, distinction between leaders and followers is meaningless. In every moment of life, we are simultaneously leading and following. There is never a time when our knowledge, judgment, and wisdom are not more useful and applicable than that of another.... We must examine the concept of leading and following with new eyes. We must examine the concept of superior and subordinate with increasing skepticism.
>
> —Dee Hock, founder and chief executive officer of Visa (1999, pp. 72–73)

Numerous scholars have brought to our attention that leaders and followers play an equally important role in the achievement of leadership outcomes (Lord et al., 1999; Shamir et al., 2007; Uhl-Bien et al., 2014), and that leadership and followership are fluid in nature (Uhl-Bien, 2006; Uhl-Bien & Ospina, 2012) hence, an individual commonly practices leadership in one situation and followership in another (DeRue & Ashford, 2010). While traditional theories focus on the interactions between these two roles as represented by two separate individuals in reciprocal relational exchanges, this book stretches the notion of leadership a step further. It does so by exploring how these two roles are coenacted by one individual—the connecting leader—who embodies concurrently the roles, identities, and positions, of *both* leader *and* follower. It seeks to extend the way we think about leadership in recognition of the fact that most individuals in organizations are never only just a "leader" or just a "follower," but are both (Collinson, 2020, DeRue & Ashford, 2010; Jaser, 2017; Uhl-Bien & Ospina, 2012). As such, they sway between the two roles to respond to relational demands and adapt to the direction of influence in the organization (Anicich & Hirsh, 2017; DeRue, 2011; Fairhurst, 2016; Fairhurst & Uhl-Bien, 2012). We know very little about this role coenactment, intended as the "confluence of behavior, cognition and affect" developed in the two roles (Ashforth et al., 2008, p. 344). Thus, the study of the connecting leader is important both for theoretical and practical reasons.

Theoretically, the connecting leader concept responds to calls to study leadership as it evolves and develops in social contexts (Denis et al., 2010), and seeks to democratize the construct of leadership, "stripping" it of some status and prestige, in the hope to discover ways in which individuals can be effective leaders *and* followers, no matter where they sit in the hierarchy (Ashford & Sitkin, 2019, p. 456; Weick, 2007). Adopting a social constructionist approach, the notion of connecting leader rests on the definition of leadership as a process of interpersonal influence (Howell & Shamir, 2005; Meindl, 1995; Lord et al., 1999; Uhl-Bien, 2006), whereby leaders motivate others to action (Ashford & Sitkin, 2019) and followers qualify and define that influence, and in so doing, jointly coconstruct leadership (Meindl et al., 1985). This definition assumes that leader and follower *both* carry the responsibility for leadership outcomes (Meindl, 1995). In turn, connecting leaders carry the responsibility of *both* roles, in bridging and linking individuals, and concurrently coconstructing relationships with both their own followers and their own leaders (DeRue & Ashford, 2010). As such, connecting leaders are key for the process of leadership to unfold (Fairhurst, 2016) by enacting the two roles in everyday balancing of relationships (Uhl-Bien, 2006) through a web of activities, practices, actions that take place in daily working lives. In short, the connecting leader approach focuses on individuals practicing leadership and followership in context, rather than qualifying them for their behaviors, traits, or attitudes of leader or follower.

Conceptualizing leadership in this way offers cues for the development of more modern theory of leadership which, on the footsteps of previous scholarship (Ashford & Sitkin, 2019; DeRue & Ashford, 2010; Lipman-Blumen, 2000; Meindl,1995), distances itself from accounts of leaders as power houses (Sturm & Antonakis, 2015), or "good guys" (servant leadership, Van Dierendonk, 2011; authentic leadership, Avolio & Gardner, 2005; transformational leadership, Bass et al., 1996). By considering the two roles of leader and follower as enacted by one person, the lens of connecting leader adds followers' preoccupations to a leader's agenda. It illuminates the vulnerability, doubts, and fragility stemming from the careful balancing of the demands of the two roles. In doing so, it provides a ground to develop theory about the interconnectedness of the two roles, and the tensions faced in the coenactment process. As elegantly said by Karl Weick, in a previous book of this series:

> To treat leading and following as simultaneous is to distribute knowing and doubting more widely, to expect ignorance and fallibility to be similarly distributed, and to expect that knowledge is what happens between heads rather than inside a single leader's head. (Weick, 2007, p. 281).

This chapter develops insights about theoretical perspectives both at the individual and relational level. At the *individual level* it explores the interpersonal process of alternating roles. This theoretical lens raises new and interesting questions such as, how does a connecting leader juggle the identity of leader and follower? What are the psychocognitive processes through which a connecting leader sways between roles? How does the enactment of one role influence the enactment of the other? What are the contextual characteristics that affect individuals' effective coenactment of the roles? In addition, at *relational level*, it explores the intrapersonal process of relationship construction with different leadership partners concurrently, and the tensions that might arise from this juggling act, resulting in questions like: How does a connecting leader build leadership and followership with different partners, who might have different needs, beliefs, and demands on the leadership outcomes? How does one create plausibility of meanings with their own leaders and followers, who might have different interpretations of the same phenomena? And what are the consequences of incompatible beliefs about leadership and followership with the other relational partners?

This chapter recognizes also that the phenomenon of the connecting leader is central to organizations under different leadership assumptions: whether we consider leadership as *formal* (based on authority differentials), or *informal* (based on shared competences and knowledge). In the first case, connecting leaders are represented by those individuals like heads of departments, teams and units, who operate as "linking pins" at the juncture between hierarchical layers (Likert, 1961; 1967). In this case, the overall system depends on the coenacted roles of leader and follower. Even a chief executive officer can now be seen not just a leader, but also as a follower of the board or of other stakeholders (e.g., shareholders, regulators). Hence his/her actions as a leader can now also be appraised as a response, a reflex, or a reaction to his/her actions as a follower of these bodies. In the second case, lacking formal authority (as employees, or members of teams), connecting leaders are more likely to represent those acts of shared or group leadership (see Denis et al., 2012, for a review) where leadership and followership rely on expertise, knowledge and social capital, and where the enactment of roles of leader and follower is constantly emergent and time bound (Day et al., 2004).

If the phenomenon of a connecting leader is so pervasive under multiple leadership assumptions, and is both theoretically and practically relevant, it remains to be asked why we do not know more about it. This chapter theorizes this is due to the overreliance on two traditions in the study of leadership, the dyadic and the romantic. A methodological overreliance on dyads is underpinned by a conceptualization of the two roles as juxtaposed and enacted by separate individuals facing one other (Dansereau et al., 1973; Grahen & Uhl-Bien; 1995; Likert, 1961). Further, from the over reliance on dyads ensues a tendency to romanticize leaders (Meindl, 1995; Meindl et al., 1985), and see them as "sacred" heroes (Grint, 2010) who can through authentic (Avolio & Gardner, 2005), charismatic (Howell & Shamir, 2005), and transformational behavior (Bass et al., 1996) play a major role in the attainment of leadership outcomes. In short, so far, the theoretical and methodological lenses used in the study of leadership seem to have ignored the fact that leaders are very often also followers, who are negotiating, responding to, and managing their own leaders' agendas. In contrast, this chapter proposes to study leadership in alternative configurations, like leadership triads (Jaser, 2017), under different ontological lenses, like leadership in practice (Nicolini, 2012), or, more provocatively, to study the leader and follower roles as one (Peters & Haslam, 2018).

This book aims at expanding this new area, through the perspective of many scholars, contributing from different traditions, and writing under different leadership assumptions. This introductory chapter will proceed in the following way: first it will present a theoretical section that hopes to unpack further our understanding of the concept of connecting leader. This part will provide an initial exploration of the roles interconnectedness and the tensions arising from the roles' coenactment. Secondly, this introductory chapter will propose alternative ways of seeing the connecting leader: leadership triads; leadership in practice; and considering leader and follower as one. Lastly, the chapter will present a summary of the chapters in the volume, highlighting how each is contributing to a better understanding of connecting leaders.

UNDERSTANDING THE CONNECTING LEADER

This section sets the stage for this book, first, by exploring the role interconnectedness through various identity theories, and analyzing inter- and intrapersonal approaches to leader and follower role identity construction. Second, it explores the tensions deriving from the role coenactment by reviewing previous empirical evidence. In particular it scans the management literature, which has historically focused on individuals who bridge different parts of the organization, embodying both roles of leader and follower.

Role Interconnectedness

While the leadership literature recognizes that the same individual must embrace both roles (DeRue, 2011; DeRue & Ashford, 2010; Sluss & Ashforth, 2007; Uhl-Bien et al., 2014), our understanding of how an individual effectively performs both roles in concert is an underexplored area (Epitropaki et al., 2017; Sy & McCoy, 2014). However, a number of role identity approaches, relying on different assumptions about leadership relationships, can help the exploration of this phenomenon (Jaser, 2017). On one hand, when leadership relationships are underpinned by informality, the roles of leaders and followers are conceptualized as coconstructed through relational exchanges (DeRue & Ashford, 2010; Uhl-Bien, 2006). On the other, when leadership roles are pegged to formal positions (e.g., manager versus reportee; Graen & Uhl-Bien, 1995), roles can be seen as given. Individuals can be conceptualized as undergoing microrole transitions (Ashforth et al., 2000), depending on who they are facing in their leadership relationship. These two approaches are explored later.

Under Assumptions of Informal Leadership

Perspectives that frame leader and follower roles as coexisting fluidly within a single individual (Uhl-Bien, 2006; Hosking, 2007), tell us that, in embodying both roles, an individual coconstructs leadership relationships with other organizational members (Fairhurst & Uhl-Bien, 2012). The relational leadership literature in particular (Cunliffe & Eriksen, 2011; Uhl-Bien, 2006; Uhl-Bien & Ospina, 2012) provides an appropriate theoretical backdrop to this way of thinking. However, other literatures also allow us to think about this fluidity, for example the shared leadership tradition (see Denis et al., 2012; Pearce & Sims, 2002), which highlights how individuals embody both roles and leadership and followership are constantly emergent. Depending on the expertise needed by the wider team at a certain time, individuals embody the role of leader or of follower (Day et al., 2004). For example, in a cross-functional team engineers and marketers take turns in defining an idea for a new product, alternating roles of leader and follower depending on the need for input at a particular time (Jassawalla & Sashittal, 1999). Under these assumptions, a connecting leader codetermines what role to enact through reciprocal interactions with other organizational members. DeRue and Ashford (2010) advance theory in this area by proposing a relational process of role identity coconstruction through claiming and granting acts between prospective leaders and followers. This can be illustrated for example by a group of department heads, who during a strategy meeting alternate roles of leader and follower of one another; in this case different roles emerge through discursive signaling, body language, or more broadly through relational exchanges among peers (Holm & Fairhurst, 2018). The connecting leader approach allows us to explore the social construction of leadership from the perspective of one individual who enacts concurrently leader and follower roles, identities, self-concepts in a group. It allows us to develop insights on the tensions that might arise when a connecting leader coconstructs leader and follower roles with individuals who hold fundamentally different beliefs about leadership. These can include different assumptions about leader prototypicality (i.e., about those attributes recognized to be prototypic of a leader, van Knippenberg & Hogg, 2003) or about what constitutes good leader and follower behavior (i.e., implicit leadership and followership theories; Epitropaki et al., 2013; Lord & Maher, 1990; Medvedeff & Lord, 2007; Sy, 2010). Yet, how a connecting leader engages in roles coconstruction with reciprocal others, or addresses conflicting perspectives, is still largely unexplored. Adriasola and Lord, in Chapter 2 of this book explore these issues, proposing that context aids or hinders these processes of shared leadership construction for those individuals who, as connecting leaders, bridge the emergence of shared leadership relationships.

Under Assumptions of Formal Leadership

Other perspectives see the two roles as less fluid, but pegged to manager-reportee positions (i.e., what historically have been called superior-subordinate positions: Dansereau et al., 1973; Dansereau et al., 1975; Graen & Uhl-Bien, 1995; Likert, 1961). So that, a manger is seen as a leader of his/her reportees, at the same time as a follower of his/her own boss, and:

> to be effective in leading his own work group ... must be able to influence his own boss; that is, he needs to be skilled both as a supervisor and as a subordinate. (Likert, 1961, p. 114)

Questions arise regarding how connecting leaders transition from one role to the other through microroles switching or "how does a manager enact the role of boss toward her subordinates, and then enact the role of subordinate toward her boss?" (Ashforth et al., 2000, p. 261; Sy & McCoy, 2014). For example, this literature explores how an individual transitions from discussing strategy with his boss, to appraising the performance of his reportee, how he/she access and activates leader and follower self-concepts in sequence, and how one self-concept informs the other. It captures an individual's intrapersonal psychological process used to "wear different hats" or "shift gears" in crossing an imaginary boundary line between roles (Ashforth et al., 2000, p.261; Sluss & Ashforth, 2007; Sy & McCoy, 2014). However, crossing the line might cause tensions when the roles of leader and follower epitomize asymmetry of power, status and control over resources (Kelley, 1992; Sturm & Antonakis, 2015; Uhl-Bien et al., 2014). In discussing cost-cutting measures with his own boss (as a follower), a manager may be given the confidential information that people who do not meet sales target are marked for an imminent lay-off program. The same manager (as a leader) would then address sales targets in a reportee's appraisal meeting by displaying stress and urgency, without being able to share the full picture. It is unclear how the coenactment unfolds in these cases, and what strategies a connecting leader might adopt to balance and buffer the needs and demands from groups at different (higher and lower) hierarchical levels. This is an important area of exploration, as a connecting leader appears as a mediator between different, even diverging agendas, and as such can behave as a unifier or an arbitrageur between the other two leadership partners (Obstfeld, 2005). Hence questions arise on how connecting leaders develop multiple identities when they need to identify with multiple groups (Haslam, 2004). In Chapter 3, Fladerer, Steffens and Haslam address these issues by presenting connecting leaders as identity entrepreneurs, who develop a series of strategies to understand and build identities of different groups.

Janusian Tensions Arising From the Role Coenactment

The above conceptualization of the connecting leader highlights how, when leadership is underpinned by formality, the connecting leader is likely to occupy positions of management (e.g., a head of a team, a department, a unit). Historically, since Zaleznick's (1977/1992) seminal piece in the *Harvard Business Review*, the concept of leader and manager have been broadly treated as separate, with leaders largely defined as fulfilling the role of visionary influencers (Kotter, 1990) and managers that of strategic administrators (Mintzberg 1971). However, the relationship between these two concepts is not clear-cut, with a number of debates among scholars still taking place (Ashford & Sitkin, 2019; Bedeian & Hunt, 2006). The treatment of the two terms has been wide ranging with: some considering leaders and managers as interchangeable (e.g., manager = superior, follower = subordinate; Grahen & Uhl-Bien, 1995; Likert, 1961); some suggesting that managers can grow into leaders (Bennis & Townsend, 1989); some considering leadership as the "extraordinarization" of management (Alvesson & Svenningson, 2003); and others noticing the similarity of these two terms, providing evidence on how they come in scholarly focus in waves, depending on societal events (Czarniawska-Joerges & Wolff, 1991), or changes in linguistic norms (Mautner & Learmonth, 2020). What is sure is that, more than 40 years later, questions on whether these terms are "synonyms or separate?" are still trending (Kniffin et al., 2019). In this unclear landscape, most leadership scholars are cautious in mentioning the word "manager" or "management," as much as management scholars are careful not to mention the word "leader" or "leadership."

It is from this awareness that I bring the management literature into this book, which is mostly about leadership. I believe that the definition of the connecting leader, under the assumption of formality of leadership, is narrow enough to allow these two literatures to speak to each other. The connecting leader in a hierarchical context links different layers of an organization (Likert, 1961), embodying authority and power differentials (Sturm & Antonakis, 2015) reflecting the predicament of a middle manager. Like middle managers, connecting leaders are "enmeshed in a web of relationships generating relentless and conflicting demands"

(McKinney et al., 2013, p. 4), continuously involved in "vertical code switching" (Anicich & Hirsh, 2017), and are more likely to experience role conflict than individuals at any other level of the organization (Floyd & Lane, 2000). Therefore, connecting leaders face idiosyncratic challenges comparable to those of managers who link organizational units. These challenges stem from the duality of their leader-follower predicament. This point is nicely illustrated by a manager studied in the LEGO company (Lüscher & Lewis, 2008, p231), who said: "How can I follow executive mandates, when I have been told to make my own decisions?"

Given the asymmetrical nature of power and authority in the two relationships contended by a connecting leader across the hierarchy, we need to know more about the consequences of juggling the two roles, and how these affect leadership and followership. The management literature provides a good starting point for this investigation as historically it has adopted a role-set approach (Pfeffer & Salancik, 1975; Toegel et al., 2013; Tsui, 1984), useful to appraise the simultaneous pressures from different relationships. For instance, scholars have highlighted how a manager:

> is not simply selecting that set of leadership behaviors that he prefers, or that he thinks will be the best for him to use, but selects his behaviors subject to the social influence coming from his subordinates, ... and his boss. (Pfeffer & Salancik, 1975, p. 142)

Hence, for the purpose of this book, the research on middle managers in particular (Dutton & Ashford, 1993; Dutton et al., 1997; Floyd & Wooldridge, 1992, 1997; Huy, 2002; 2011; Huy et al., 2014) offers a resourceful library of challenges faced by connecting leaders who are sandwiched between units (Gjerde & Alvesson, 2020). I identify two main kind of tensions: about material resources, for example with the allocation and distribution of pay and promotion (Woolridge et al., 2008); or about intangible resources like distribution of knowledge (Nonaka, 1994; Nonaka & Takeuchi, 1995), and the expression of contrasting emotions (Huy, 2002, 2011) to different audiences. These janusian tensions pertaining to connecting leaders are explored in Chapter 4, through a paradox lens by Pradies, Delaghe and Lewis, and in Chapter 5, through a processual lens that captures middle managers as "yo-yos" moving between leading and following, by Alvesson and Gjerde. Further, I provide a sample of the management literature to build an informed picture of the challenges and tensions enmeshed within leader-follower role coenactment.

Tensions About Material Resources

Tensions surrounding material resources can be latent in situations of business as usual, but become salient when a situation of stability is disturbed, like when change occurs (Balogun & Johnson 2004; Rouleau, 2005), when new strategies are implemented (Rouleau & Balogun, 2011), when a program of cost cutting, involving redundancies, is taking place (Norman et al., 2010), or even when innovation is harvested from the bottom of the company (Burgelman, 1983; Burgelman & Sayles, 1983; Mainemelis, 2010). In the latter case, for example, managers have been found to have to perform the opposite actions of compliance and deviance (Burgelman, 1983a,b; Floyd & Woolridge, 1992; Mainemelis, 2010): complying with their leaders' strategy to save resources, to gain their trust, and deviating from the same strategy to allow their followers to scavenge for resources and conduct "skunk" work to test new products/processes. Burgelman's study (1983) provides insights on the existential value of this double game, showing that connecting leaders work though "hiding their [own team's] efforts until they could show positive results clearly had survival value" (Burgelman, 1983, p. 233). In other instances of change implementation for example, when change is decided at the top and incontrovertibly implemented downward, managers manifest their frustration about the fact that some routines are modified, limiting their capacity to make decisions about the team, ultimately constraining leadership behaviors (Balogun & Johnson, 2004, p. 541): "The power is at the top. If you want things signing, you want things to happen, you go upwards" (engineering, interview).

Tensions About Intangible Resource

Tensions surrounding intangible resources are often representative of meaning discrepancies, arising from different interpretations of the same events by the connecting leader's stakeholders. Let us think for example about a connecting leader who empathizes with the excitement of change implementation at the top, and with the opposite emotions of resistance to the same change at the bottom (Aheame et al., 2014; Huy, 2002). In these cases, connecting leaders "experience a wide range of conflicting emotions and ... need to manage their own emotional ambivalence" (Huy, 2002, p. 36) before interacting with the top management, who has designed the change, and subordinates, who are the recipients of the change. Nonaka and Takeuchi (1995) seminal study of knowledge in organizations provides another useful illustration. Connecting leaders, as heads of units and departments, play a key role in the formation of knowledge, have to understand and master contrasting types of knowledge, as well as integrate "abstract concepts" from the top with the "practical" and experience-led ones at the shop-floor level. Again, these individuals have been found to have to use opposite social influence tactics (where social influence can be considered as an intangible resource) in the relationships with senior managers and with their own team. They adopt impression management in one relationship (Dutton & Ashford, 1993), and authentic and transformational leadership in the other (Beatty & Lee, 1992).

While theoretically I have unpacked some aspects of the connecting leader, the remainder of this chapter explores emerging avenues for the empirical study of connecting leaders.

WAYS OF SEEING THE CONNECTING LEADER

In dyads the connecting leader disappears. As mentioned in the introduction, the over reliance on dyads obfuscates the fact that most leaders are also followers and vice versa. Implicit or explicit dyadic assumptions reinforce the sacred elements of leadership: the separation and the distance between leader and follower roles (Bligh et al., 2011; Grint, 2010). Under these assumptions, leaders and followers are caught in entitative positions facing each other (Crevani et al., 2010; Uhl-Bien et al., 2014,), where we are bewitched by the leader role, and bemused by the follower one (Kelley, 1992). In dyads the issues that prevent us from "seeing" connecting leaders are threefold: first, the narrowing of the focus of analysis to two individuals; second, the pegging of roles to hierarchical positions; and lastly, the implication that those who are leaders have different skills, characteristics, behaviors, and even identities than those who are followers.

In order to overcome these assumptions, which constrict a full view of the phenomenon of the connecting leader, this chapter will explore three novel directions which could facilitate the empirical study of connecting leaders: (1) the widening of the dyadic configuration to a leadership triad; (2) the focus on leadership in practice; and (3) treating leading and following as one.

Leadership Triads

The first avenue to see the connecting leader consists in widening the focus of analysis of how we study leadership. So far, in alternative to dyads, scholars have used other units of analysis in the study of leadership, such as groups (Gronn, 2002) to explore leadership as distributed or shared (Day et al., 2004; Gronn, 2015) and networks, to explore patterns of leadership across the wider organization (Contractor et al., 2012). These units of analysis, however, do not allow us to zoom into the intra- and interpersonal issues of a connecting leader, and the tensions of the coenactment, and are more apt to capture the collective dynamics of leadership in the plural (Denis et al., 2012). For this reason, this chapter proposes *leadership triads* as an alternative configuration, "a pattern of leadership" (Gronn, 2015, p. 547) which illuminates unique leadership phenomena, like the connecting leader. Situated between dyads (Dansereau et al., 1975), and groups (Gronn, 2002), triads allow us to focus on interpersonal relationships, while capturing group dynamics, like part-taking and coalitions, mystifying the mechanisms of reciprocity at the core of most dyadic theories (Graen & Uhl-Bien, 1995). Since Simmel's *Soziologie* (1908/1950) we know that going from dyads to triads has a greater impact on relational dynamics than any other change in group size. Hence the change from dyads to triads is not just relative to the number of participants. Rather, it is one "of quality, of dynamics, and of stability" of the relationships (Krackhardt, 1998, p. 23), as said by Szimmel (1908/1950, p. 141):

> The sociological situation between the superordinate and the subordinate is completely changed as soon as a third element is added. Party formation is suggested instead of solidarity; that which separates servant and master is stressed instead of what binds them, because now common features are sought in the comrade and, of course, are found in their common contrast to the superordinate of them both.

Leadership triads are defined as three people connected by relationships of authority (Contractor et al., 2012), a leader, his/her own boss, and his/her own reportee. The leader (henceforth defined as a *connecting leader;* CL) is involved in two formal leadership relationships, with his/her boss (henceforth the *leader of the triad;* L) and with his/her reportee (the *follower of the triad;* F; see Figure 1.1).

Studying triads allows us to see past the separation of the two roles, as now the person in the middle can be studied in his/her concurrent enact-

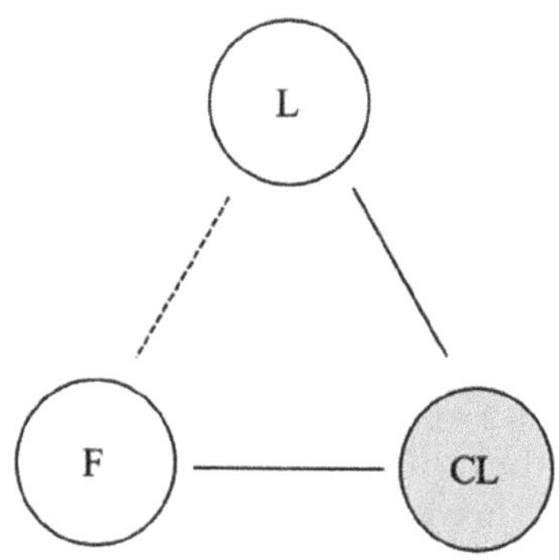

Figure 1.1. The connecting leader.

ment of the two roles. It also permits us to move toward internally consistent accounts of vertical and horizontal relationality by utilizing readily available theoretical considerations pertaining to triads (quality of relationships, Krackhardt, 1999; the role of connecting leaders in bridging "structural holes," Burt, 1992; types of triads, Granovetter, 1973; Simmel, 1908/1950; coalitions, Caplow, 1956; balance of relationships, Heider, 1958). Studying leadership in triads allows us to revise existing leadership theories in new directions. For example, below I provide a postromantic perspective on transformational leadership, through a triadic focus.

Theorized since the 1970s (Burns, 1978; Bass, 1999), transformational leadership (TL) is based on the idea that the more a leader is inspirational, charismatic, intellectually stimulating, and value driven, the better he/she can motivate followers. Transformational leaders have been connected to followers' performance, job satisfaction (Taklaeb et al., 2008), organizational commitment, organizational citizenship behavior (Felfe & Heinitz, 2010), and even innovation (Kark et al., 2003). In initial studies, dating back to the 1980s, scholars expressed caution in attributing TL behavior to leaders' individual qualities. Bass and colleagues highlighted that "the degree of transformational leadership behavior observed at one level of management tended also to be seen at the next lower level of management. The leadership patterns of subordinate superior dyads somehow tended to match each other" (Bass et al., 1987, p. 83). Nonetheless, TL research became dominated by dyadic perspectives, reinforcing the image of a charismatic leader as a mythological hero able to rescue both followers and organizations in distress (Tourish, 2013). The somewhat oversimplistic, often decontextualized, reliance on leaders' behavior has also moved critics to decry TL models as inductively derived: "a grounded taxonomy more than anything else" (van Knippenberg & Sitkin, 2013, p.10).

By taking a triadic view the heroic aspects are now downplayed, and TL becomes much more complex to understand, or explain. In being a follower and a leader, the CL is now with and without authority, with and without power (Sturm & Antonakis, 2015), and has to master remarkably different tactics to exert influence up and down the triad. While he/she can use charismatic devices, typical of TL, to influence F, he/she needs also to master ingratiation, impression management, to influence L (Dutton & Ashford, 1993). "Switching hats" to transitions between two such different roles and communication tactics can have a high psychoaffective costs (Ashforth et. al, 2000). In this social interaction with both triad's constituents, CL will form a nuanced identity, more multifaceted than that of an able and charismatic leader. His/her identity in a triad can be seen as one of a leader and a follower concurrently.

Previous TL studies have highlighted an interplay between leaders' and followers' identity formation. Followers play a role in reinforcing a leader's charismatic identity (Howell & Shamir, 2005), and leaders play a role in deeply influencing their followers' sense of selves (Kark et al., 2003). In a triad the claiming and granting mechanisms through which leaders and followers defined each other's role identities (DeRue & Ashford, 2010) acquire a further level of complexity. A CL might be negatively impacted by divergence of the beliefs on leadership (Epitropaki, et al., 2013; Medvedeff et al., 2007), between the other two triad constituents. For example, in referring back to Bass (1987) and colleagues' comments about the link between leadership styles throughout different levels of management, it can be said that if CL's boss (L) embraces nontransformational models of leadership this would influence CL, in his/her ability to internalize models of transformational leadership and behave as a transformational leader him/herself. Similarly, it is possible to hypothesize that divergent leadership beliefs (e.g., implicity leadership theories, Epitropaki, et al., 2013; Medvedeff et al., 2007) in the dyad L-CL and CL-F, might make it more difficult for CL to harmonize or separate (Obstfeld, 2005; Simmel, 1908/1950) ambiguities, tensions, or different agendas, between L and F (Burgelman, 1983; Burgelman & Sayles (1983); Floyd & Woolridge, 1992). In this situation CL might find that being inspirational, intellectually stimulating and even charismatic, might be more stressful than previously theorized. In other words, the triad magnifies TL's dark sides for leaders themselves, resonating with recent findings that a transformational leadership style is connected to depletion of leaders' emotional resources, with negative effects on their turnover intentions (Lin et al., 2018). These considerations help situating TL models into complex organizations, where dyadic charismatic model might be seen as too simplistic or unrealistic, and when TL behavior becomes much more dependent on relationships across the hierarchy.

More theorizing needs to take place before triads can be recognized as another configuration to study leadership next to dyads, groups and networks (Contractor et al., 2012). However, thinking through the lens of the connecting leader forces the boundaries of what is possible to explore through common configurations of leadership.

Leadership in Practice

A second way in which we can explore empirically the concept of connecting leader consists in dropping the assumption that leadership is pegged to roles. This view of leadership conceptualizes it as coconstructed in interactions through practices that form leadership (Crevani et al.,

2010; Nicolini, 2012; Larsson, 2017). To overcome dyadic role-pegged, entitative assumptions, these emergent approaches consider leadership not as a role specific activity of a leader, or a follower, but as a collective set of practices. The attention is directed to how coordinated leadership action is constructed (Crevani et al., 2010; Drath et al., 2008; Larsson & Lundholm, 2013). What makes this approach distinctive is "its commitment to release leadership from a role-driven, entitative influence relationship" (Raelin, 2017, p. 216). For this reason, at a first glance, this way of looking at leadership might seem at odds with the definition of the connecting leader (as an individual coenacting the roles of leader and follower) because it relinquishes the importance of roles in determining leadership. However, from an empirical perspective, the study of leadership in practice is often underpinned by interactionist and ethnomethodological approaches (Larsson, 2017; Nicolini, 2012), which emphasize the fluid sequencing of activity and talk of "leaders" and members' micro-practices over time' (Holm & Fairhurst, 2018, p. 695).

This perspective reflects the coordinated action in which connecting leaders engage in building leadership by engaging in multiple relationships. In their empirical study of leadership in an executive team, Holm and Fairhurst (2018) interestingly compare this sequencing of microactivities to DeRue and Ashford's (2010) claiming and granting. Where leadership is constructed by a relational recognition of authority, with leaders claiming authority and followers granting it. Therefore, by considering leadership as emerging from situated interaction, practices of leadership are often seen as alternance of leading and following. Under this perspective, everyone in the organization is a potential connecting leader.

In other words, by focusing on leadership as a collective, this approach emancipates everyone in the organization as a coconstructor of leadership (Collinson, 2006, 2020) through dialectic processes of interaction. In doing so it suggests that leaders (and followers) are everywhere, and they are distinguished by their actions. Two chapters provide empirical insights on the connecting leader from an interactionist perspective, Chapter 7 by Walker, who in exploring middle managers identifies a set of leadership practices, calling them "managerial stances" and Chapter 8 in which Wåhlin-Jacobsen and Larsson provide us with insights emerging from the analysis of conversations.

Leader and Follower as One

Finally, one last recent trend in the literature that supports the empirical exploration of the concept of connecting leader is the treatment of leaders and followers as one. This approach focuses on similarities, overlaps and affinities between characteristics which are attributed to effective leaders and effective followers. It echoes early findings in peer nomination studies conducted by Hollander and Web (1955), where navy cadets were likely to nominate the same people as their leaders or followers for a mission.

Despite these early findings, romantic and dyadic-focused literature still consider leaders and followers as embracing "separate mindsets" (Bradberry, 2015). This belief is accentuated by ideas that in order to become an effective leader, individuals may need to develop a plethora of social, cognitive, and psychological skills through training and experience (Day & Halpin, 2004; Lord & Hall, 2005). There is therefore a widespread understanding that leader identity is different from follower identity, and that individuals embrace one and suppress the other as they progress in their careers (Epitropaki et al., 2017). However, recent studies provide evidence that exemplary leaders' and followers' behaviors, skills and identities are more interconnected than previously thought. Agho's (2009) study of a group of 302 executives found that they valued the possibility that effective followership is a precondition of effective leadership. Baker and colleagues (2011) found that exemplary followers possess the characteristics of both exemplary followers and leaders, especially at testing times, like during organizational change. More recently, Peters and Haslam (2018) found that military recruits who embraced the follower identity were more likely to be perceived as effective leaders by their peers.

When appraised from a connecting leader perspective, these studies suggest that the general assumptions that leader and follower identities and behaviors are fundamentally different, and embraced at different times, might be overplayed, and that leaders to be effective need to have the ability to be effective followers too, and vice versa. The findings from these studies may also suggest that those leaders who are also effective followers might accumulate more information, contextual understanding or social capital from their own leaders, and hence might be more likely to emerge as good leaders of their own team. In short, the effective enactment of a role, the one of follower, results in a positive synergy which makes the role of leader more effective. The conceptualization of the connecting leader, as an individual who enacts both roles, is well suited to be explored with similar approaches. Two chapters of this book bring examples of how this can be done: Chapter 8 by Robinson, Bérubé, and Langley, brings us an exploratory qualitative study of military recruits who are in the position of being both leaders and followers. And finally, in Chapter 9 Riggio, Liu, Reichard, and Walker, stretch the concept of leader and follower outside formal organizations, to everyday life through a study of leadership in the community, catching leadership behaviors of people with no formal leadership position (hence often considered as followers by some leadership literature).

To sum up, understanding leadership from a perspective of a connecting leader pushes us to stretch theoretical boundaries and embrace novel ways of exploring leadership empirically, bringing the study of leadership closer to the contextual complexity that leaders (and followers) need to navigate in practice. This book includes a series of theoretical and empirical chapters that offer suggestions on how this can be done, these are testament to the need for a greater exploration of the phenomenon of the connecting leader.

INTRODUCTION TO THE BOOK CHAPTERS

The chapters included in this book are not intended to provide an exhaustive explanation of the phenomenon of the connecting leader, rather they are the beginning of an investigation of a phenomenon that is so pervasive, yet so underexplored. They exemplify the challenges and implications of trying to understand the leader and follower roles as coenacted. The fact that so many perspectives are involved is testament to the complexity we are faced with in attempting to transcend implicit and explicit romantic assumptions of the juxtaposition of these two roles. The chapters reflect a variety of ontologies and scholarly traditions, and hope to represent the start of an exploration of a new territory in leadership.

The first two chapters represent identity perspectives which to some extent have been reviewed earlier in the introduction: leader and follower identity coconstruction in situations of shared leadership, and in more formal situation through social identity theory. Largely influenced by theories of identity construction (Ashford & Schinoff, 2016; Lord et al., 2017), in Chapter 2, Elisa Adriasola and Robert Lord lay out an identity-based structural model which explain how identities and associated cognitive, motivational, and emotional processes at different identity levels can foster the emergence of shared leadership. They provide novel theoretical insights on how connecting leaders sway between identities in the shared leadership and followership processes. Their framework explains the dynamic adjustments that connecting leaders undergo as they construct leader or follower situated identities as part of their role. This chapter contributes to a better understanding of the complexity and dynamism of the identity construction process as individuals engage in processes with dyadic partners and as part of relevant groups. The chapter is highly theoretical and delivers a complex model, while at the same time being enriched by practical examples, of individuals who juggle identities in situation of shared leadership, and by insightful illustrative tables.

In Chapter 3, Martin Fladerer, Niklas Steffens, and Alexander Haslam, in contrast, explore the issue of the role coenactment from a social identity theory perspective (Haslam, 2004). A connecting leader is theorized as occupying gaps in organizations, and bridging the link between teams, departments, or units. This social identity perspective illuminates the multiple "we" and "us" that he/she encounters in the leader and follower roles' coenactment. In belonging to multiple groups (the one he/she leads, and the one he/she follows) successful connecting leaders are theorized as able to shape though rhetoric and action, the identity of multiple groups. The ability to understand and listen to multiple relevant groups identities emerges as crucial for connecting leaders to identify with different groups. This chapter provides insights on how practically a connecting leader can adopt different strategies through which achieve the multiple identification with different groups.

The following two chapters offer insights on the tensions connecting leaders face in the leader follower role coenactment. In Chapter 4, Camille Pradies, Marieke Delanghe, and Marianne Lewis unpack these tensions by using the theoretical lens of paradox. The chapter starts by recognizing that connecting leaders are in a structural position that exposes them to at least one (i.e. being a leader and a follower) but more likely to a multitude of paradoxes. The fact that connecting leaders face multiple and intensifying tensions, makes their ability to grasp and lead through paradoxes all the more critical. The chapter provides a systematic literature review capturing the breadth and depth of the study of leaders who face paradox. It unpacks paradoxes as inherent to leadership, but also as stemming from the environment. In doing so it illustrates not only how connecting leaders through particular behavior and skills can engage with paradoxes, but also how paradox can be used as a leadership resource. Finally, the chapter provides further insights by using two case studies as illustration of how connecting leaders are affected by paradoxical tensions.

The tensions surrounding a connecting leader are also the main topic of Chapter 5 in which Alvesson and Gjerde provide a colorful account of middle managers sandwiched between others, and therefore strained by the middle levelness of their position. This is a good example of how management literature can enrich and complement our understanding of leadership. They highlight the double relationality where the middle manager has to operate as a leader and a follower. However, the authors point out that this multiple dynamic relationality is underexplored and attempt to fill this lacuna by analyzing three aspects of what is uniquely "middle" about connecting leaders: doings (tasks), self-understanding (identities) and ways of relating to significant others in the organization (relationality). They contribute to the literature of management and leadership that challenges static dichotomies of Superior/Leader and Subordinate/Follower and suggest a messier and more dynamic understanding of life in the middle.

While the above chapters provide great theoretical insights on the conceptualization of connecting leaders, the last four chapters are empirical in nature. These are divided in two sections. The first section comprises Chapter 6 and 7, which embrace a practice ontology (Nicolini, 2012). In particular Chapter 6, by Christian Dyrlund Wåhlin-Jacobsen and Magnus Larsson, present further complexity in the study of connecting leaders. In recognizing that organization members sometimes hold many different roles that can be invoked to the effect of leading and following, they focus not only on members relationships with their immediate superiors and subordinates, but with others as well. From microconversation analysis of meetings in a bank, the roles and their meaning in the organizational context emerge as continuously enacted and negotiated during organization members' interactions. From this perspective, leadership is not only performed by invoking one's role-based authority as a leader, but also through the management of meaning in interactions: the authors address this phenomenon as connecting leadership. This chapter presents us with a lens through which everyone holds the promise of a connecting leader, fluidly swaying between leading and following independently from their formal role.

On the same ontological vein in Chapter 7, Roddy Walker presents us with the concept of managerial stances offering a theorization of the situated identities of connecting leaders and their managerial work, concurrently leading and following, influencing and being influenced within the wider organization. Through an ethnographic study of a leadership development program in the Danish public sector, it documents the fluctuating orientation of the work of connecting leaders in practice. By investigating the organizational influences, it highlights how successful connecting leaders gain a middle ground, a capacity to perceive situations from different perspectives, informed by their different rationales, broadening their repertoire of actions of leading and following. An interesting analysis distinguishes connecting leader as following their subordinates and their superiors as well. The author gives us insights on the process through which a middle manager can act as a connecting leader, as a threading needle who brings differing interests of organizational subordinates and superiors together.

The last section of the book is also dedicated to empirical studies, the two chapters in this section stand in contrast to each other as one studies leadership and followership interconnectedness in the military, known for its formal hierarchical structure, and the other in the community, characterized by the lack of hierarchy and formality of roles. However, they have in common a vision which I introduced above as the notion of "leader and follower as one." Chapter 8 by Melanie Robinson, Nicole Bérubé, and Ann Langley is an exploratory qualitative study of members of the Royal Military College of Canada in formal positions who requested them to enact both leader and follower roles. This study illuminates how the two roles are perceived as fused together and difficult to disentangle, recognized as equally important, and more similar to each other than previously theorized. It was also found that through mentoring and modeling, leaders demonstrate desired behaviors and reinforce the expectations for followers, bridging the distance between leaders and followers. The participants would describe the roles as being so closely construed that they almost seemed to merge into one. Further, effective leaders emerged as those who were more agile in moving between leadership and followership. In such a hierarchical context, known for its emphasis on hierarchy and obedience, these findings might come as a surprise. Yet they reinforce the need to study more closely the interconnectedness between leadership and followership. Despite this study is exploratory in nature it opens up questions on whether leader and follower as analytical labels are sufficient to define the activity of connecting leaders.

In keeping the best for last, Chapter 9 by Ronald Riggio, Zhengguang Liu, Rebecca Reichard, and Dayna Walker, attempt to establish a new construct, proposing everyday leadership and engaged followership as two sides of the same coin. They start by asking the provocative question of how we can study leadership in people who do not necessarily have an identifiable leadership position. They conceptualize everyday leadership as multidimensional and propose two strategies for assessing it: self-report survey measures, and assessment centers. They capture five dimensions of everyday leadership (leadership work duties, taking charge, voice, individual innovation, and civic engagement), and four behavioral dimensions to be assessed in simulations (pathways, people and place, problem solving, and positive persuasion). Their methodological rigor has to be praised in attempting to measure such a difficult to capture phenomenon. This chapter shows the flexibility of the concept of the connecting leader, which has been so far theorized as one person who occupies the role as a leader to some, and a follower to others, but could be also viewed as an individual who, regardless of formal title or authority, influences others to achieve shared objectives for the good of the collective, i.e. someone who would typically be consider as a follower (positionally, i.e. not having formal leadership), yet who behaves as a leader (e.g. by influencing, forming a collective vision, taking action, etc.). In this chapter, the authors portray everyday leadership as one form of connecting leadership to capture how everyone, in their daily lives, is both a leader and a follower in unexpected ways.

CONCLUSION

In this introductory chapter I have presented the emergent concept of a connecting leader. I have defined this as an individual that coenacts both roles, behaviors, identities of a leader and a follower, as he/she is embedded in a multitude of leadership relationships across the organization. I have suggested that an understanding of connecting leaders can help us advance theory in the field of leadership, by proposing that a connecting leader is a key tassel in the unfolding of leadership processes in organizations. I have also advocated that the advancement of our understanding of connecting leader is important practically, as managers who contend with multiple relationships would benefit from understanding how the two roles could be coenacted more effectively. However, I submitted that connecting leaders are at best undertheorized, with the leadership literature mostly focused on the interaction between leader and followers as enacted by separate individuals facing each other. I proposed that in order to advance our understanding of connecting leaders we could focus on three areas:

- role coenactment and the interconnectedness under both formal and informal assumptions of leadership (study of identity formation or microrole switching; personal, relational and contextual characteristics which favor the coenactment);
- Janusian tensions arising from the coenactment (different kind of tensions, and those leadership and followership strategies to overcome them); and
- new ways of seeing the connecting leader (whether through new leadership configurations, like triads; ontological perspectives like leadership practices; or through the exploration of the similarities between the roles of leaders and followers).

Understanding leadership from a perspective that acknowledges that many individuals in organizations are not just leaders or followers, but both, democratizes the way we theorize leadership. It challenges the sequence of influence that the two roles have on each other, when we normally think that even when leadership is coproduced, the role of leader has more weight than the one of follower. In some cases, this perspective allows us to envision that the connecting leader's actions *as a leader*, can only be understood after him/her, *as a follower*, has processed and enacted his/her own leader's action. In other words, the connecting leader hints at the possibility that, in some instances, the inception of leadership stems from the process of following. To sum this up, treating following as a consequence of leading, as customary in the leadership literature (Uhl-Bien et al., 2014), does not take into account that there was following before. For the connecting leader, in a hierarchical organization, the enactment of the role of leader can depend upon and be informed by the role of follower having already taken place. The connecting leader opens up new considerations for the possibility that following actions establish, or at least influence, what finally becomes leading actions. These considerations help us understanding further the promise for theory development held by the emerging concept of the connecting leader.

REFERENCES

Agho, A. O. (2009). Perspectives of senior-level executives on effective followership and leadership. *Journal of Leadership & Organizational Studies, 16,* 159–166.

Ahearne, M., Lam, S. K., & Kraus, F. (2014). Performance impact of middle managers' adaptive strategy implementation: The role of social capital. *Strategic Management Journal, 35*(1), 68–87.

Alvesson, M., & Sveningsson, S. (2003). Managers doing leadership: The extra-ordinarization of the mundane. *Human relations, 56*(12), 1435–1459.

Anicich, E. M., & Hirsh, J. B. (2017). The psychology of middle power: Vertical code-switching, role conflict, and behavioral inhibition. *Academy of Management Review, 42*(4), 659–682.

Ashford, S. J., & Sitkin, S. B. (2019). From problems to progress: A dialogue on prevailing issues in leadership research. *The Leadership Quarterly, 30*(4), 454–460.

Ashforth, B. E., Harrison, S. H., & Corley, K. G. (2008). Identification in organizations: An examination of four fundamental questions. *Journal of Management, 34*(3), 325–374.

Ashforth, B. E., Kreiner, G. E., & Fugate, M. (2000). All in a day's work: Boundaries and micro role transitions. *Academy of Management Review, 25*(3), 472–491.

Ashforth, B. E., & Schinoff, B. S. (2016). Identity under construction: How individuals come to define themselves in organizations. *Annual Review of Organizational Psychology and Organizational Behavior, 3,* 111–137. https://doi.org/10.1146/annurev-orgpsych-041015-062322

Avolio, B. J., & Gardner, W. L. (2005). Authentic leadership development: Getting to the root of positive forms of leadership. *The Leadership Quarterly, 16*(3), 315–338.

Balogun, J., & Johnson, G. (2004). Organizational restructuring and middle manager sensemaking. *Academy of Management Journal, 47*(4), 523–549.

Baker, S. D., Mathis, C. J., & Stites-Doe, S. (2011). An exploratory study investigating leader and follower characteristics at US healthcare organizations. *Journal of Managerial Issues, 8,* 341–363.

Bass, B. M. (1999). Current developments in transformational leadership: Research and applications. *The Psychologist-Manager Journal, 3*(1), 5–21.

Bass, B. M., Avolio, B. J., & Atwater, L. (1996). The transformational and transactional leadership of men and women. *Applied psychology, 45*(1), 5–34.Bass, B. M., Waldman, D. A., Avolio, B. J., & Bebb, M. (1987). Transformational leadership and the falling dominoes effect. *Group & Organization Studies, 12*(1), 73–87.

Beatty, C. A., & Lee, G. L. (1992). Leadership among middle managers: An exploration in the context of technological change. *Human Relations, 45*(9), 957–989.

Bedeian, A. G., & Hunt, J. G. (2006). Academic amnesia and vestigial assumptions of our forefathers. *The Leadership Quarterly, 17*(2), 190–205.

Bennis, W. G., & Townsend, R. (1989). *On becoming a leader* (Vol. 36). Addison-Wesley.

Bligh, M. C., Kohles, J. C., & Pillai, R. (2011). Romancing leadership: Past, present, and future. *The Leadership Quarterly, 22*(6), 1058–1077.

Bradberry, T. (2015). *Are you a leader or a follower?* Forbes.com. https://www.forbes.com/sites/travisbradberry/2015/08/18/are-you-a-leader-or-a-follower/#8635dd560915

Burgelman, R. A. (1983). A process model of internal corporate venturing in the diversified major firm. *Administrative Science Quarterly*, 28, 223–244.

Burgelman, R. A., & Sayles, L. R. (1983). *Inside corporate innovation: Strategy, structure, and managerial skills.* Free Press.

Bums, J. M. (1978). *Leadership.* Harper & Row.

Burt R. S. (1992) *Structural holes*. Cambridge, MA: Harvard University Press.

Caplow, T. (1956). A theory of coalitions in the triad. *American Sociological Review 21*(8), 489–493.

Collinson, D. (2006). Rethinking followership: A post-structuralist analysis of follower identities. *Leadership Quarterly, 17*(2), 179–189.

Collinson, D. L. (2020). 'Only connect!': Exploring the critical dialectical turn in leadership studies. *Organization Theory, 1*(2). https://doi.org/10.1177/2631787720913878

Contractor, N. S., DeChurch, L. A., Carson, J., Carter, D. R., & Keegan, B. (2012). The topology of collective leadership. *The Leadership Quarterly, 23*(6), 994–1011.

Crevani, L., Lindgren, M., & Packendorff, J. (2010). Leadership, not leaders: On the study of leadership as practices and interaction. *Scandinavian Journal of Management, 26,* 77–86.

Cunliffe, A. L., & Eriksen, M. (2011). Relational leadership. *Human Relations, 64*(11), 1425–1449.

Czarniawska-Joerges, B., & Wolff, R. (1991). Leaders, managers, entrepreneurs on and off the organizational stage. *Organization Studies, 12*(4), 529–546.

Dansereau, F., Cashman. J., & Graen, G. (1973). Instrumentality theory and equity theory as complementary approaches in predicting the relationship of leadership and turnover among managers. *Organizational Behavior and Human Performance, 10,* 184–200.

Dansereau, F., Jr., Graen, G., & Haga, W. J. (1975). A vertical dyad linkage approach to leadership within formal organizations: A longitudinal investigation of the role making process. *Organizational Behavior and Human Performance, 13*(1), 46–78.

Day, D. V., Gronn, P., & Salas, E. (2004). Leadership capacity in teams. *The Leadership Quarterly, 15*(6), 857–880.

Day, D. V., & Halpin, S. M. (2004). Growing leaders for tomorrow: An introduction. In D. V. Day, S. J. Zaccaro, & S. M. Halpin (Eds.), *Leader development for transforming organizations: Growing leaders for tomorrow* (pp. 3–22). Routledge.

Denis J. L., Langley, A., & Rouleau, L. (2010). The practice of leadership in the messy world of organizations. *Leadership, 6*(1), 67–88.

Denis, J. L., Langley, A., & Sergi, V. (2012). Leadership in the plural. *The Academy of Management Annals, 6*(1), 211–283.

DeRue, D. S. (2011). Adaptive leadership theory: Leading and following as a complex adaptive process. *Research In Organizational Behavior, 31*125–150.

DeRue, D. S., & Ashford, S. J. (2010). Who will lead and who will follow? A social process of leadership identity construction in organizations. *Academy of Management Review, 35*(4), 627–647.

Drath, W. H., McCauley, C. D., Palus, C. J., Van Velsor, E., O'Connor, P. M., & McGuire, J. B. (2008). Direction, alignment, commitment: Toward a more integrative ontology of leadership. *The Leadership Quarterly, 19*(6), 635–653.

Dutton, J. E., & Ashford, S. J. (1993). Selling issues to top management. *Academy Of Management Review, 18*(3), 397–428.

Dutton, J. E., Ashford, S. J., O'Neill, R. M., Hayes, E., & Wierba, E. E. (1997). Reading the wind: how middle managers assess the context for selling issues to top managers. *Strategic Management Journal, 18*(5), 407–423.

Epitropaki, O., Kark, R., Mainemelis, C., & Lord, R. G. (2017). Leadership and followership identity processes: A multilevel review. *The Leadership Quarterly, 28*(1), 104–129.

Epitropaki, O., Sy, T., Martin, R., Tram-Quon, S., & Topakas, A. (2013). Implicit leadership and followership theories "in the wild": Taking stock of information-processing approaches to leadership and followership in organizational settings. *The Leadership Quarterly, 24*(6), 858–881.

Fairhurst, G. T. (2016). Leadership process. In A. Langley & H. Tsoukas (Eds.), *The SAGE handbook of process organization studies* (pp. 497–511). SAGE.

Fairhurst, G. T., & Uhl-Bien, M. (2012). Organizational discourse analysis (ODA): Examining leadership as a relational process. *The Leadership Quarterly, 23*(6), 1043–1062.

Felfe, J., & Heinitz, K. (2010). The impact of consensus and agreement of leadership perceptions on commitment, organizational citizenship behaviour, and customer satisfaction. *European Journal of Work and Organizational Psychology,* 19, 279 – 303

Floyd, S. W., & Lane, P. J. (2000). Strategizing throughout the organization: Managing role conflict in strategic renewal. *Academy of Management Review, 25*(1), 154–177.

Floyd, S. W., & Wooldridge, B. (1992). Middle management involvement in strategy and its association with strategic type: A research note. *Strategic Management Journal, 13,* 153–167.

Floyd, S. W., & Wooldridge, B. (1997). Middle management's strategic influence and organizational performance. *Journal of Management studies, 34*(3), 465–485.

Gjerde, S., & Alvesson, M. (2020). Sandwiched: Exploring role and identity of middle managers in the genuine middle. *Human Relations, 73*(1), 124–151.

Graen, G. B., & Uhl-Bien, M. (1995). Relationship-based approach to leadership: Development of leader-member exchange (LMX) theory of leadership over 25 years: Applying a multi-level multi-domain perspective. *The Leadership Quarterly, 6*(2), 219–247.

Granovetter, M. S. (1973). The strength of weak ties. *American Journal of Sociology 78*(6), 1360–1.

Grint, K. (2010). The sacred in leadership: Separation, sacrifice and silence. *Organization Studies, 31*(1), 89–107.

Gronn, P. (2002) Distributed leadership as a unit of analysis. *Leadership Quarterly, 13*(4), 423–451.

Gronn, P. (2015) The view from inside leadership configurations. *Human Relations, 68*(4), 545–560.

Haslam, S. A. (2004). *Psychology in organizations: The social identity approach*. London: SAGE.

Heider, F. (1958) *The psychology of interpersonal relations*. WILEY.

Hock, D. (1999). *Birth of the chaordic age*. Berrett-Koelher

Hollander, E. P., & Webb, W. B. (1955). Leadership, followership, and friendship: an analysis of peer nominations. *The Journal of Abnormal and Social Psychology, 50*(2), 163–167.

Holm, F., & Fairhurst, G. T. (2018). Configuring shared and hierarchical leadership through authoring. *Human Relations, 71*(5), 692–721

Hosking, D. M. (2007) Not leaders, not followers. In B. Shamir, R. Pillai, M. C. Bligh, & M. Uhl-Bien (Eds.), *Follower-centered perspectives on leadership: A tribute to the memory of James R. Meindl* (pp. ix–xxxix). Information Age

Howell, J. M., & Shamir, B. (2005). The role of followers in the charismatic leadership process: Relationships and their consequences. *The Academy of Management Review, 30*(1), 96–112.

Humborstad, S. W., & Kuvaas, B. (2013). Mutuality in leader–subordinate empowerment expectation: Its impact on role ambiguity and intrinsic motivation. *The Leadership Quarterly, 24*(2), 363–377.

Huy, Q. N. (2002). Emotional balancing of organizational continuity and radical change: The contribution of middle managers. *Administrative Science Quarterly, 47,* 31–69.

Huy, Q. N. (2011). How middle managers' group-focus emotions and social identities influence strategy implementation. *Strategic Management Journal, 32*(13), 1387–1410.

Huy, Q. N., Corely, K. G., & Kraatz, M. S. (2014). From support to mutiny: Shifting legitimacy judgments and emotional reactions impacting the implementation of radical change. *Academy of Management Journal, 57*(6), 1650–1680.

Jaser, Z. (2017). Pulled in two directions: Being in concert a leader to some and a follower to others. In *Academy of Management Proceedings, 2017*(1), 16660.

Jassawalla, A. R., & Sashittal, H. C. (1999). Building collaborative cross-functional new product teams. *Academy Of Management Executive, 13*(3), 50–63.

Kark, R., Shamir, B., & Chen, G. (2003). The two faces of transformational leadership: Empowerment and dependency. *Journal of Applied Psychology, 88*(2), 246–255.

Kelley, R. E. (1992). *The power of followership: How to create leaders people want to follow, and followers who lead themselves*. Broadway Business.

Kotter, J. P. (1990). What leaders really do. *Harvard Business Review, 68*(3), 103–111.

Kniffin, K. M., Detert, J. R., & Leroy, H. L. (2019). On leading and managing: Synonyms or separate (and unequal)? *Academy of Management Discoveries*. https://journals.aom.org/doi/10.5465/amd.2018.0227

Krackhardt, D. (1999). The ties that torture: Simmelian tie analysis in organizations. *Research in the Sociology of Organizations, 16*(1), 183–210.

Larsson, M. (2017). Leadership in interaction. In J. Storey, J. Hartley, J.-L. Denis, P. Hart, & D. Ulrich (Eds.), *The Routledge companion to leadership* (pp. 173–193). Routledge.

Larsson, M., & Lundholm, S. E. (2013). Talking work in a bank: A study of organizing properties of leadership in work interactions. *Human Relations, 66*(8), 1101–1129.

Likert, R. (1961) *New patterns of management*. McGraw-Hill.

Likert, R. (1967). *The human organization: Its management and values*. McGraw-Hill.

Lin, S. H., Scott, B. A., & Matta, F. K. (2019). The dark side of transformational leader behaviors for leaders themselves: A conservation of resources perspective. *Academy of Management Journal, 62*(5), 1556–1582.

Lipman-Blumen, J. (2000). *Connective leadership: Managing in a changing world*. Oxford University Press.

Lord, R. G., Brown, D. J., & Freiberg, S. J. (1999). Understanding the dynamics of leadership: The role of follower self-concepts in the leader/follower relationship. *Organizational Behavior and Human Decision Processes, 78*(3), 167–203.

Lord, R. G., Day, D. V., Zaccaro, S. J., Avolio, B. J., & Eagly, A. H. (2017). Leadership in applied psychology: Three waves of theory and research. *Journal of Applied Psychology, 102*(3), 434–451.

Lord, R. G., & Hall, R. J. (2005). Identity, deep structure and the development of leadership skill. *The Leadership Quarterly, 16*(4), 591–615.

Lord, R. G., & Maher, K. J. (1990). Alternative information-processing models and their implications for theory, research, and practice. *Academy of Management Review, 15*(1), 9–28.

Lüscher, L. S., & Lewis, M. W. (2008). Organizational change and managerial sensemaking: Working through paradox. *Academy of Management Journal, 51*(2), 221–240.

Mautner, G., & Learmonth, M. (2020). From administrator to CEO: Exploring changing representations of hierarchy and prestige in a diachronic corpus of academic management writing. *Discourse & Communication*. https://doi.org/10.1177/1750481319893771

Mainemelis, C. (2010). Stealing fire: Creative deviance in the evolution of new ideas. *Academy of Management Review, 35*(4), 558–578.

McKinney, R., McMahon, M., & Walsh, P. (2013). Danger in the middle: Why mid-level managers aren't ready to lead. *Harvard Business School Publishing*, pp. 50–62.

Medvedeff, M. E., & Lord, R. G. (2007). Implicit leadership theories as dynamic processing structures. In B. Shamir, R. Pillai, M. C. Bligh, & M. Uhl-Bien (Eds.), *Follower–centered perspectives on leadership: A tribute to the memory of James R. Meindl* (pp. ix–xxxix). Information Age.

Meindl, J. R. (1995). The romance of leadership as a follower-centric theory: A social constructionist approach. *The Leadership Quarterly*, *6*(3), 329–341.

Meindl, J. R., Ehrlich, S. B., & Dukerich, J. M. (1985). The romance of leadership. *Administrative Science Quarterly*, *30*, 78–102.

Mintzberg, H. (1971). Managerial work: Analysis from observation. *Management science*, *18*(2), B–97.

Nicolini, D. (2012). *Practice theory, work, and organization: An introduction*. Oxford University Press.

Nonaka, I. (1994). A dynamic theory of organizational knowledge creation. *Organization Science*, *5*(1), 14–37.

Nonaka, I., & Takeuchi, H. (1995). *The knowledge–creating company: How Japanese companies create the dynamics of innovation*. Oxford University Press.

Norman, S. M., Avolio, B. J., & Luthans, F. (2010). The impact of positivity and transparency on trust in leaders and their perceived effectiveness. *The Leadership Quarterly*, *21*(3), 350–364.

Obstfeld, D. (2005). Social networks, the tertius iungens orientation, and involvement in innovation. *Administrative Science Quarterly*, *50*(1), 100–130.

Pearce, C. L., & Sims, H. J. (2002). Vertical versus shared leadership as predictors of the effectiveness of change management teams: An examination of aversive, directive, transactional, transformational, and empowering leader behaviors. *Group Dynamics: Theory, Research, and Practice*, *6*(2), 172–197.

Peters, K., & Haslam, S. A. (2018). I follow, therefore I lead: A longitudinal study of leader and follower identity and leadership in the marines. *British Journal of Psychology*, *109*(4), 708–723.

Pfeffer, J., & Salancik, G.R. (1975). Determinants of supervisory behavior: A role set analysis. *Human Relations*, *28*, 139–154.

Raelin, J. A. (2017). Leadership-as-practice: Theory and application—An editor's reflection. *Leadership*, *13*(2), 215–221.

Rouleau, L. (2005) Micro-practices of strategic sensemaking and sensegiving: How middle managers interpret and sell change every day. *Journal of Management Studies*, 42(7), 0022–2380.

Rouleau, L., & Balogun, J. (2011). Middle Managers, Strategic Sensemaking, and Discursive Competence. *Journal Of Management Studies*, *48*(5), 953–983.

Shamir, B., Pillai, R., Bligh, M. C., & Uhl-Bien, M. (2007). *Follower–centered perspectives on leadership: A tribute to the memory of James R. Meindl*. Information Age

Simmel, G. (1950). *The sociology of Georg Simmel* (K. H. Wolff, Trans.) Collier McMillan. (Original work published 1908)

Sluss, D. M., & Ashforth, B. E. (2007). Relational identity and identification: Defining ourselves through work relationships. *Academy of Management Review*, *32*(1), 9–32.

Sturm, R. E., & Antonakis, J. (2015). Interpersonal power: A review, critique, and research agenda. *Journal of Management, 41*(1), 136–163.

Sy, T. (2010). What do you think of followers? Examining the content, structure, and consequences of implicit followership theories. *Organizational Behavior & Human Decision Processes, 113*(2), 73–84.

Sy, T., & McCoy, T. (2014). Being both leaders and followers: Advancing a model of leader and follower role switching. In L. M. Lapierre & M. K. Carsten (Eds.), *Followership: What is it and why do people follow?* (pp. 121–140). Emerald Group.

Tekleab, A. G., Sims, H. P., Yun, S., Tesluk, P. E., & Cox, J. (2008). Are we on the same page? Effects of self-awareness of empowering and transformational leadership. *Journal of Leadership & Organization Studies, 14,* 185–201.

Toegel, G., Kilduff, M., & Anand, N. (2013). Emotion helping by managers: An emergent understanding of discrepant role expectations and outcomes. *Academy of Management Journal, 56*(2), 334–357.

Tourish, D. (2013). *The dark side of transformational leadership: A critical perspective.* Routledge.

Tsui, A. S. (1984). A role set analysis of managerial reputation. *Organizational Behaviour and Human Performance, 34,* 64–96.

Uhl-Bien, M. (2006). Relational leadership theory: Exploring the social processes of leadership and organizing. *The Leadership Quarterly, 17*(6), 654–676.

Uhl-Bien, M., & Ospina, S. (Eds.). (2012). *Advancing relational leadership research: A dialogue among perspectives.* Information Age.

Uhl-Bien, M., Riggio, R. E., Lowe, K. B., & Carsten, M. K. (2014). Followership theory: A review and research agenda. *Leadership Quarterly, 25*(1), 83–104.

van Dierendonck, D. (2011). Servant leadership: A review and synthesis. *Journal of management, 37*(4), 1228–1261.

van Knippenberg, D., & Hogg, M. A. (2003). A social identity model of leadership effectiveness in organizations. *Research in Organizational Behavior, 25,* 243–295.

van Knippenberg, D., & Sitkin, S. B. (2013). A critical assessment of charismatic—transformational leadership research: Back to the drawing board? *The Academy of Management Annals,* 7(1), 1–60.

Weick, K. E. (2007). Romancing, following and sensemaking: James Meindl's legacy. In B. Shamir, R. Pillai, M. C. Bligh, & M. Uhl-Bien (Eds.), *Follower–centered perspectives on leadership: A tribute to the memory of James R. Meindl* (pp. 187–209). Information Age.

Wooldridge, B., Schmid, T., & Floyd, S. W. (2008). The middle management perspective on strategy process: Contributions, synthesis, and future research. *Journal of Management, 34*(6), 1190–1221.

Zaleznik, A. (1992). Managers and leaders: are they different? *Harvard Business Review, 70*(2), 126–135.

PART 1

INTERCONNECTED LEADER-FOLLOWER IDENTITIES

CHAPTER 2

FROM A LEADER AND A FOLLOWER TO SHARED LEADERSHIP

An Identity-Based Structural Model for Shared Leadership Emergence

Elisa Adriasola
Universidad Adolfo Ibanez, Chile

Robert G. Lord
Durham University, United Kingdom

ABSTARCT

In this chapter, we develop an identity-based structural model to understand how identity processes at the individual, dyadic, and team level can partially explain shared leadership emergence. We differentiate between the level at which an identity is represented (individual, relational, collective) and levels of analysis (individual, dyadic, collective) to explain how interrelated identities provide a structure for shared leadership. Using this framework, we focus mainly on individual and dyadic processes to explore how team members' identity composition (i.e., leader and follower) and the

The Connecting Leader: Serving Concurrently as a Leader and a Follower
pp. 31–65

processes regarding individual self can affect (and be affected by) dyadic- and team-level processes and partially explain shared leadership emergence. Throughout this chapter we address the dynamic and process-oriented role of identity as it becomes contextualized, and how cognitive, motivational and learning processes impact the team, the dyad, and the individual. This chapter provides a rich perspective for understanding shared leadership in its complexity, and it develops a framework that can help organize theory and research, particularly that which explains the connection between seeing oneself as a leader and as a follower.

Modern organizations rely on a variety of teams at all levels including: boards, consultancy, knowledge-based, informal, departments/functional, problem-solving, leadership, self-directed, and virtual teams (Carson et al., 2007; Morgeson et al., 2009; Zaccaro et al., 2001). Leadership continues to be considered one of the most critical factors predicting team performance (Day, Gronn, & Salas, 2004; Morgeson et al., 2009; Wang et al., 2014; Yammarino et al., 2012; Zaccaro et al., 2001). However, such teams operate in a context of growing complexity in which "feedback is all over the place and in all kinds of directions" (Hazy & Uhl-Bien, 2014, p. 711), coming from multiteam processes (Carter & DeChurch, 2014); technology, global competition, and sustainability demands; as well as creative processes within organizations.

To address such complexity and uncertainty, team leadership structures are often dynamic, with a team member needing to lead at some points and follow at others as context and functional demands change. Thus, the theme of this book, which focuses on processes that connect leadership and followership, is central to understanding these dynamic adjustments. In this chapter we develop a framework for understanding these connections by delving deeper into identity processes, which may be grounded in individual, relational, or collective representations. We use this framework to understand dynamic shifts in active identities—from follower to leader to follower again—recognizing that this can be a collective or dyadic as well as an individual identity process. Such dynamics are particularly important to shared or collective leadership, which is often viewed as a type of team process that has high potential to effectively manage complex and challenging team contexts.

Consistent with this emphasis, over the last decades, there has been a shift toward a collective approach to team leadership (Cullen-Lester & Yammarino, 2016; Yammarino et al., 2012), and a recognition that leadership processes, which form, sustain, and grow the systems (Hazy & Uhl-Bien, 2014) are also adapting and evolving. As a consequence, leadership paradigms are shifting from a focus on characteristics of specific individuals in hierarchical leadership positions to an emphasis on leadership processes which are more dynamic and flexible in work teams (Acton et al., 2018; DeRue, 2011; Foti et al., 2017).

To illustrate these issues, consider the demands on Mary, a member of a strategic management team in a retail organization. At time she works alone, as she develops marketing plans, her unique area of expertise, but still being aware of the multiple demands on her organizations. Here she exhibits self-leadership, as she draws on marketing experience and adjust to the current retailing context (Manz & Sims, 1980; Sims & Lorenzi, 1992). However, at other times she works closely with Bill, who leads the purchasing department. In interactions with Bill, she frequently leads, but also often follows his suggestions, particularly when the focus shifts to purchasing opportunities. Other times, Mary and Bill are both part of a larger team that also addresses growth, financial, sales, as well as personnel issues. Here leadership moves all over the team depending on the task at hand, but both Marry and Bill follow more than lead. In all these instances, Mary has the potential to lead, but also the potential to follow, and identities related to both roles may be relatively salient. But Mary is also aware of how she is perceived by others, and how she evaluates their leadership activities. We will return to this example many times to illustrate key points in the chapter.

Because, team structures are grounded in social perception processes, as well as the active identities of team members (Acton et al., 2018), the dynamic aspect of team leadership creates a corollary demand for flexibility in the activation of perceptual schema and active identities, particularly when leadership is shared. Moreover, the underlying dynamics of emergence and acquiescence depend on the interplay between leadership and followership behaviors at a surface level and the activation of leader and follower identities at a deeper level (Acton et al., 2018; DeRue, 2011). For this reason, in this chapter we emphasize the interrelation of leader and follower identities in understanding shared leadership, but we also recognize that this is part of a social, perceptual process.

Epitropaki et al. (2017) explained that individuals hold both enduring leader and follower self-schemas which, when adjusted to specific momentary contexts, translate into leader and follower identities, respectively. Identities, which are situated self-construals (Ashforth & Schinoff, 2016; Lord & Chui, 2018), are therefore dynamic and provide an underpinning for many context-dependent processes associated with shared leadership. Our focus in this chapter is on the more dynamic and situated, self-identity rather than on the more enduring self-schemas. But we should note that self-schema, which vary across individuals, serve as attractors around which identities emerge in the dynamic, social systems associated with leadership. Thus for both Mary and Bill, their sense of who they are at a particular moment changes, but it is also grounded in their core identities—which include both leader and follower self-schema —as well as their current task and social context.

Epitropaki et al. (2017) emphasize the multilevel nature of identity and the related processes which can reflect two dimensions which must be distinguished: the *level of analysis* (individual, dyadic, or collective) (Yammarino et al., 2005; Yammarino & Gooty, 2017) involved in statistical analysis or theorizing and the *level of self* (individual, relational, or collective) (Brewer & Gardner, 1996) at which a person's self-construal occurs. The level at which the self is represented often changes within individuals over time, and thus would be nested under the individual level of analysis. As our example described, Mary's identity may be represented at an individual level as she addresses marketing concerns, or at a dyadic level as she works with her colleague Bill, or at a collective level when engaged with the larger management team. Epitropaki et al. also highlighted the pressing need for further research at the different levels of analysis to improve understanding of the leadership phenomenon. Consequently, to add precision to our coverage, Table 2.1 uses this 3 x 3 framework to organize our theoretical analysis and to understand connective leadership. Although the current chapter addresses this need by proposing a theoretical framework for understanding the emergence of shared leadership at the team and dyadic level of analysis, we emphasize the activation and contextual adjustment of individual-level identities (as shown by the shaded areas in Table 2.1). More specifically, this chapter will address the ways in which team members' identity composition (i.e., leader versus follower) and processes regarding individual selves can affect dyadic- and team-level processes and partially explain shared leadership emergence.

In this chapter we lay out a model of the dynamic aspects of the intrapersonal and interpersonal identity and their relationship to shared leadership. This is important as it helps address not only the heretofore neglected intra-individual-level antecedents of shared leadership but also set up a framework to further understand the mechanisms and boundary conditions under which shared leadership is most effective (Bolden, 2011; Drescher & Garbers, 2016; Paunova, 2015; Wang et al., 2014). We then proceed to addressing the dynamics that underlie shared leadership processes.

This chapter contributes to the literature on emerging team and leadership processes in several ways. First, it suggests a framework that can help organize and analyze theory and research related to identity and identity dynamics that address both levels of representation of the self as well as levels of analysis. Second, it takes a multilevel approach to explore the emergence of shared leadership assessing individual level and dyadic level identity processes that can enhance the likelihood of shared leadership emergence in teams. Third, it addresses how social interaction in

Table 2.1. Conceptual Model for Shared Leadership Process Studies

	Level of Analysis for Theory or Statistics		
Level of Identity Representation	*Individual* 	*Dyadic* 	*Collective/Team* 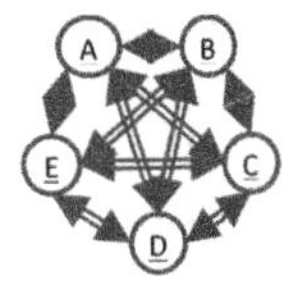
Individual	1 The self is represented as a distinct individual who is unique and separate from others, and the unit for theory and analysis is the individual.	2 The self is represented as a distinct individual who is unique and separate from others, but the unit for theory and analysis is the dyad.	3 The self is represented as a distinct individual who is unique and separate from others, but the unit for theory and analysis is the collective.
Relational	4 The self is represented in terms of role relations with specific others, but the unit for theory and analysis is the individual.	5 The self is represented in terms of role relations with specific others, and the unit for theory and analysis is the dyad.	6 The self is represented in terms of role relations with specific others, but the unit for theory and analysis is the collective.
Collective	7 The self is represented as being part of a group or larger collective such as an organization, but the unit for theory and analysis is the individual.	8 The self is represented as being part of a group or larger collective such as an organization, but the unit for theory and analysis is the dyad.	9 The self is represented as being part of a group or larger collective such as an organization, and the unit for theory and analysis is the collective.

Notes: Shaded area is our emphasis. Each cell represents the way the subject of analysis represents him or herself in combination with how researchers theorize and analyze this representation. Over time an individual's self-representation can change (vertical movement in table), and this differences is independent of the way researchers theorize and analyze phenomena (horizontal differences in table). Cells 1, 5, and 9 reflect theory and analyses that are consistent with the way an individual represents the self. Cells 2, 3, and 6 reflect analyses that are at a level higher than subjects represent the self, aggregating distinct representations; whereas Cells 4, 7, and 8 reflect analyses that are lower than the way individuals represent themselves, thus reflecting the effects of an individual's own representation of higher level units (e.g., group).

teams and dyads affect the development of identity on individuals in order to make them more (or less) complex. Altogether, this chapter contributes to the understanding of identity dynamics that can impact the capacity of individuals like Bill and Mary to concurrently serve as a leader and a follower.

SHARED LEADERSHIP AND MULTILEVEL IDENTITY DYNAMICS

Shared leadership—also referred to as distributed leadership—is an emergent phenomenon in which leadership is performed collectively by multiple members of a team, but at different times (Carson et al., 2007; Nicolaides et al., 2015). Thus, shared leadership is inherently dynamic and sensitive to context. Morgeson et al. (2009) conceptualize shared leadership as an informal and internal source of team leadership with the potential to fulfill all functions of leadership and thereby achieve effective team performance. Consistent with this perspective, three meta-analyses from 2014 and numerous studies published after them (D'Innocenzo et al., 2014; Drescher & Garbers, 2016; Marion et al., 2016; McHugh et al., 2016; Nicolaides et al., 2014; Serban & Roberts, 2016; Wang et al., 2014; White et al., 2016) have consistently demonstrated that shared leadership is associated with team effectiveness and other desirable outcomes such as satisfaction.

Although shared leadership is likely to be complemented by other forms of leadership, it has the potential to be the main source of leadership for effective teams. As such, it is critical to understand *how* to foster shared leadership emergence in teams, and we argue that issue is closely related to the dynamic that activate leader or follower identities. Identity serves this function as it can be applied at individual, dyadic, and group levels (Acton et al., 2018; DeRue, 2011); is contextualized (Ashforth & Schinoff, 2016; Lord & Chui, 2018; Lord et al., 2016; Markus & Wurf, 1987); and has important self-regulatory as well as social perception functions (Johnson et al., 2017; Kihlstrom & Klein, 1994). Further, scholars have highlighted the importance of exploring the processes occurring at all identity levels to obtain a more complete and accurate understanding of the social processes that allow leadership to emerge in teams, as is the case of shared leadership (Day & Dragoni, 2015; Hall et al., 2009). In addition, it is well established that shifts from follower to leader self-identities (or vice versa) may precede changes in social behavior related to leadership (Epitropaki et al., 2017). Consequently, changes in how individuals represent their identity or in the level at which identity dynamics occur are potentially critical to understanding shared leadership.

Therefore, we need a framework such as the one provided in Table 2.1, to help organize and add precision to the literature addressing shared leadership dynamics. Henceforth, we will simply use cell numbers to tie specific articles or theories to this organizing framework and we will move from individual to relational to collective identity representations (down the rows of Table 2.1) as we address each level of analysis (columns in Table 2.1). Note that as one moves down the rows, self-representation are different, often reflecting developmental trends as independent self-representations coalesce into dyadic and then group identities. But they can also reflect momentary changes as illustrated by our example of Mary and Bill's changing roles.

The work by DeRue and colleagues is exceptional in its emphasis on the multi–level dynamic aspects of identity as they related to leadership emergence in groups and movement across the rows of Table 2.1. Hence, we begin with their work to illustrate the value of our framework. DeRue and Ashford (2010) highlighted the role of the leader and the follower identity in the leadership claiming and granting process. In their model, this identity work develops over time, differentiates leader and follower roles in a dyad, has cognitive consequences in terms of the use of implicit theories relating to leadership and followership, and organizes social and work roles in a team. By emphasizing the mutual recognition of role relationships, they explain a movement from the first to the second rows in Table 2.1, that is from individual to dyadic identity representations. Extending this theorizing, DeRue (2011) proposed a theoretical model of how dyadic individual identities develop into double interacts that are stable and based on relational identities (cell 2 in Table 2.1 becomes cell 5). He then examined how these relationships functioned within group structures (cell 6), eventually developing into shared leadership pattern within a team or collective identities (cell 9). Thus, he explains movement from the individual to the dyadic and eventually to the collective rows in Table 2.1. Further, mirroring these developments, the basis of social exchanges often moves from being self-centered to group centered (Flynn, 2005) and trust in the dyad, and then in the collective, solidifies the group structure. Take the example of a recently hired chief financial officer joining the executive team in an organization. As her social exchanges with the chief executive officer and chief operating officer accumulate, she may start changing her self-representation from an expert in the financial area that has experience that differentiates her form the rest of the team (cell 2), to a representation that includes her relationship with the chief executive officer and in her relationship with the chief operating officer (cell 5). With further experience, she may also emphasize her role as part of the executive team (cell 9), with corresponding shifts in motivation and behavior.

Several subsequent empirical works have investigated this process of moving across the rows in Table 2.1 as the unit for theory and analysis changes from individuals to dyads to teams and differences among these social units are addressed. In a study based on the shared leadership structure, DeRue et al. (2015) investigated the individual and team level mechanisms through which trust and competence predict density and centralization of leadership structure (DeRue et al., 2015). It found that individuals' perceptions of team warmth made their identification with their team more salient, which in turn resulted in leadership being provided by multiple individuals within the team, implying a team-level structure and process (cell 9). In other words, between individual differences in perceptions cumulated to affect team-level processes. Taking a similar perspective, Chrobot-Mason et al. (2016) studied how identification with the team or organization influence leadership ties between individuals working in teams (cell 8). Their findings indicated that individual's identification with the organization but not with the team, predicted reciprocation of a leadership relationship. These researchers set a precedent in theorizing how identity level relates to shared leadership, approaching this issue from multiple levels of analysis and illustrating the intricacies of this complex emergent phenomenon. Based on both studies we see how collective level represented identities affected dyadic level and team level processes (cells 8 and 9 in Table 2.1—e.g., individual self is represented at the collective level and that will impact his behaviors toward dyadic partners as well as his behaviors as a member of the team). Though not studied, collective identities likely also changed the basis for individual level cognitions and affect (cell 7 in Table 2.1—i.e., salient collective representation of the self, impact the individual's behaviors when working independently, such as it could with ethical or moral decisions). What these studies addressed was an aggregation process through which individual differences cumulated to create higher level structures but what they missed was the within-person dynamics associated with whether individual, relational, or collective self-representations were more available.

This within-person approach is suggested by Sy and McCoy (2014) in their theoretical proposition of the construct *leader-follower switching*, which they define as an "intrapersonal process of dynamically switching between leader and follower role" (p. 124), and differentiated from shared leadership based on its intrapersonal nature as compared to the interpersonal nature of the latter. This theoretical proposition focuses principally on one level (i.e. within-person), although it recognizes importance of the context and dyads. However, to our knowledge, there is still no research that address the dynamics involving interrelated processes at the individual, dyad and team levels of analysis, which we have argued are necessary to develop a thorough understanding of shared leadership emergence.

Identity and Dynamic Systems

Individual Level of Analysis. Identities influence the way individuals perceive their surroundings, their affective responses, and their behaviors. As such, the individual level processes associated with leader and follower identities play a key role in understanding not only *who* will emerge as a leader and as a follower, but also *how* and *when* they will do it (Epitropaki et al., 2017). Identity and the associated process of identity construction that translates self-schemas into contextualized identities are essential part of the sensemaking and enactment that individuals do in order to understand who they are and how they fit in their environment. Indeed, neuroscience research has established that there are specific integrative networks in the brain which are concerned with the self, which are called *default network* (Gusnard et al., 2001; Spreng & Grady, 2010). When activated, default networks allow the individual to access stored information relevant for the task at hand, and thus guide perception and action planning process leading to behavior (Gusnard et al., 2001). As such, events from the past (stored in memory) become paramount for the meaning the individual assign to current events and their vision of the future; however, the accessed, self-relevant memories need to be recombined and integrated in a meaningful way (Addis & Schacter, 2012; Spreng & Grady, 2010). Therefore, the sensemaking occurring through activated identities acts as the link that interprets the past from the perspective of the present while also providing the building blocks for the future (Addis & Schacter, 2012).

In short, the leader and follower self-identities that individuals construct will constitute sources of relevant information and self-regulatory processes for team events and will, therefore, influence the likelihood individuals engage in leader and follower behaviors while working with their team. Thus, individual-level behavior will differ across the rows of Table 2.1 (cells 1, 4, or 7—e.g., behaviors oriented to self-preserve, turn into behaviors that aims at satisfy the dyad needs, which then turn into behaviors that aim to benefit "us all" as part of the collective); and leadership processes that move individuals from one row to another can have profound consequences (Lord & Brown, 2004). In terms of shared leadership, it will be much more difficult to establish a collective or shared form of leadership if individuals' level of identity tends to be at the individual (cell 1), than at the relational (cell 4) or collective (cell 7) levels. Setting the stage for effective shared leadership may then require behaviors and process that promote collective individual level identities such as leadership behaviors that are prosocial rather than being proself (De Cremer, 2002).

In addition to this "row" effect associated with the level at which identity is represented, the specific content of one's identity (whether a leader or follower identity is activated) will affect the likelihood of engaging in leader or follower behaviors. This effect is independent of the row or column in Table 2.1, as individual-level leadership identities could be activated for a person whose identity was predominantly individual, relational, or collective. Here past histories and the centrality of leader as compared to follower self-schema would be important. Yet as shown in Figure 2.1, it is the identity that is active at a particular moment that will affect individual A's leader- or follower-related behaviors, and these dynamics change over time. As we will discuss later, and as shown in the bottom panel of Figure 2.1, it may also be possible to have interrelated leader and follower self-schemas as leaders gain extensive experience with shared leadership situations.

> ***Proposition 1.*** Active leader and follower individual-level self-schemas will influence the contextualized identity that is constructed, social and self-perceptions, and leader (follower) behavior.

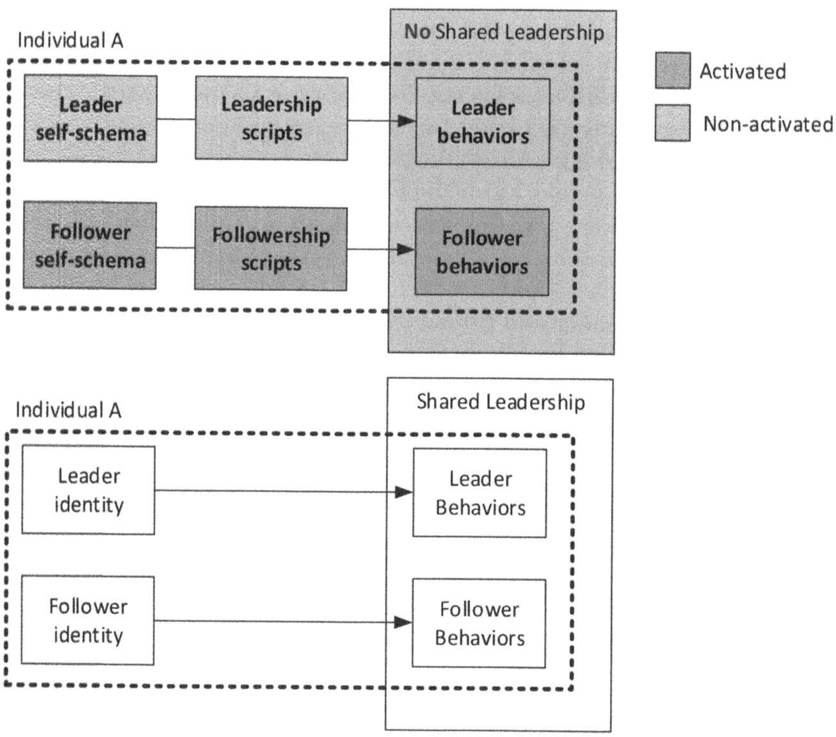

Figure 2.1. Individual level interplay between leader and follower self-schema activation.

> ***Proposition 2.*** As one moves from individual to relational to collective identity levels (e.g., from cell 1 to cell 4 to cell 7), activation of leader or follower self-schema will also tend to change.

Dyadic Level of Analysis. Acton et al. (2018) develop an identity-based, dynamic model of leadership emergence which is grounded in the self-identities of group members. They argue that group structures emerge as an individual's leadership schema is activated and is paired with another group member's follower self-schema. In combination these processes allow a leadership identity to emerge with respect to this dyad. Thus, there are both within-person and between-person social processes involved in the emergence of a leadership structure, and because this structure is contextualized, it can change over time. As already noted, DeRue (2011) develops a very similar argument.

Following this line of thought, a unique aspect of shared leadership is that members taking leader roles also take follower roles at some stage while working with their teams (DeRue & Ashford, 2010). In other words, both leader and follower self-identities can emerge for the same individual, but at different times, when teams share leadership. One critical determinant of which schema becomes a stable attractor is the role of others in helping one construct an identity (Ashforth & Schinoff, 2016). The presence of a leader self-schema makes an individual more likely to emerge as a leader (Day, 2000; Hannah et al., 2009; Lord & Hall, 2005); however, leader emergence only occurs effectively when it is recognized and accepted by others (Day, 2000; Gerstner & Day, 1997; Lord et al., 1999). That is, the activated leader self-schema becomes a contextualized leadership identity.

This process may be momentary, however, when the exchange becomes solidified by situated identities of both leaders and followers, a more stable dyadic structure emerges, which has been labeled a double interact (Acton et al., 2018; DeRue, 2011; Weick, 1979). *Double interacts* reflect a reciprocal interrelation of leaders and followers, that can be thought of in terms of behavior, but at a deeper level can also be thought of in terms of the interlocking of leader and follower identities (Acton et al., 2018; DeRue, 2011). Such interlocking occurs because individuals typically elicit a unique identity in others who view them as being important (Andersen & Chen, 2002; Shah, 2003), and this identity transference process applies to leadership as well (Ritter & Lord, 2007). When this transference occurs, identity activation becomes dyadic as both individuals contribute to the process, and we have moved from the individual to the dyadic column of Table 2.1.

Within the double interact units, the identities of both individuals become salient. Although one might typically think of this as a role making process in which individual role differentiation occurs over time as the early LMX literature suggested (cell 2), the LMX literature developed into a more dyadic perspective (cell 5) in which both leader and follower characteristics were considered within a dyadic relationship that developed over time as both parties focus on dyadic-level functioning (Graen & Uhl-Bien, 1995). Movement from leader- or follower-based to relationship-based dyadic representations (from cell 2 to 5 in Table 2.1) changes the nature of interactions so that trust, mutual obligation, accommodation, and mutual learning describe underlying processes (see Graen & Uhl-Bien, 1995, Table 2, p. 224).

However, in shared leadership situations, dyadic relations must allow each party to be both a leader and follower, albeit at different times. Thus, greater identity and social complexity need to characterize both individuals and dyadic social units (see Lord et al., 2011, for a discussion of complexity). Returning to our example or Mary and Bill, their repertoire of identities needs to include not only individual leader and follower identities, but also double interacts in which Mary leads and Bill follows and double interacts where Bill leads and Mary follows. This allows switching form leader to follower roles to be part of a familiar, stable structure, rather than a disruptive event.

> ***Proposition 3.*** Movement to a dyadic level of analysis in which both dyadic members contribute to schema-activation and identity construction, requires greater complexity in individual identities and double-interacts for shared leadership to be effective.

> ***Proposition 4.*** Relevant domains for understanding leadership and followership change as one moves from individual to relational level identities (Cells 2 to 5): Leader and follower self-schema are more critical when individual level identities predominate, but relational history and dyadic dynamics predominate when relational levels are salient.

Team/Collective Level of Analysis. Movement to a collective level of theory and analysis as reflected in the third column of Table 2.1 complicates issues further. Here individual, relational, or collective level of identities could exist within a team structure, but we expect that effective teams will move toward relational and collective level identities (cells 6 and 9). This would change the nature of social exchanges (Flynn, 2005) so that the focus is on group processes and group-level outcomes. As the social identity literature has clearly indicated, this change also shifts the nature of implicit leadership theories to emphasize group prototypes (Hogg, 2001; van Knippenberg & Hogg, 2018), although general leadership prototypes are still important (Lord et al., 2019). Hence, leaders emerge and are sustained by conforming to group prototypes as well as contributing to group-related rather than self-serving outcomes. One relevant type of group norm may be for shared as opposed to hierarchical leadership structures (DeRue et al., 2015).

One important aspect of shared leadership is that, because individuals can fulfill multiple roles, they need more complex identities and double interacts, in which both leadership and followership roles are compatible and are easily constructed. Group structures are also more complex and dynamic. Consequently, both individually and collectively, requisite complexity is needed (Hannah et al., 2011), and that complexity can come either from experience or it can be created on the spot through individual and group processes (Lord et al., 2011). Complexity also arises at a behavioral level, in that the behaviors that address needed task or socioemotional functions can vary across members and across time. Hence, each group member needs greater behavioral complexity (Hooijberg, 1996).

In shared leadership systems, dynamic processes can be explained by the functional leadership approach, where leadership needs are addressed by different individuals during the performance cycle (Lord et al., 2017; Stogdill & Shartle, 1949; Zaccaro et al., 2001). For example, the needs of structuring and defining tasks or problems, provision of information used in problem solving, providing material resources, and managing personnel resources are likely to be addressed by different team members. The advantage of shared leadership is that different individuals may have unique skills or resources related to these functions. From this functional perspective, team leadership is oriented toward the satisfaction of team needs and is aimed at team performance. As such, the leadership role should go to whoever—inside or outside the team—can best undertake the responsibility of satisfying team needs (Lord et al., 2017; Morgeson et al., 2009).

As a consequence of this dynamic functional allocation, teams may experience leadership from more than one source at any one time and, the sources of leadership are dynamic and can change over time (DeRue, 2011). This occurs within complex adaptive systems, and it may involve the emergence of attractors at individual, dyadic, or team levels of analysis that link identities with relevant task or social elements. For example, the emergence of a momentary attractor could be affected by individual level-factors such as the salience of a leader self-schema when individual holds specialized knowledge for a task. Alternatively, dyadic-level factors such as doing a task with a dyadic partner with whom one worked previously and for which stable double interacts already exist, or collective-level factors such as having team norms for shared leadership could also affect the emergence of shared leadership roles. In the following section, we are more specific as to what such attractors may look like from a structural perspective and how they are linked to shared leadership.

AN IDENTITY-BASED, STRUCTURAL MODEL FOR SHARED LEADERSHIP

Interrelated Identities as a Structure for Shared Leadership

We know how shared leadership looks like at the team level of analysis, but then how does it look at the dyad and individual level of analysis? Understanding all three levels could help us understand what an appropriate intervention would be to increase the likelihood of shared leadership emergence. Figure 2.2 depicts a structure for identities in which individuals can be isolates, part of a single dyad, or members of multiple dyads that occur within a team structure. When people are isolated, the identity that is activated is likely to be dependent on chronic self-schemas, which tend to be active in most situations or in some instances are cued by task contexts or momentary needs (Lord et al., 2016; Markus & Wurf, 1987). In single double-interacts dyads, each individual can elicit an identity in others (Andersen & Chen, 2002; Ritter & Lord, 2007), and over time, a stable double-interact, and perhaps multiple double interacts are likely to provide structure to their relationship. This relational identity serves as an attractor in a dynamic system (Acton et al., 2018). However, in team contexts, there are multiple dyads and many double interacts as

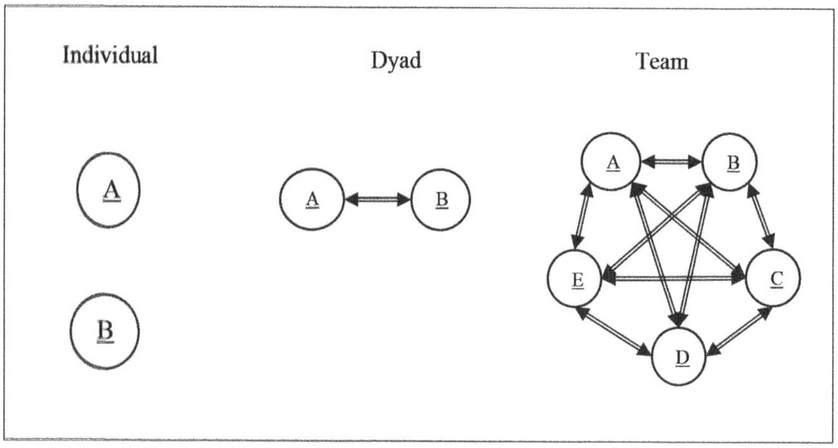

Figure 2.2. Multilevel nature of shared leadership.

well as an enduring team climate and momentary task demands, which further contextualize individual identities.

Multilevel Nature of Shared leadership: Importance of Individual and Dyadic Levels

As shown in Table 2.2, the different definitions of shared leadership found in the literature reflect different levels of analysis. For instance, the definition most popularly used refers to an emergent team property of mutual influence and shared responsibility among team members (Pearce & Conger, 2002), which is conceptualized as the basis for processes originated from the team as a whole rather than an individual level of analysis. Operationally, team members perception about leadership behaviors being shared by the team as a whole (individual perceptions are aggregated at the team level of analysis) are influenced by team-level norms as social identity theory maintains. In short, as ideally conceived, shared leadership operates in cell 9 of Table 2.1.

However, there are alternative aspects that point to the subcomponents of shared leadership, and thus to the dyadic level and to the individual level of analysis (see Table 2.2). But the functioning of identities under the collective column is different than under the individual or dyadic level columns of Table 2.1, and it would be described as individuals within groups or dyads within groups, respectively (Hall & Lord, 1995; Klein et al., 1994). To understand this difference, consider that under normal team processes, tasks and responsibilities are often completed by specific individuals or specific dyads rather than by the group as a whole. When this happens, individual (cell 3) or relational (cell 6) level identity representations may be temporarily salient, but they are influenced by the group context. When functioning as an individual or dyad, one is still motivated by group-level goals and behavior is still guided by group level values and culture, although individual or dyadic level factors may also be important.

Ultimately, the phenomenon we are looking at with shared leadership, is indeed that complex. It relies—or ideally does so—on the team as a whole (cell 9), the dyads available in the team (cell 6), as well as each individual of a dyad and of a team as having a potential for leadership and followership (cell 2 and 3). And over time tasks and responsibilities flexibly move among these levels as different subsets of group members are engaged in group-related functional activities. As such, ignoring the subcomponents and the complexity of the phenomenon would limit the full understanding of the underlying processes allowing shared leadership to emerge and guide group processes. The following

Table 2.2. Multilevel Nature of Shared Leadership: The Whole and its Parts

Level of Analysis	*Relevant Definition*	*Conceptualization*	*Operationalization*	*Sample Papers*
Team 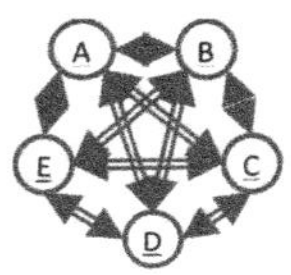 	• "An emergent team property of mutual influence and shared responsibility among team members whereby they lead each other toward goal achievement" (Carson et al., 2007; Hoch & Kozlowski, 2014; Pearce & Conger, 2003; Wang et al., 2014) • "An emergent phenomenon in which leadership is performed collectively by multiple members of a task group" (Paunova, 2015, p. 936) • "Process of influencing others and facilitating goal-related efforts, implying nothing about the number of people who perform these functions" (Yukl, 2002)	• Leadership (task and or relationship specific) behaviors shared by the team	• Aggregation: each member's perception about team behaviors shared by the team rather than resting on individual is aggregated	• Wood (2005) • Avolio et al. (2003) • Pearce and Ensley (2004) • Hiller et al. (2006)
		• Influence is shared and distributed within the team	Social network: Density of leadership ties	• Carson et al., 2007; Wang et al., 2014) • Chiu et al. (2016)
			• Descentralization of leadership ties	• Mehra et al. (2006)
			• Density and decentralization of leadership ties within a team	• DeRue et al. (2015)
Relational (dyad) 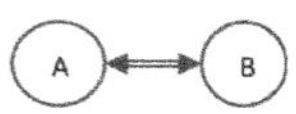 	• "A set of *interactive influence processes* in which team leadership functions are voluntarily shared among internal team members in the pursuit of team goals" (Nicolaides et al., 2014)	• Dynamically changing relationship ties claiming and granting of leadership or followership without precluding the chances of changing role while working as a team (DeRue & Ashford, 2010)	• Exchange of leader and follower role within a dyad—leadership ties change structure	• DeRue and Ashford 2010; DeRue et al. (2015)
Intraindividual  	• "Shared leadership reflects pattern where multiple group *members are engaging in both leadership and followership*" (DeRue, 2011, p. 135) • Shared leadership can be viewed in terms of how different individuals enact leader and follower roles at different points in time (Lord et al., 2017, p. 444)	• Engaging on both *leader and follower associated functions* while interacting with others/ within a dyad	• An individual is able to shift and engage in both leadership and followership behaviors	• Addressed conceptually, DeRue (2011) • Acton et al. (2018) • Sy & McCoy (2014) • Empirically, Coluccio et al. (2019)

section, we build upon this complexity and explore the role of identity in the emergence of shared leadership in teams from this dynamic, multilevel framework, paying particular attention to individual- and dyadic-level functioning within the context of an overall collective identity associated with shared leadership.

Identity at the Individual Level of Analysis and Shared Leadership

Identities involve different elements that comprise our self-concept, which will include attributes, roles, defining experiences, and even future forms of our self. The identities of a leader and follower are complex in that they are multilayer, context bounded and socially construed (DeRue et al., 2009; Epitropaki et al., 2017). At the individual level of analysis, the leader and the follower identity will be associated with specific self-schema that might be more or less integrated with the overall self-construct of an individual (Epitropaki et al., 2017). Each of these self-schemas will have a typical form, with characteristics that will act as an attractor for activating leader or the follower self-schema. It is how individuals construe these self-schemas within their self-concept, and how their self-definition as leaders or followers interacts with the context and others that bears on identity construction and shared leadership emergence.

As discussed in Proposition 1, the activation of a leader or follower self-schema is required for the perception and decisionmaking process leading to a leader or follower behavior. However, there are multiple aspects relative to leader and follower self-schemas that might influence the extent to which they become activated. For instance, Acton et al. (2018) argue that activation of a leader or follower self-schema at a specific time will depend on the situation at that time, the knowledge stored from past experiences in similar situations, and motivational states. That is, the probability of an individual emerging as a leader is dependent on the activation of a leader self-schema being greater than the follower self-schema at a specific time, and vice versa for follower emergence. Applying this logic then to a shared leadership perspective—we are concerned about the conditions that might increase the probabilities for individual to easily shift activation from one self-schema to the other, allowing for a leader-follower role switching (Sy & McCoy, 2014).

> ***Proposition 5:*** The dynamic shift of activation from a leader to a follower self-schema and vice versa in a particular situation will depend on both leader and follower self-schemas being easily accessible at that particular situation.

> ***Proposition 6:*** The probability that an individual is able to fulfill both leadership and followership associated functions in a specific situation or context, will depend on the capacity to dynamically shift between construction of a leader and follower self-schema in that context.

Content of ILT and IFT and Schema Activation. Recent theory and research indicate that the construction of leader or follower identity is context specific (Ashforth & Schinoff, 2016; Lord & Chui, 2018; Lord et al., 2016). Although context can include many variables related to leadership (Lord et al., 2001), the level at which self-representations are defined (Brewer & Gardner, 1996) and the nature of relevant roles (Stets & Burke, 2000) are critical factors, as is expertise, or the amount of experience with relevant roles (Lord & Hall, 2005). In general, assuming collective group identities are salient, roles would be dynamic, changing over time in both their definition and who best fulfills the functional requirements of a role. Adopting a role likely depends on a self-categorization processes, in which the context provides fast and relatively automatic adjustments of social categories like "leader" or "follower," and individuals self-categorize with respect to these roles. Self-categorization, in turn, is based on one's momentary assessment of functional roles and their fit with one's self-perceived characteristics, skills, and recent experience in the social context. For this reason, it is helpful to examine both the definition of leader and follower categories, as well as the processes by which these definitions are adjusted to context.

Social categories often lack clear boundaries and thus are defined in terms of central characteristics or a prototype (Rosch, 1978), which because they are used automatically in self and social categorization, are thought to provide an explanation of implicit leadership and implicit followership theories (ILT and IFT correspondingly, Lord et al., 1984; Sy, 2010). One's perceived fit with these categories would then affect self-categorization, as well as the tendency of others to validate this self-construal (Acton et al., 2018; DeRue & Ashford, 2010). As already noted, with shared leadership this process occurs in the context of identification with a group, so that ILTs and group prototypes (van Knippenberg & Hogg, 2018) are likely to both influence self-categorization as a leader or follower.

As we previously noted, the self-categorization of an individual as belonging—or not—to a leader or follower category depends on a relatively automatic matching of personal characteristics to the relevant prototype. Assessment of one's own attributes as being descriptive of a leader or follower prototype depends on fit with active self-schema (e.g., I am intelligent) which may be central or peripheral to the self (Markus &

Wurf, 1987). The critical question is whether activation spreads from one's active self-schema, as adjusted to context, to a leader or follower prototype. In line with our Proposition 5, individuals' capacity to easy access both leader and follower self-schema might impact their likelihood of sharing leadership. As such, the similarity of ILTs and IFTs would impact the capacity to access and swiftly switch between activating leader and follower self-schema.

Centrality of Leader and Follower Self-Schema. When ILTs and IFTs closely match self-schemas, these self-schemas will be clearer and will tend to be more central to the self, and thus, will be activated frequently as part of the working self-concept. When that occurs, one would expect both the self-schema and the relevant prototype to mutually activate each other and to guide thoughts and behaviors. In other words, if one's ILT and self-schema agree, and this self-schema is central to one's self, then when tasks or contexts make leadership needs salient, self-categorization as a leader should occur eliciting leadership activities. Similar reasoning would activate follower schemas and role when they are familiar and appropriate to context. On the contrary, if the content of ILTs and IFTs do not match self-schema, these self-schemas will tend to be more ambiguous and more peripheral in the self-concept. A more peripheral position will reduce activation and accessibility. Further, peripheral schemas are likely to require more cues to become activated than central self-schema.

What this means in the context of shared leadership is that when a contextualized leadership prototype does not fit one's central self-schema, leadership identities will be slow to form, will lack clarity, and one will not have high leadership self-efficacy (confidence). Follower identities may be activated more easily and more frequently in such situations. Consequently, others are more likely to initiate leadership, and double interacts would tend to develop with others as leaders and oneself as a follower, even if one is more capable than one's dyadic partner at fulfilling a leadership need. However, this is not an entirely passive or automatic process. Individuals will also select situations in which they feel comfortable, and they can alter contexts (and choices of others), so that there are more opportunities to construct and enact leadership identities (Serpe & Stryker, 1987; Stets & Burke, 2000). However, in this context environmental cues gain relevance, as they might activate more peripheral schemas.

One important consequence of shared leadership contexts (being in cell 9) is that all group members are motivated to develop as leaders and help others do the same, so that over time, leadership becomes more central to self-schema. This would be particularly likely if one has a strong identification with a group because she or he would define leadership in terms of a group prototype and see themselves as fitting this prototype (van Knippenberg & Hogg, 2018). They would also be more motivated to move a group toward its goals. DeRue et al. (2015) also found that identification with a group is associated with leadership activities.

Integration of Leader and Follower Self-Schema. The extent to which ILTs and IFTs share elements, and thus the extent to which leader and follower category prototypes match each other, is critical in understanding whether one can move back and forth between leader and follower self-schema activation. A high overlap between the leader and follower self-schemas implies that both tend to be activated by the same context, and that activation of one schema will activate the other as well. In contrast, if ILTs and IFTs are substantially different, then leader and follower category prototypes will not be activated by the same context and thus, activation of one self-schema will inhibit activation of the other. For instance, when a leader prototype includes "dominance" whereas the follower prototype includes "subordination," it is likely that when a situational cue triggers 'subordination' only follower self-schema will become activated, and the leader self-schema activation will be inhibited. However, if both schemas include characteristics such as "caring," then situations that cue such an attribute will facilitate access to both self-schemas. Thus, we argue that the extent to which ILTs and IFTs and leader and follower category prototypes overlap, will impact the compatibility between the leader and follower self-schema, facilitating easy access to both and thus, the capacity of individuals to shift between leader and followers' self-schema activation.

Therefore, the capacity of an individual to move back and forth between leader and follower identity activation will be improved when an integration between leader and follower self-schemas exist, as activation of one schema will make salient and spread activation to the other. Furthermore, the likelihood of activation in different situations will increase if one or both the self-schemas are central to the self-concept, whereas more peripheral self-schemas as leader and follower might increase the reliance on more environmental cues (such as team norm). This theory based on self-categorization processes and ILT/IFTs is summarized in Propositions 7–9.

> ***Proposition 7.*** The similarity of ILTs and self-schemas will promote clarity and centrality in leader identities and increase the probability that one will self-categorize as a leader and assume leadership roles; whereas similarity of IFTs and self-schemas will promote clarity and centrality in follower identities, increasing the probability of self-categorization as followers and assuming follower roles.

> ***Proposition 8:*** Similarity in ILTs and IFTs (and leader and follower prototypes) will facilitate integration between leader and follower self-schema, allowing flexible shifting between these schemas.

Proposition 9. Shared leadership and collective identities will promote ILT and self-schema congruence, clarifying leadership roles, and fostering development of leadership identities in a larger proportion of group members than in hierarchical leadership situations.

Expertise and Schema Activation. Lord and Hall (2005) explained how information is processed differently by novice, intermediate and expert leaders. These differences involve the content of knowledge that is used, how it is used, and what triggers access to that knowledge. While these researchers explore expertise from a development perspective associated with leaders' skills, the overarching stages and characteristics of such stages also inform our thinking with respect to self-schema activation and use in the context of shared leadership. For instance, a novice leader is more dependent on working memory to adapt generic knowledge (such as that associated with ILTs or IFTs) to a specific situation, which narrows attention and limits available cognitive resources. This focusing of attention likely decreases activation of other schemas and thus access to knowledge and resources associated with them, which likely reduces the behavioral flexibility of novice leaders. In contrast, expert leaders are less tied to the specific situation, and the knowledge they access has developed from a systematic organization of previous experiences around specific principles. Reliance on this type of knowledge frees working-memory processing resources, allowing these more expert leaders to broaden attention and access other self-schemas and as a consequence, increasing their behavioral flexibility.

In a context relevant for shared leadership where easy access to both leader and follower self-schemas are needed, the reduced behavioral flexibility of a novice leader may be tied to difficulties in accessing and contextualizing alternative self-schema. As such, context might impact which self-schema is activated in novice leaders. For example, a novice leader, who likely experiences high working-memory demands, may be locked into the need to demonstrate leadership and conform to ILTs or group prototypes, and therefore would have difficulty ceding leadership to someone with more skills regarding a specific task, whereas an expert leader would more easily grasp a broader perspective increasing the probability of shared leadership. This reasoning helps us understand how the tendency of an individual to engage in shared leadership can change as experience develops.

Proposition 10: Expertise and use of principled knowledge by leaders will reduce working-memory demands and increase the extent to which their leader and follower self-schema are both easily accessible. Thus, the likelihood of being able to shift easily between competing schema should be higher for experts than novices.

In sum, our analysis of how individual level self-schema are activated and translated into situated identities depends on their fit with general prototypes (Lord et al., 1984) or group prototypes (Hogg, 2001; van Knippenberg & Hogg, 2018) that guide self-categorization. Thus, we can see how a shared leadership context can move one from an individual to a collective level of identity representation (cells 1 to 7) and can change their likelihood of exhibiting leadership (or followership) in a shared leadership situation. However, this change also depends on dyadic level processes that are represented in the dyadic column of Table 2.1, which are addressed in the next section.

IDENTITY AT THE DYADIC LEVEL OF ANALYSIS AND SHARED LEADERSHIP

Moving to the dyadic level, we need to keep in mind that all the heretofore discussed processes are contingent on the dyadic partner as a cue, and also as a dynamic, semi-independent entity that is part of a double interact. Further, as shown in Table 2.3, most propositions developed for the individual levels of analysis have close analogs at the dyadic (and team) levels. However, what is unique and critically important at the dyadic level is the role of the level of the situated identity has in the motivation for exchanges within the dyad, and how this can shape the structure that develops over time within the dyad.

As previously discussed, a critical change in the meaning and expectations of the role occur when moving from individual to relational or collective levels of identity as the former's need to differentiate will motivate individuals solely on personal interests (Brewer & Gardner, 1996; Flynn, 2005). In contrast, significant "others" are incorporated to the sense of self in relational and collective defined identities, thus in the aim of preserving self, the needs of others are also included (Aron & Aron, 1986). This fundamental motivational shift is likely to result in greater positive affect for each individual, which reinforces social roles and also creates greater capacity to learn and adapt (Fredrickson, 1998). Structurally, dyads develop into double-interacts, which creates stability (movement from cells 2 to 5) but may inhibit shared leadership unless it is strongly reinforced by team-level norms and unless complexity develops in terms of multiple types of double interacts develops (e.g., Mary leads and Bill follows and Bill leads and Mary follows are both common double inter-

Table 2.3. Propositions Relating Leader/Follower Identity Dynamics to Shared Leadership Processes

<table>
<tr><th>Individual Level</th><th>Dyadic Level</th><th>Team Level</th></tr>
<tr><td>Proposition 1. Active leader and follower individual-level self-schemas will influence the contextualized identity that is constructed, social and self-perceptions, and leader (follower) behavior.</td><td>Generalizes to dyad, which provides additional activation cues, structure, and history.</td><td>Generalizes to team levels, except that team norms become important.</td></tr>
<tr><td colspan="3">Proposition 2. As one moves from individual to relational to collective identity levels (e.g., from cell 1 to cell 4 to cell 7), activation of leader or follower self-schema will also tend to change.</td></tr>
<tr><td colspan="2">Proposition 3. Individual identities will stabilize as double-interacts, which involves movement to a dyadic level of analysis in which both members contribute to schema-activation and identity construction.</td><td>Dyads and double-interacts are affected by team identities under which they are nested.</td></tr>
<tr><td colspan="2">Proposition 4. Relevant domains for understanding leadership and followership change as one moves from individual to relational level identities (Cells 2 to 5): Leader and follower self-schema are more critical when individual level identities predominate, but relational history and dyadic dynamics predominate when relational levels are salient.</td><td>Generalizes to team level, but team norms and prototypes become relevant.</td></tr>
<tr><td>Proposition 5. The dynamic shift of activation from a leader to a follower self-schema and vice-versa in a particular situation will depend on both leader and follower self-schemas being easily accessible at that particular situation.</td><td colspan="2">Generalizes to dyads and teams which both provide additional structures and cues that affect schema accessibility.</td></tr>
<tr><td>Proposition 6. The probability that an individual is able to perform both leadership and followership behaviors in a specific situation or context, will depend on the capacity to dynamically shift between construction of a leader and follower self-schema in that context.</td><td colspan="2">Generalizes to dyads and teams which both provide additional structures and cues that affect schema accessibility.</td></tr>
<tr><td>Proposition 7. The similarity of ILTs and self-schemas will promote clarity and centrality in leader identities and increase the probability that one will self-categorize as a leader and assume leadership roles; whereas similarity of IFTs and self-schemas will promote clarity and centrality in follower identities, increasing the probability of self-categorization as followers and assuming follower roles.</td><td colspan="2">Generalizes to dyads and teams which both add additional constraints on identity construction.</td></tr>
</table>

(Table continues on next page)

Table 2.3. (Continued)

Individual Level	*Dyadic Level*	*Team Level*
Proposition 8. Similarity in ILTs and IFTs (and leader and follower prototypes) will facilitate integration between leader and follower self-schema, allowing flexible shifting between these schemas.	Generalizes to dyads and teams which both affect identity construction through transference from dyadic partner or salient aspects of group prototypes.	
Proposition 9. Shared leadership and collective identities will promote ILT and self-schema congruence, clarifying leadership roles, and fostering development of leadership identities in a larger proportion of group members than in hierarchical leadership situations.		
Proposition 10. Expertise and use of principled knowledge by leaders will reduce working-memory demands and increase the extent to which their leader and follower self-schema are both easily accessible. Thus, the likelihood of being able to shift easily between competing schema should be higher for experts than novices.		

Note: Columns indicate levels of analysis for which proposition applies.

acts) Also, when team identification is also strong, we have dyads within groups level of analysis, which would be characterized by cell 8. What this means then is at a specific moment, we have a double interact with associated identities guiding processes, and over time we have dyadic processes operating to create stability, however, a team-level norm may promote flexibility and development.

Dynamics also reflect the claiming and granting activities of both partners, and when this produces positive responses, relational identities would tend to be strengthened. The motivational changes associated with individuals shift to more relational or collective identities in teams where opportunities for interaction are more available, can increase the goal-related interdependence (Fitzimons et al., 2015). Thus, social identities are the base for social goals and hence will impact not only action but also interpretation of feedback from goal attainment. Therefore, both the experience of social goal pursues and the claiming and granting processes will provide information to individuals that can also affect the dynamic moves of level of identity representation.

In sum, as dyads might represent their identity at the individual, relational and collective level, the nature of exchanges (Flynn, 2005) become a critical dyadic process to explore as it sets expectations for the interplay between dyadic partner's identities. Exchange can not only reinforce schema-based tendencies, they also can induce movement from individual to relational and collective level for dyads.

Identity at the Collective Level of Analysis and Shared Leadership

At the team level, both motivational and cognitive aspects change, with motivation being directed at benefiting the team as a whole (Flynn, 2005) and self-categorization being based on match to a group prototype. Further, at this level, the team context influences dyadic and individual level processes, which continue to operate but under a team norm which ideally promotes shared leadership. For example, claiming and granting of leadership would depend on matching group prototypes rather than on conforming to identities elicited by one's dyadic partner. Further, groups provide greater complexity (see Figure 2.2), with any particular individual being part of multiple dyads as well as the overall team. With a strong team identification, these multiple dyadic structures would tend to evolve into a structure that is consistent with group norms and histories. Yet, with shared leadership norms, we would expect roles to change as task and organizational contexts change and individuals with the most relevant resource address the momentary functional leadership demands of a group.

IMPLICATIONS

In this section, we list several implications that follow from our theoretical development. Rather than completely restating the logic we have developed, we simply number the propositions supporting each implication where relevant. However, we will not deal extensively with the team level since we have not gone into developing propositions other than to recognize that teams form a context for people and dyads to the extent there is a coherent identity and people identify with the team.

Individual-Level Implications

At the individual level, it becomes critical to recognize that complexity of teams comes from interactions, not just the addition of their parts (i.e., compilational aggregation, Koslowski & Klein, 2000). Furthermore, this complexity reflects processes involving both the rows and columns in Table 2.1. Shared leadership typically involves movement from individual to collective self-representations, but also research moves from individual to dyads to groups levels of theory and analysis, and as groups constrain the ways dyads operate and constrain the ways individuals operate in that dyadic context. Therefore, in shared leadership structures, researchers recognized that processes are inherently more complex and people need to develop more complex identity dynamics and representations to be effective.

Several of our propositions (1, 2, 3, 5, 6, 10) address the extent to which schema and process complexity are interrelated. Collectively, they imply that the required complexity for shared leadership is dynamically constructed as dyads and teams evolve (Lord et al., 2011). Further, this evolution involves changes in both how people represent the self (rows of Table 2.1) and shifts in the nature of theory regarding dyadic and group level processes (columns of Table 2.1). Shared leadership involve complex processes that require more complex schemas. This complexity involves not only the capacity to easily access different schemas (i.e., leader and follower), but also the ability to move across levels responding to environmental cues, especially as sometimes people work as individuals, sometimes as dyads and sometimes as a whole team.

In terms of implicit leadership and followership theories (propositions 7, 8 and 9), it becomes critical for leader and follower schemas to share elements and to be central to the self. This reflects individual level differences in readiness for shared leadership. But it is also important for these schemas to fit with group norms which are clear and widely accepted among group members. When the team norm is not clear, structure is likely to come from an individual's own ILTs and IFTs, and it will reflect the different histories and beliefs of group members, leading to confusion and potential conflict in claiming and granting processes. However, with clear group-level norms that are shared, structure ideally will develop in a coherent way as individuals move from individual level (cell 1) to group level (cell 9) self-representations. In other words, the basis for flexible collaboration and coordination in assuming leadership functions then lies in the way that group norms can shape identity construction in the team context. Norms can also extend to emotions and affect, and groups that emphasize warm social relations may foster greater group identification which then leads to more shared leadership (DeRue et al., 2015).

Team member's implicit theories are an important part of this identity adjustment process, but learning and adjusting to a group prototype are also needed for an effective shared leadership structure to emerge. As social identity theory (Hogg, 2001; van Knippenberg & Hogg, 2018) explains, identification with the group fosters reliance on group prototypes, but individual level structures are also important (Lord et al., 2019). It is important to recognize that the dynamics involved in shared leadership development also occur at the level of goals that guide specific behavioral and learning processes. Identities constrain goal emergence (Lord et al., 2011), but actions and interpretation of task progress typically occurs at the level of task goals. Jokassari and Adriasola (2018) emphasize that both personal and social goals guide leadership identity development. We would add to their assessment the expectation that social goals would be more prominent as one moved from cells 1 to 5 to 9 in Table 2.1. Further, it may be the setting and successful completion of social goals that explains the microlevel dynamics in shared leadership development. Yet goal setting and pursuit are interrelated with identities. There is a top down effect, where represented levels of the self will impact the goals that are set (i.e., set goals will change as a person moves from individual to dyad level or collective levels), but also bottom up effect, where feedback from personal and social goals attainment will impact development of identity. Learning is also likely to occur in conjunction with goals setting and attainment, as specific productions are learned in conjunction with goal progress (Lord & Hall, 2005; Newell, 1990). For example, one may learn to trust the skills and values of specific dyadic partners or team members in a particular functional domain, because doing so has previously resulted in goal attainment. Such learning then builds routines for automatically sharing leadership in similar future situations.

Dyadic-Level Implications

At the dyadic level, the interactions process becomes critical both at the level of identities and at the levels of goals. At the identity level, one adjusts identities based on transference processes (Andersen & Chen, 2002) as dyadic partners elicit specific identities and become included in one's identity (Aron & Aron, 1986). At the goal level, significant others influence the goals we set and pursue (Shah, 2003). Consequently, motivational and emotional processes occur at the level of identities and at the level of goals as one responds to the situational demands of shared leadership contexts. In terms of motivation, it is the welfare of the dyad that predominates at this level, and social rather than personal strivings should predominate. In terms of emotions, we would expect that positive emotions, which are typically associated with goal achievement, would form a potent basis for dyadic development through the broaden and build processes described by Fredrickson (1998). Not all goals are easily attained, and positive emotions also can be a source of resilience when difficulties are encountered. Thus, positive dyadic (and group) emotional climates could be expected to facilitate continued development of shared leadership capacity.

A relational identity could be expected to support the motivational and emotional processes needed to flexibly respond to momentary functional demands of shared leadership. This is basically what Hooijberg (1996) describes as behavioral complexity. However, it must be supported by complexity in social and identity processes to fully address task demands for individuals (Lord et al., 2011) and teams (Hannah et al., 2011). Complexity in double interacts is one illustration of this increased complexity. In this chapter we have explained how this process occurs as identity representations change over time and as mutuality moves one from individual to dyadic levels of analysis, and then on to team levels of analysis where group identification is common. Social self-regulatory process within teams can also provide the context to foster the flexibility within dyads, as social aspects of goals are defined at dyadic or team level. Successful history of shared goals attainment can foster relational identities as well as identification with the team.

Interventions at a dyadic level might be oriented at strengthening relationships, such that healthy and positive situated identities are developed which elicit commitment and positive affect within dyads. Here a critical approach would be to promote shared goals for dyadic members, which can lead to effective coordination, social reinforcement, and positive affect as goals are flexibly pursued. Related to this strategy would be the type of incentives that are set for dyads, as they can strengthen or weaken the level at which the identity is constructed or the affective climate of a team (DeRue et al., 2015). Interventions might also involve role playing in which roles are reversed as a way to foster alternative double interacts.

CONCLUSIONS

To summarize, we laid out an identity-based structural model for shared leadership in which we explain how identities and associated cognitive, motivational, and emotional processes at different identity levels can foster the emergence of shared leadership. A crucial point is that in shared leadership for each person the *potential* to be a leader and a follower should always be available, but which identity is manifest at a particular moment depends on the nature of active identity representations and the team context. We explored how individual identity processes provide the basis for dyadic processes to develop that can enhance or inhibit shared leadership emergence. We also explained how team identity processes become more than the addition of the parts (i.e. team member and dyads) through interactions that develop over time. Further, we showed how the focus on individual, dyadic and team processes can enrich the understanding of how shared leadership unfolds in teams. While this understanding provides future avenues to development of theory and research on shared leadership, it also informs the identity process that involve different identity representations (e.g., the rows in Table 2.1). Similarly, our theory extends research on identity representations to encompass their different qualities when theory and analyses focus on individuals, compared to dyads or groups.

We maintained that identity underlies leadership and followership processes, and we developed a framework that explaining the dynamic adjustments that connecting leaders undergo as they construct a leader or a follower situated identities as part of their role. This chapter provides a base to explore the complexity and dynamism of such process, as individuals represent their identity at the individual, relational or collective level, but also as they engage in processes individually, with dyadic partners and as part of relevant groups. This framework has implications for theory, research, practice and development of individuals who are expected to shift in active identities from follower to leader and, to follower again.

ACKNOWLEDGMENT

This research was supported by the Comisión Nacional de Investigación Científica y Tecnológica de Chile, CONICYT FONDECYT/INI11160859 and the Advancing Leadership Research grant (W911NF-18-2-0049) from the U.S. Army Research Institute for the Behavioral and Social Sciences awarded to R.G.L. The views, opinions, and/or findings contained in this chapter are those of the authors and shall not be construed as an official Department of the Army position, policy, or decision, unless so designated by other documents.

REFERENCES

Acton, B. P., Foti, R. J., Lord, R. G., & Gladfelter, J. A. (2019). Putting emergence back in leadership emergence: A dynamic, multilevel, process-oriented framework. *The Leadership Quarterly*, *30*(1), 145–164. https://doi.org/10.1016/j.leaqua.2018.07.002

Addis, D. R., & Schacter, D. L. (2012). The hippocampus and imagining the future: Where do we stand? *Frontiers in Human Neuroscience*, *5*, 1–15. https://doi.org/10.3389/fnhum.2011.00173

Andersen, S. M., & Chen, S. (2002). The relational self: An interpersonal social-cognitive theory. *Psychological Review*, *109*(4), 619–645. https://doi.org/10.1037/0033-295X.109.4.619

Aron, A., & Aron, E. N. (1986). *Love and the expansion of self: Understanding attraction and satisfaction*. Hemisphere/Harper & Row.

Ashforth, B. E., & Schinoff, B. S. (2016). Identity under construction: How individuals come to define themselves in organizations. *Annual Review of Organizational Psychology and Organizational Behavior*, *3*, 111–137. https://doi.org/10.1146/annurev-orgpsych-041015-062322

Avolio, B. J., Sivasubramaniam, N., Murry, W. D., Jung, D., & Garger, J. W. (2003). Development and preliminary validation of a team multifactor leadership questionnaire. In C. L. Pearce & J. A. Conger (Eds.), *Shared leadership: Reframing the hows and whys of leadership* (pp. 143–172). SAGE.

Bolden, R. (2011). Distributed leadership in organizations: A review of theory and research. *International Journal of Management Reviews*, *13*(3), 251–269.

Brewer, M. B., & Gardner, W. (1996). Who is this "We"? Levels of collective identity and self representations. *Journal of Personality and Social Psychology*, *71*, 83–93.

Carson, J. B., Tesluk, P. E., & Marrone, J. A. (2007). Shared leadership in teams: An investigation of antecedent conditions and performance. *Academy of Management Journal*, *50*(5), 1217–1234.

Carter, D. R., & DeChurch, L. A. (2014). Leadership in multiteam systems: A network perspective. In D. V. Day (Ed.), *The Oxford handbook of leadership and organizations* (pp. 482–502). Oxford University Press.

Chiu, C. Y., Owens, B. P., & Tesluk, P. E. (2016). Initiating and utilizing shared leadership in teams: The role of leader humility, team proactive personality, and team performance capability. *Journal of Applied Psychology, 101*(12), 1705–1720. https://doi.org/10.1037/apl0000159

Chrobot-Mason, D., Gerbasi, A., & Cullen-Lester, K. L. (2016). Predicting leadership relationships: The importance of collective identity. *Leadership Quarterly, 27*(2), 298–311. https://doi.org/10.1016/j.leaqua.2016.02.003

Coluccio, G., Adriasola, E., & Espejo, A. (2019). Untangling the role of agreeableness and conscientiousness in shared leadership emergence: A multilevel approach. Manuscript sumbitted for publication.

Cullen-Lester, K. L., & Yammarino, F. J. (2016). Collective and network approaches to leadership: Special issue introduction. *Leadership Quarterly, 27*(2), 173–180. https://doi.org/http://dx.doi.org/10.1016/j.leaqua.2016.02.001

D'Innocenzo, L., Mathieu, J. E., & Kukenberger, M. R. (2014). A meta-analysis of different forms of shared leadership–team performance relations. *Journal of management*. https://doi.org/10.1177/0149206314525205

Day, D. V. (2000). Leadership development: A review in context. *The Leadership Quarterly, 11*(4), 581–613. https://doi.org/10.1016/S1048-9843(00)00061-8

Day, D. V., & Dragoni, L. (2015). Leadership development: An outcome-oriented review based on time and levels of analyses. *Annual Review of Organizational Psychology and Organizational Behavior, 2*(1), 133–156. https://doi.org/10.1146/annurev-orgpsych-032414-111328

Day, D. V., Gronn, P., & Salas, E. (2004). Leadership capacity in teams. *Leadership Quarterly, 15*(6), 857–880.

De Cremer, D. (2002). Charismatic leadership and cooperation in social dilemmas: A matter of transforming motives? *Journal of Applied Social Psychology, 32*(5), 997–1016.

DeRue, D. S. (2011). Adaptive leadership theory: Leading and following as a complex adaptive process. *Research in organizational behavior, 31*, 125–150.

DeRue, D. S., & Ashford, S. J. (2010). Who will lead and who will follow? A social process of leadership identity construction in organizations. *Academy of Management Review, 35*(4), 627–647.

DeRue, D. S., Ashford, S. J., & Cotton, N. C. (2009). Assuming the mantle: Unpacking the process by which individuals internalize a leader identity. In L. M. Roberts & J. E. Dutton (Eds.), *Exploring positive identities and organizations: Building a theoretical and research foundation* (pp. 213–232). Taylor & Francis.

DeRue, D. S., Nahrgang, J. D., & Ashford, S. J. (2015). Interpersonal perceptions and the emergence of leadership structures in groups: A network perspective. *Organization Science, 26*(4), 1192–1209.

Drescher, G., & Garbers, Y. (2016). Shared leadership and commonality: A policy-capturing study. *Leadership Quarterly, 27*(2), 200–217. https://doi.org/10.1016/j.leaqua.2016.02.002

Epitropaki, O., Kark, R., Mainemelis, C., & Lord, R. G. (2017). Leadership and followership identity processes: A multilevel review. *The Leadership Quarterly, 28*(1), 104–129. https://doi.org/10.1016/j.leaqua.2016.10.003

Fitzsimons, G. M., Finkel, E. J., & VanDellen, M. R. (2015). Transactive goal dynamics. Psychological Review, 122(4), 648–673. https://doi.org/10.1037/a0039654

Flynn, F. J. (2005). Identity orientations and forms of social exchange in organizations. *Academy of Management Review, 30*(4), 737–750.

Fredrickson, B. L. (1998). What good are positive emotions? *Review of General Psychology, 2,* 300–319.

Foti, R. J., Hansbrough, T. K., Epitropaki, O., & Coyle, P. T. P. (2017). Dynamic viewpoints on implicit leadership and followership theories: Approaches, findings, and future directions. *Leadership Quarterly, 28,* 261–267.

Gerstner, C. R., & Day, D. V. (1997). Meta-analytic review of leader-member exchange theory: Correlates and construct issues. *Journal of Applied Psychology, 82*(6), 827–844.

Graen, G. B., & Uhl-Bien, M. (1995). Relationship-based approach to leadership: development of leader-member exchange (LMX) theory of leadership over 25 years: Applying a multi-level multi-domain perspective. *Leadership Quarterly, 6*(2), 219–247.

Gusnard, D. A., Akbudak, E., Shulman, G. L., & Raichle, M. E. (2001). Medial prefrontal cortex and self-referential mental activity: Relation to a default mode of brain function. *Proceedings of the National Academy of Sciences, 98*(7), 4259–4264.

Hall, R. J., & Lord, R. G. (1995). Multi-level information-processing explanations of followers' leadership perception. *Leadership Quarterly, 6*(3), 265–287.

Hall, R. J., Lord, R. G., & Foster, K. E. (2009). Considerations in applying the social relations model to the study of leadership emergence in groups: A leadership categorization perspective. *Research in Multi-Level Issues, 8,* 193–213. https://doi.org/10.1108/S1475-9144(2009)0000008009

Hannah, S. T., Lord, R. G., & Pearce, C. L. (2011). Leadership and collective requisite complexity. *Organizational Psychology Review, 1*(3), 215–238.

Hannah, S. T., Woolfolk, R. L., & Lord, R. G. (2009). Leader self-structure: A framework for positive leadership. *Journal of Organizational Behavior, 30*(2), 269–290.

Hazy, J. K., & Uhl-Bien, M. (2014). Changing the rules: The implications of complexity science for leadership research and practice. In D. V. Day (Ed.), *The Oxford handbook of leadership and organizations* (pp. 709–732). Oxford University Press.

Hiller, N. J., Day, D. V., & Vance, R. J. (2006). Collective enactment of leadership roles and team effectiveness: A field study. *Leadership Quarterly, 17*(4), 387–397. https://doi.org/10.1016/j.leaqua.2006.04.004

Hoch, J. E., & Kozlowski, S. W. J. (2014). Leading virtual teams: Hierarchical leadership, structural supports, and shared team leadership. *Journal of Applied Psychology, 99*(3), 390–403. https://doi.org/10.1037/a0030264

Hogg, M. A. (2001). A social identity theory of leadership. *Personality and Social Psychology Review, 5*(3), 184–200.

Hooijberg, R. (1996). A multidirectional approach toward leadership: An extension of the concept of behavioral complexity. *Human Relations, 49*(7), 917–946. https://doi.org/10.1177/001872679604900703

Johnson, R. E., Muraven, M., Donaldson, T. L., & Lin, S.-H. J. (2017). Self-control in work organizations. In D. L. Ferris, R. E. Johnson, & C. Sedikides (Eds.), *The self at work* (pp. 119–144). Routledge.

Jokisaari, M., & Adriasola, E. (2020). *The role of new leaders' personal and shared goals in identity development.* Unpublished working paper.

Kihlstrom, J. F., & Klein, S. B. (1994). The self as a knowledge system. In R. S. Wyer & T. K. Srull (Eds.), *Handbook of social cognition* (Vol. 1, pp. 153–208). Erlbaum.

Klein, K. J., Dansereau, F., & Hall, R. J. (1994). Levels issues in theory development, data collection, and analysis. *Academy of Management Review, 19*(2), 195–229.

Kozlowski, S. W. J., & Klein, K. J. (2000). A multilevel approach to theory and research in organizations: Contextual, temporal, and emerging processes. In K. J. Klein & S. W. J. Kozlowski (Eds.), *Multilevel theory, research and methods in organizations: Foundations, extensions, and new directions* (pp. 3–90). Jossey-Bass.

Lord, R. G., & Brown, D. J. (2004). *Leadership processes and follower self-identity.* Routledge.

Lord, R. G., Brown, D. J., & Freiberg, S. J. (1999). Understanding the dynamics of leadership: The Role of follower self-concepts in the leader/follower relationship. *Organizational Behavior and Human Decision Processes, 78*(3), 167–203.

Lord, R. G., Brown, D. J., Harvey, J. L., & Hall, R. J. (2001). Contextual constraints on prototype generation and their multilevel consequences for leadership perceptions. *Leadership Quarterly, 12*(3), 311–338.

Lord, R. G., & Chui, S. L. M. (2018). Dual process models of self-schemas and identity: Implications for leadership and followership processes. In D. L. Ferris, R. E. Johnson, & C. Sedikides (Eds.), *The self at work* (pp. 341–361). Routledge.

Lord, R. G., Day, D. V., Zaccaro, S. J., Avolio, B. J., & Eagly, A. H. (2017). Leadership in applied psychology: three waves of theory and research. *Journal of Applied Psychology, 102*(3), 434–451.

Lord, R. G., Epitropaki, O., Foti, R. J., & Hansbrough, T. K. (2020). Implicit leadership theories, implicit followership theories, and dynamic processing of leadership information. *Annual Review of Organizational Psychology and Organizational Behavior,* 7(1), 49–74. https://doi.org/10.1146/annurev-orgpsych-012119-045434

Lord, R. G., Foti, R. J., & De Vader, C. L. (1984). A test of leadership categorization theory: Internal structure, information processing, and leadership perceptions. *Organizational Behavior and Human Performance, 34*(3), 343–378.

Lord, R. G., Gatti, P., & Chui, S. L. M. (2016). Social-cognitive, relational, and identity-based approaches to leadership. *Organizational Behavior and Human Decision Processes, 136,* 119–134.

Lord, R. G., & Hall, R. J. (2005). Identity, deep structure and the development of leadership skill. *Leadership Quarterly, 16*(4), 591–615.

Lord, R. G., Hannah, S. T., & Jennings, P. L. (2011). A framework for understanding leadership and individual requisite complexity. *Organizational Psychology Review, 1*(2), 104–127.

Manz, C. C., & Sims, H. P., Jr. (1980) Self-management as a substitute for leadership: A social-learning theory perspective. *Academy of Management Review, 5*(3), 361–367. https://doi.org/10.5465/amr.1980.4288845

Marion, R., Christiansen, J., Klar, H. W., Schreiber, C., & Akif Erdener, M. (2016). Informal leadership, interaction, cliques and productive capacity in organizations: A collectivist analysis. *Leadership Quarterly, 27*(2), 242–260. https://doi.org/10.1016/j.leaqua.2016.01.003

Markus, H., & Wurf, E. (1987). The dynamic self-concept: A social psychological perspective. *Annual Review of Psychology, 38*(1), 299–337.

McHugh, K. A., Yammarino, F. J., Dionne, S. D., Serban, A., Sayama, H., & Chatterjee, S. (2016). Collective decision making, leadership, and collective intelligence: Tests with agent-based simulations and a field study. *Leadership Quarterly, 27*(2), 218–241. http://doi.org/10.1016/j.leaqua.2016.01.001

Mehra, A., Smith, B. R., Dixon, A. L., & Robertson, B. (2006). Distributed leadership in teams: The network of leadership perceptions and team performance. *Leadership Quarterly, 17*(3), 232–245.

Morgeson, F. P., DeRue, D. S., & Karam, E. P. (2010). Leadership in teams: A functional approach to understanding leadership structures and processes. *Journal of Management, 36*(1), 5–39. https://doi.org/10.1177/0149206309347376

Newell, A. (1990). *Unified theories of cognition*. Harvard University Press.

Nicolaides, V. C., LaPort, K. A., Chen, T. R., Tomassetti, A. J., Weis, E. J., Zaccaro, S. J., & Cortina, J. M. (2014). The shared leadership of teams: A meta-analysis of proximal, distal, and moderating relationships. *Leadership Quarterly, 25*(5), 923–942. https://doi.org/10.1016/j.leaqua.2014.06.006

Paunova, M. (2015). The emergence of individual and collective leadership in task groups: A matter of achievement and ascription. *Leadership Quarterly, 26*(6), 935–957.

Pearce, C. L., & Conger, J. A. (2002). *Shared leadership: Reframing the hows and whys of leadership*. SAGE.

Pearce, C. L., & Conger, J. A. (2003). All those years ago. In C. L. Pearce & J. A. Conger (Eds.), *Shared leadership: Reframing the hows and whys of leadership* (pp. 1–18). SAGE

Pearce, C. L., & Ensley, M. D. (2004). A reciprocal and longitudinal investigation of the innovation process: The central role of shared vision in product and process innovation teams (PPITs). *Journal of Organizational Behavior, 25*(2), 259–278.

Ritter, B. A., & Lord, R. G. (2007). The impact of previous leaders on the evaluation of new leaders: An alternative to prototype matching. *Journal of Applied Psychology, 92*(6), 1683–1695. https://doi.org/10.1037/0021-9010.92.6.1683

Rosch, E. (1978). Principles of categorization. In E. Rosch & B. Lloyd (Eds.), *Cognition and categorization* (pp. 27–48). Erlbaum.

Serban, A., & Roberts, A. J. B. (2016). Exploring antecedents and outcomes of shared leadership in a creative context: A mixed-methods approach. *Leadership Quarterly, 27*(2), 181–199. https://doi.org/10.1016/j.leaqua.2016.01.009

Serpe, R. T., & Stryker, S. (1987). The construction of self and reconstruction of social relationships. *Advances in Group Processes, 4*, 41–66.

Shah, J. (2003). Automatic for the people: How representations of significant others implicitly affect goal pursuit. *Journal of Personality and Social Psychology, 84*(4), 661–681. https://doi.org/10.1037/0022-3514.84.4.661

Sims, H. P., Jr., & Lorenzi, P. (1992). *The new leadership paradigm: Social learning and cognition in organizations.* SAGE.

Spreng, R. N., & Grady, C. L. (2010). Patterns of brain activity supporting autobiographical memory, prospection, and theory of mind, and their relationship to the default mode network. *Journal of Cognitive Neuroscience, 22*(6), 1112–1123.

Stets, J. E., & Burke, P. J. (2000). Identity theory and social identity theory. *Social Psychology Quarterly, 63*(3), 224–237. https://doi.org/10.2307/2695870

Stogdill, R. M., & Shartle, C. L. (1949). Methods for determining patterns of leadership behavior in relation to organization structure and objectives. *Journal of Applied Psychology, 32*, 286–291.

Sy, T. (2010). What do you think of followers? Examining the content, structure, and consequences of implicit followership theories. *Organizational Behavior and Human Decision Processes, 113*(2), 73–84.

Sy, T., & McCoy, T. (2014). Being both leaders and followers: Advancing A model of leader and follower role switching. In L. LaPierre & M. Carsten (Eds.), *Followership: Why is it and why do people follow?* (1st ed., pp. 121–139). Emerald.

van Knippenberg, D., & Hogg, M. A. (2018). Social identifications in organizations. In D. L. Ferris & R. E. Johnson (Eds.), *The self at work: Fundamental theory and research* (pp. 72–90). Routledge.

Wang, D., Waldman, D. A., & Zhang, Z. (2014). A meta-analysis of shared leadership and team effectiveness. *Journal of Applied Psychology, 99*(2), 181–198. https://doi.org/10.1037/a0034531

Weick, K. E. (1979). *The social psychology of organizing* (Topics in social psychology series). McGraw-Hill Humanities.

White, L., Currie, G., & Lockett, A. (2016). Pluralized leadership in complex organizations: Exploring the cross network effects between formal and informal leadership relations. *Leadership Quarterly, 27*(2), 280–297. https://doi.org/10.1016/j.leaqua.2016.01.004

Wood, M. S. (2005). Determinants of shared leadership in management teams. *International Journal of Leadership Studies, 1*(1), 64–85.

Yammarino, F. J., Dionne, S. D., Chun, J. U., & Dansereau, F. (2005). Leadership and levels of analysis: A state-of-the-science review. *Leadership Quarterly, 16*(6), 879–919.

Yammarino, F. J., & Gooty, J. (2017). Multi-level issues and dyads in leadership research. In B. Schyns, R. J. Hall, & P. Neves (Eds.), *Handbook of methods in leadership research* (pp. 229–255). Edward Elgar.

Yammarino, F. J., Salas, E., Serban, A., Shirreffs, K., & Shuffler, M. L. (2012). Collectivistic leadership approaches: Putting the "we" in leadership science and practice. *Industrial and Organizational Psychology, 5*(4), 382–402. doi:10.1111/j.1754-9434.2012.01467.x

Yukl, G. (2002). *Leadership in organizations* (5th ed.). Prentice Hall.

Zaccaro, S. J., Rittman, A. L., & Marks, M. A. (2001). Team leadership. *Leadership Quarterly, 12*(4), 451–483. https://doi.org/10.1016/S1048-9843(01)00093-5

CHAPTER 3

BRIDGING GAPS IN ORGANIZATIONS

Leaders as Entrepreneurs of Identity

Martin P. Fladerer
Ludwig Maximilian University of Munich and Technical University of Munich

Niklas K. Steffens and S. Alexander Haslam
The University of Queensland

ABSTRACT

Modern organizations are complex social systems that provide their members with a range of different social identities (e.g., as a member of a work team). Social identities (i.e., people's sense of "we" and "us" derived from group memberships) determine *who* collaborates as well as *how* they collaborate and *what* they collaborate on. Social identities have the capacity not only to make organizations efficient and productive, but also to make them innovative and dynamic. In this chapter, we draw on the social identity approach to develop an analysis of the role leaders play as *identity entrepreneurs* in bridging gaps between individuals and groups in organizations. We examine how leaders' rhetoric and actions serve to define both group boundaries and the meaning associated with those groups and explore the

The Connecting Leader: Serving Concurrently as a Leader and a Follower
pp. 67–96

impact of this on organizational functioning. We also discuss various strategies that leaders can employ to create connections among individuals and groups by harnessing the power of shared social identity. We conclude by discussing how these efforts are more likely to be successful to the extent that leaders work with, and build upon, the social realities of those they want to lead.

Groups are a prominent feature of organizational life. Importantly, they also furnish their members with a sense of social identity—a sense of the self as "we" and "us" not just "me" and "I" (Haslam, 2004; Hogg & Terry, 2001). Modern organizations are complex social systems that provide their members with a range of different social identities (e.g., as a member of a work team, a department and the organization as a whole; Ashforth & Johnson, 2001). Importantly, when, and to the extent that, people identify with a social group they will generally align their understanding of the world and their behavior with the norms, beliefs and ideals of that group (Turner, 1982). Social identity theorizing (e.g., Postmes & Branscombe, 2010) argues that individuals' internalization of those social identities is then the psychological process that makes coordinated and cooperative group behavior (Turner, 1982) as well as organizational life (Haslam et al., 2003) possible. Social identities determine *who* collaborates as well as *how* they collaborate and *what* they collaborate on (Haslam et al., 2011). They have the capacity not only to make organizations efficient and productive, but also to make them innovative and dynamic (Haslam, 2004; Haslam et al., 2013; Hogg & Terry, 2001; van Knippenberg & Hogg, 2003b).

Yet, to capitalize on this potential, those who seek to create and encourage collaboration need to proactively define and shape identity (Haslam et al., 2011; Reicher et al., 2005). The process by which they do this has been referred to as *identity entrepreneurship* (Reicher & Hopkins, 2001, 2003). Generally speaking, *identity entrepreneurs* "seek to create an inclusive category which embraces all those they seek to mobilize, whose values and priorities are realized in their proposals and of which they themselves are representative" (Reicher et al., 2005, p. 557). As outlined in the social identity approach to leadership (Haslam et al., 2011; Hogg & Terry, 2001; van Knippenberg & Hogg, 2003a), by speaking and acting for "us," people can define and shape who belongs to the group (and who does not) and what the group wants (and does not want) to achieve. In this regard, creating and shaping shared identities becomes an essential dimension of organizational functioning and success (e.g., Fladerer et al., 2020; Millward & Postmes, 2010; van Dick et al., 2018).

Identity entrepreneurship is not bound to a formal role within groups or organizations (Haslam et al., 2011). Regardless of whether or not they are a formal leader, provided that they are understood to represent the group, any member of a group has the capacity to engage in behaviors that shape what the group is about and help to mobilize it in a specific direction. Nevertheless, as we will discover in this chapter, not all efforts to shape "who we are" and "what we want to do" will be equally successful when it comes to inspiring followership.

In this chapter, we develop an analysis of the role leaders play as identity entrepreneurs in bridging the gaps between individuals and groups in organizations. We start by outlining the social identity approach to organizations and leadership and clarifying why social identities are central to the dynamics of organizational life. We then go on to examine how leaders' rhetoric and actions serve to define both category boundaries and category content and explore the impact of this on organizational functioning, as well as how their capacity to do this is contingent on them being seen to represent and promote the interests of group. We continue by discussing various strategies that leaders can employ to create connections among individuals through harnessing the power of social groups. We conclude by discussing how these efforts are more likely to be successful to the extent that they work with, and build upon, the social realities of those they want to lead.

THE SOCIAL IDENTITY APPROACH TO ORGANIZATIONAL LIFE AND LEADERSHIP

The social identity approach (Haslam, 2004; Postmes & Branscombe, 2010) is comprised of two theories that have been explored in 50 years of theoretical and empirical research: *social identity theory* (Tajfel & Turner, 1979) and *self-categorization theory* (Turner et al., 1987; Turner et al., 1994). Social identity theory (Tajfel & Turner, 1979) observes that in a range of social contexts people's sense of self, and hence their behavior, is informed not so much by their individuality (their personal identity; Turner, 1982) as by their sense of themselves as group members (their social identity; Tajfel, 1972). In a bank, for example, people may define themselves as members of groups based on their profession (e.g., "us accountants") or their department (e.g., "us members of the finance department") or as members of a particular team (e.g., "us members of the audit unit"). Among other things, being a member of a group is important for its members because it gives them a sense of orientation, efficacy and connection (Reicher & Haslam, 2006).

Moreover, when people self-define themselves as members of a group this leads to forms of behavior that are qualitatively distinct from behavior based on their personal identity (Turner, 1991). Not least, this is because it leads people to seek to positively differentiate their (in)group (us) from meaningful other (out)groups (them) on relevant dimensions of comparison (Tajfel & Turner, 1979). In simple terms, this means that group members want their group to be unique and special and to be set apart from other groups—so that we are different from, and better than, them.

As Tajfel showed in the famous *minimal group studies*, this motivation is evidenced even in situations where groups have little a priori meaning for their members (Tajfel et al., 1971; for a comprehensive review, see Spears & Otten, 2012). In these studies, schoolboys were categorized into groups on the basis of an arbitrary criterion (e.g., their supposed preference for the abstract painters Klee and Kandinsky). Importantly, they knew nothing about, and did not interact with, other members of their group. Nevertheless, when asked to distribute money or other resources between two other participants—one a member of their own group (the *ingroup*) and the other a member of another group (the *outgroup*)—they reliably favored ingroup members over outgroup members (i.e., giving more money or resources to the ingroup member). In this way, Tajfel (1970) noted that the boys sought to differentiate their ingroup from the outgroup through a strategy of *ingroup favoritism*. This involved reward allocations that served to positively differentiate the ingroup from the outgroup, even if this meant allocating less to the ingroup in absolute terms. More specifically, it became clear that the boys preferred a strategy of maximum positive differentiation in favor of the ingroup over one that maximized absolute benefits for the ingroup (Spears & Otten, 2012).

Beyond the minimal group studies, a rich body of evidence speaks to the general motivation for positive distinctiveness in the form of ingroup differentiation and favoritism. This motivation also becomes stronger the more a given group membership (e.g., as a member of an organization or a particular organizational unit) becomes an important part of a person's self-concept (e.g., as a result of their long tenure in an organization or organizational unit).

Self-categorization theory (Turner, 1991; Turner et al., 1987) focuses on the cognitive mechanisms that underpin social identity processes of this form (for a comprehensive review, see Haslam, 2004). In particular, it argues that individuals' internalization of a shared social identity—a sense of "we-ness"—is the "cognitive mechanism that makes group behavior possible" (Turner, 1982, p. 21). Applying this to the organizational domain, scholars have argued that a sense of shared organizational identity (i.e., a sense of "we-ness' with other organizational members at a given level of inclusiveness; e.g., the organization, the department, the team) is what makes organizational life possible (Haslam, Postmes, et al., 2003).

Turner (1982) argues that the cognitive process underlying the transition from behavior which is motivated by personal identity to that which is motivated by social identity is *self-stereotyping* (or depersonalization). Through this "the self comes to be seen in terms of a category membership that is shared with other in-group members" (Haslam et al., 2011, p. 52). As a result, people see themselves and others, not as individual persons that are different from other individuals, but as members of the group which they belong to. As a result, they will incorporate the norms and goals that define the group as part of who they are, in ways that have important consequences for the way they think, feel, and behave. For example, in contexts where a person sees itself as part of a project team, he or she will be motivated not so much to pursue personal goals (e.g., to get a personal reward, to outperform other team members) as to pursue the collective goals of that team (e.g., by helping other team members, by working toward the team's shared goals). This ability to define the self, and hence to think and behave, in terms of we and us and not just I and me is in turn a basis for a range of organizational behaviors. Among other things, then, research shows that people are more willing (a) to share information with, (b) to trust, and (c) to support those that they define as members of a their ingroup (rather than an outgroup; Greenaway et al., 2015; Levine et al., 2005).

Importantly, social categories are defined in relation to the perceived social reality (Oakes et al., 1994). This means that they (and the meanings attached to them) are not set in stone, but rather are context dependent and evolving. For example, after an organizational restructuring process, two formerly separate departments (e.g., sales and communications) may become one department (e.g., outreach) and hence form a new relevant social category for its members. At the same time, social categories can shape social reality. Indeed, this was seen in the minimal group studies where researchers created a social category (i.e., Klee or Kandinsky lovers) and the subsequent self-categorization of participants as members of those categories shaped the way they behaved in their social world (i.e., who they favored and who they did not). In this way, (cognitive) conceptions of social identities are not static, but responsive to changes in social context (Levine et al., 2005; Oakes et al., 1994). By the same token they can be shaped through proactive constructions (Reicher & Hopkins, 2001, 2003).

Again, self-categorization theory (Turner et al., 1987; Turner et al., 1994) specifies the conditions under which a social category (e.g., a department) becomes psychological operative for its members (i.e., *salient*). More specifically, the theory argues that self-categorization is a context-sensitive process which depends on a person's *readiness* to use a particular self-categorization in interaction with its *fit* (Oakes et al., 1994). This means that a person is more likely to self-categorize as member of a specific group (e.g., as "us sales people"), if (a) this group has been a basis for their self-definition in the past and (b) this self-categorization makes sense of the perceived similarities and differences between people in the specific situation that they find themselves. So, for example, a person is more likely to self-categorize as a member of their organization when representing that organization at an award ceremony than when at a football game because in the former (but not the latter) context this group membership serves to define meaningful similarities with, and differences from, the people around them.

This idea is elaborated in self-categorization theory's principle of *comparative fit* (Oakes et al., 1994). This suggests that a person is more likely to define themselves in terms of a particular self-category (e.g., as a member of Organization X) to the extent that the differences between members of that category on a given dimension of judgment are perceived to be smaller than the differences between members of that category and others that are salient in a particular context (i.e., meta-contrast principle; Turner, 1985). For example, as Figure 3.1 suggests, if two employees of Organization X—one from the Sales Department and one from the Legal Department—find themselves in a context with members of another organization (e.g., Organization Y) present (Case 1), it is more likely that they will define themselves in terms of their organizational identity than would be the case in situations with only them present (Case 2). Because the former context directs the focus on their shared group membership, the two members of Organization X are more likely to see themselves as similar to each other and as having common interests and purpose. Importantly, by restructuring who people perceive themselves to be, changes in comparative context have the capacity to change their behavior (e.g., Levine et al., 2005), a point that has been confirmed in a large number of empirical studies (e.g., Haslam & Turner, 1992, 1995).

Beyond comparative fit, the content of a social category must also be consistent with a person's expectations about the category in order for it to become salient (i.e., it must have high *normative fit*). If the category-related expectations are not met, the social categorization will not be invoked to make sense of the situation. For example, if members of a Sales Team act in ways that violate expectations about this group (e.g., by being introverted and reserved) this social categorization is less likely to be used by others as a basis for social interaction with them.

However, this process can be proactive as well as reactive. This means that, if one is interested in promoting a sense of shared identity between organizational members one does not have to sit and wait for situations to arise in which a specific shared identity is comparatively and normatively fitting. Instead, one can take steps to *define the social context* in ways that make this outcome more likely. For example, if someone is interest in having members of the different departments in Organization X work

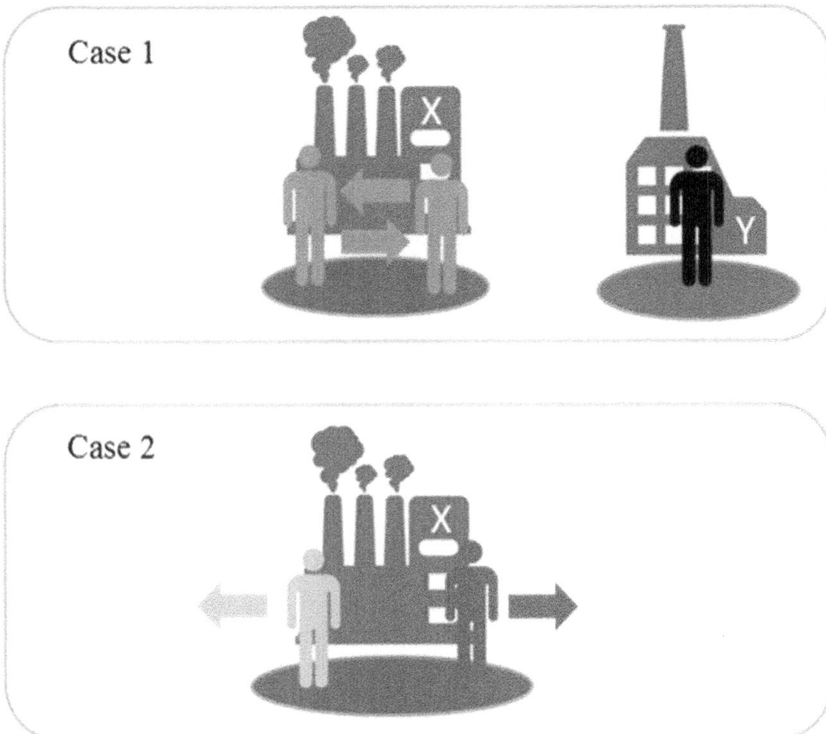

Note: Other things being equal, the meta-contrast principle (Turner, 1985) suggests that two employees of the same Organization X but different departments (e.g., the sales and legal department) are more likely to define themselves in terms of their shared organizational identity in a situation where members of another Organization Y are present (Case 1) than would be the case in a situation where only they are present (Case 2).

Figure 3.1. Variation in self-categorization as a function of comparative context.

together, then he or she may strive to make comparison (out)groups more salient (e.g., by drawing attention to threats posed by Organization Y) with a view to bringing this about.

Taking this forward, in what follows we will consider the role that leaders and other organizational members can play—as identity entrepreneurs—in shaping people's self-categorizations—and hence their behavior—in precisely this way. Here we will argue that leaders have two key tools that they can deploy for this purpose: their rhetoric and their actions (Haslam & Reicher, 2007; Reicher & Hopkins, 2003). The key idea here, then, is that effective group mobilization rests upon a leader's capacity not only to talk the talk that creates shared social identity but to walk the walk.

EFFECTIVE LEADERS NEED TO BE IDENTITY ENTREPRENEURS

Based on the theoretical knowledge derived from the social identity approach, researchers have argued that shared group membership is a basis for mutual social influence (Turner, 1991) and hence *leadership* (Haslam et al., 2011; Hogg, 2001; van Knippenberg & Hogg, 2003a). Not least, this is because "no leader can represent us when there is no 'us' to represent" (Haslam et al., 2011, p. 75). More specifically, it is argued that leadership is a process of *identity management* (Haslam et al., 2011; Steffens, Haslam, Reicher et al., 2014; van Dick et al., 2018) in which would-be leaders (i.e., group members who are looking to shape the behavior of other group members) actively create and shape what it means to be "one of us." In this regard, successful leaders do not simply accept existing social identities as given (or take for granted that there are none) but instead seek actively to create shared identities and promote a particular version of group identity for those they want to lead. This process has been termed identity entrepreneurship (Reicher & Hopkins, 2001, 2003).

As identity entrepreneurs, leaders can use words and actions to win followers over to adopt their version of identity and to motivate them to pursue those actions that are aligned with that version of "who we are." In particular, they can create new identities or shape existing identities by working to define their inclusiveness (i.e., category boundaries) and meaning (i.e., category content). By shaping category boundaries, leaders can define who acts together, who supports each other, and who we care about, while by shaping category content (i.e., the values, ideas, and goals) they can influence what the group is mobilized for (Haslam et al., 2011). A metaphor used by Haslam and colleagues underscores this point: "identity works less as an object than as a container that carries the fuel for journeys to countless different social destinations" (Haslam et al., 2011, p. 162). For example, in times of the *energiewende*, energy companies might change their ideals and strategic goals from "delivering energy" to "delivering *renewable* energy." In the former case, members of the organization may be motivated to guarantee stable delivery of energy and to minimize the costs for customers; while in latter, they are likely to be more motivated to work hard to discover how to incorporate sustainable energy sources into their energy mix and to educate costumers about energy-saving strategies.

It is important to note that the meanings associated with a social identity will constrain leaders' range of influence (Turner, 1991). Groups members can only be persuaded to do things that they see as manifestations of who they are and what they believe in—they won't do anything just because someone tells them to (Haslam et al., 2011). This can be seen in organizational merger and acquisitions activities (e.g., Giessner et al., 2011): Whilst these are often heavily promoted by senior executives, employees often perceive mergers as threat to their organizational identity (e.g., understanding of who we are as organization) and, where this is the case, it often leads to resistance and failure (Marks & Mirvis, 2001; Terry, 2003). In this way, along the lines set out in self-categorization theory (Turner et al., 1987), leadership is a recursive process in which identity shapes leadership and leadership shapes identity (Haslam et al., 2011; Steffens, Haslam, Reicher et al., 2014). For this reason, leaders need to carefully frame their rhetoric and actions to appeal to a group's understanding of "who we are," and to create and promote a version of identity that makes a case for their own group representativeness (or more formally, their group prototypicality; Hogg, 2001; Turner & Haslam, 2001).

To illustrate these points we can draw on insights gleaned from the BBC Prison Study (e.g., Haslam & Reicher, 2007; Reicher et al., 2005; Reicher & Haslam, 2006) and extrapolate their relevance to groups and organizations. The BBC Prison Study was an experimental case study in which 15 men were randomly assigned to one of two groups as prisoners and guards within a simulated prison environment. Even though the prison had certain features that were similar to those in actual prisons, the aim of the study was not so much to recreate a prison as to observe people's behavior within a hierarchical institution in which groups differed in status and power (Reicher & Haslam, 2006). The aspects of the study most relevant to the present discussion related (a) to the emergence of organization and leadership within prisoner and guard groups and (b) to the relationship between this and (changing) patterns of shared social identity within the prison. Although a prison system clearly has unique features, it has many features (e.g., hierarchical structure, status differences, existence of subgroups) that are characteristic of organizations in general. For this reason, the leadership processes observed in the study are pertinent to the analysis of leadership processes in groups and organizations more generally (Haslam et al., 2011).

Leader Rhetoric

Language is a key vehicle through which leaders cultivate and communicate a particular version of a group identity to followers (e.g., Augoustinos & de Garis, 2012; Fladerer et al., 2020; Steffens & Haslam, 2013; for a review see Haslam et al., 2011). In particular, through their use of rhetoric leaders are able to delineate the boundary between us and them and outline what we stand for and want to achieve.

This is seen in the following statement in which DM (a participant who emerged as leader of the prisoners over the course of the study) discusses the problem of the heat in the prison with one of the guards:

> DM: You and I — your group and the group I'm in–both have this problem of the heat. And I've got to sleep in this, there is no way I will. And, you know, I won't bear it. And I think collectively we should do something about it to the people who are running the experiment. Now you know in a normal, day-to-day, real life situation, that's what would happen. (Haslam & Reicher, 2007, p. 136)

Here, DM tries to define the social reality of "who belongs to us" in a way that integrates prisoners as well as guards into an inclusive group (i.e., "*collectively we* should do something about it"; Haslam & Reicher, 2007, p. 136). Instead of separating prisoners and guards, DM reconceptualizes the social structure by introducing two new categories: "us the affected" (i.e., all the participants) and "them the controllers" (i.e., the experimenters). In this way, he tries to mobilize the guards and prisoners to work together.

In this regard, we-referencing language is a particularly important tool with which leaders can create and shape a sense of shared social identity (see Fiol, 2002). This is seen in the following extract, where one of the prisoners, PB (who has stolen one of the guard's keys) discuss how to utilize this to improve their situation:

> PB: What the issue is, they want the fucking keys back and all I am saying is I want to use the keys as a lever to move us forward as a group.
>
> DM: Can I make a suggestion? What we should do is, we should suggest to them —and I suggested this to a couple of lads before, and the guards, and they were nodding—we should have a forum that meets once a day between us, all of us, the guards and us, and in the forum we'll discuss the grievances we've got. (Haslam & Reicher, 2007, p. 136)

In this extract, PB speaks of his plans to utilize his theft of the guards' keys in an individualistic manner: that is, what *he* wants to do. DM, on the other hand, speaks of his plans in a collective manner: focusing instead on what *we* should do. So, while PB suggests an individual heroic act, DM advocates collective action. The fact that this version of identity (i.e., cooperation with the guards) prevails in the group can then be seen in a discussion between PB and another prisoner, JE (Haslam & Reicher,

2007, p. 138). In the discussion, JE picks up on what has been articulated as collective vision by DM and expresses the desire to act collectively rather than individually.

Similar processes can also be observed in the world at large. For example, in a 2005 interview (Heracleous & Klaering, 2014), Steve Jobs explained why Apple moved to use Intel to provide processors for its computers:

> You know we have a good relationship with IBM and they've got a product road map and today the products are really good. But as we look out into the future where we wanna go is maybe a little bit different. We can envision some awesome products we wanna build for our customers in the next few years and as we look out a year or 2 in the future, Intel's processor road map really aligns with where we wanna go much more than any others. So that's why I think why we're gonna begin this transition now and its gonna take 2 years, but I think its gonna get us where we wanna be to build the kind of future products we wanna build. Our products today—our products today are fine, but it's really you know a year or 2 down the future where we see some issues. (cited in Heracleous & Klaering, 2014, p. 145)

In the interview we see that Jobs frames his answer around the idea that the change enables Apple to realize "who they are" in terms of what they value (i.e., innovative "awesome products"). Further evidence of the relevance of leaders' efforts to speak on behalf of the group comes from an archival study by Fladerer et al. (2020). In an analysis of the use of identity-related language of DAX chief executive officers (CEO) between 2000 and 2016, these researchers found that there was a positive relationship between CEOs' we-referencing language and indicators of organizational performance (i.e., return on assets and sales per employee). Based on these results, the authors suggest that we-referencing language serves to fulfill two core functions: (1) it signals leaders' own identification with the group to the members of that group and (2) it clarifies what the groups stands for (and what it does not stand for) and what it wants to achieve (see also Steffens & Haslam, 2013).

In sum, leaders' rhetoric—particularly, their capacity to speak on behalf of a group—plays a central role in their efforts to be *entrepreneurs of identity*. With their words, leaders can create (but also undermine) a shared sense of "us" among those they seek to lead. However, in the end, leaders not only have to "talk the talk of identity" but also to walk the walk (Haslam et al., 2011; Hogg et al., 2012).

Leader Action

Alongside rhetoric about who we are and what we want to be, leaders' ambitions to create and embody a sense of shared identity also need to be reinforced by their actions (Haslam et al., 2011). Among other things, to be effective, these need to center on the creation of structures, practices, and rituals that embody and celebrate the group. These become manifestations of "what it means to be us" and help to give substance to the group's norms, beliefs, and values. For example, in the BBC Prison Study, DM not only sought to represent the group, but also suggested the creation of a forum as a *structural solution* that would allow the prisoners to present their demands to the guards. In particular, the forum allowed the prisoners to negotiate (and improve) their situation as a group rather than as individuals. The importance of providing structure can be seen from what happened after DM was removed from the experiment by the researchers. While support for his ideas remained high—among both prisoners and guards—the group lacked the competence to implement the forum. And without a leader who would coordinate the group's efforts, conflict between the guards and prisoners flared up again (see Haslam et al., 2011; Haslam & Reicher, 2007; Reicher et al., 2005).

The question of which structures, practices and rituals will be valued by the group depends on the *content* of its shared identity (i.e., what it means to be us). Different identities are associated with different sets of norms, beliefs and values (e.g., being a doctor versus being a broker) and through the process of identification with a group, group members will base their behavior on this shared understanding (Turner, 1982). Essentially, for leaders, putting identity into action means introducing and facilitating those structures that allow group members to live out and derive meaning from their group membership, as well as to make it visible to others (Ashforth & Kreiner, 1999). In organizational contexts, there are a range of structures or rituals that serve this function. For example, a leader might introduce standing (or even walking) meetings in order for group members to live out a sense that the group values health and thereby embed this as part of their self-understanding. By the same token, in a group that values innovativeness, it might be more useful for a leader to embrace activities that signal a commitment to innovation (e.g., introducing a new app to manage projects).

EFFECTIVE LEADERS NEED TO BE INGROUP PROTOTYPES AND INGROUP CHAMPIONS

As identity entrepreneurs, leaders not only need to define meaningful groups, but they also need to represent and advance those groups. This process revolves around taking the *group* forward and therefore it is ultimately not so much about leaders as about the perception of potential followers: "Followers do not automatically accept what is put to them, rather they weigh it and evaluate it on the basis of their prior experiences and the other sources of information available to them" (Reicher et al., 2005, p. 561). Critical to this process is the question of whether a leader is perceived to be "of the group" (rather than representative only of themselves or of an outgroup) and "for the group" (rather than for themselves or for an outgroup).

Being Seen as "One of Us"

Being seen to be of the group—that is, representing the *group prototype*—is an essential asset for leaders. In essence, a prototypical group member embodies the "core attributes of the group that make this group special and distinct from others" (Steffens, Haslam, Reicher, Platow, et al., 2014, p. 1003). The degree to which an individual is seen as prototypical in part determines his or her ability to influence other ingroup members (Barreto & Hogg, 2017; van Knippenberg, 2011). For example, a prototypical leader will be seen as more charismatic (than a nonprototypical or outgroup leader) by his followers (Platow et al., 2006; Steffens, Haslam, & Reicher, et al., 2014).

This point is demonstrated by two experimental studies conducted with undergraduate students by Platow and colleagues (2006), in which potential followers were presented with in formation which indicated that the group leader was either prototypical or nonprototypical of the group. After reading a written statement by the leader asking for followers' approval and support of a campaign, potential followers then rated the leader's persuasiveness and charisma. Findings showed that the more representative a leader was of perceivers' ingroup the more they were seen as charismatic and persuasive. In this way, portraying oneself—and being perceived—as representative of the group puts leaders in a position to *redefine* the boundaries and the content of the group (e.g., Steffens et al., 2013). Coming back to Steve Jobs, he was often perceived to embody what Apple was: creative, innovative, and ambitious. Basically, Jobs was Apple. As a result, he was able to motivate followers in ways that translated his vision of Apple into material reality.

At the same time, research suggests that prototypical leaders are evaluated more leniently (than nonleader group members or outgroup members) when they deviate (i.e., innovate or transgress) from group norms (e.g., Abrams et al., 2013; Abrams et al., 2018). In the case of Steve Jobs, for example, biographers have observed that he regularly crossed the line in social interactions by being rude and disrespectful to employees (Isaacson, 2011). However, it appears that employees were forgiving of these transgressions, because he was understood to represent the best of the group in other aspects which were central to the group's identity (cf. Abrams et al., 2013). In this way, it is critical for leaders to be perceived to be "one of us" in order for followers to take their lead when they deviate from established norms and goals—both in the form of innovations as well as transgressions.

Demonstrating That One Is "Doing it for Us"

We noted above that after he had stolen the guards' keys, PB told his fellow prisoners: "What the issue is, they want the fucking keys back and all I am saying is I want to use the keys as a lever to move us forward as a group" (Haslam & Reicher, 2007, p. 136). However, this attempt to rally other prisoners behind him failed. In large part this was because, as a result of his individualistic approach, other group members did not perceive him to be an advocate for the group's interest and goals. In short, he was not seen to be an *ingroup champion* (Haslam et al., 2011; Steffens, Haslam, Reicher, et al., 2014). Steffens and colleagues (2014) define an ingroup champion as someone who advances the shared interests of the group they want to lead.

As with "being one of us," demonstrating that one is "doing it for us" helps to secure support from other group members (e.g., potential followers; e.g., Haslam & Platow, 2001; van Knippenberg & van Knippenberg, 2005). In an empirical demonstration of this point, Haslam and Platow (2001) invited students to participate in a study of attitudes toward student leaders. In one experiment (Study 2), participants were introduced to Chris—the head of the students' representative council at an Australian university—via a video interview. They then learned about a new policy that he wanted to introduce that involved erecting permanent billboard sites on campus, and about his decision to nominate six members to a council discussing government's decision to cut university funding (or tighten gun control). Participants were randomly assigned to one of three conditions depicting Chris's nomination strategy in which this was either identity affirming (i.e., nominating more representatives of the ingroup position), evenhanded (i.e., nominating an equal number of representatives of the in- and outgroup position), or identity negating (i.e., nominating more representatives of the outgroup position). After the participants saw the video and learned about Chris's decision, they were asked to indicate how fair and sensible his billboard policy was. Reactions were equally positive in the identity-affirming and even-handed conditions but significantly less positive in the identity-negating condition. However, when the participants were given an opportunity to generate ideas to back up his billboard policy, only those in the identity-affirming condition showed any enthusiasm for this task. In other words, it was only when Chris had a history of championing the group that other group members were willing to demonstrate the followership that would translate that policy into reality.

Along related lines, recent work in an organizational setting by Steffens and colleagues (2020) investigated the effect of the level of CEO pay on personal identification with the leader as well as perceptions of leadership and charisma. In an experimental as well as field study, results showed that employees identified less with a high-paid CEO than with one who was paid less. This is, in turn, fed into perceptions of the CEO's perceived identity leadership and charisma. Again then, by undermining a sense shared of identity between leaders and followers, CEO's high pay undermined their ability to secure followership.

In sum, being perceived to be of the group and for the group is critical to identity leaders' efforts to mobilize ingroup members. How though, is this to be achieved—particularly in a world in which there are typically multiple groups to represent and where intergroup division abounds? This is a question that researchers have tackled by outlining different strategies for redefining group boundaries to form superordinate groups that are more inclusive(e.g., Hornsey & Hogg, 2000a) or for shaping intergroup relations in ways that establish cooperative intergroup norms (e.g., Hogg et al., 2012; Pittinsky & Simon, 2007). In the following section, we review these strategies, which are illustrated in Figure 3.2, and present an integrated and practical model for developing a shared identity within organizations—the ASPIRe model (Haslam et al., 2003; Peters, Haslam, Ryan, & Steffens, 2015). To begin this section, however, we first explain why leaders need to focus on understanding the identity of the groups they want to lead before embarking on the journey of identity entrepreneurship.

BRINGING INDIVIDUALS AND GROUPS TOGETHER IN ORGANIZATIONS

Leaders rarely—indeed probably never—have the opportunity to perform identity leadership on a blank slate. More likely, different groups, encompassing their unique set of values, norms, and ideals, already exist within the environment in which they seek to have influence. To be able to work with these, leaders need to reflect and understand these identities. Indeed, engaging in process of understanding a group's identity is likely to be especially important when it comes to winning over low identifiers—in organizational settings, those individuals who do not identify with the organization or the groups within it or who have ambivalent feelings about these entities (Kreiner & Ashforth, 2004; Schuh et al., 2016).

In this regard, it is clear that modern organizations are differentiated in multiple hierarchically structured formal social categories (e.g., as separate work teams, departments, divisions) of the form shown on formal organizational charts. Yet alongside formal groups (e.g., project teams), cross-cutting identities, which can be both formal or informal, are often important for organizational members (Ashforth & Johnson, 2001; Ellemers & Rink, 2005). Informal categories may be based on social relationships (e.g., friendships), common interests (e.g., sports fans), or demographic characteristics (e.g., age, gender or ethnicity). As a consequence, multiple social identities are available to organizational members (Ashforth & Johnson, 2001; Ellemers & Rink, 2005). It is therefore important for leaders to be aware of the fact that formal groupings do not necessarily reflect an individual's experience of social life within an organization (Peters et al., 2013; Peters et al., 2015). For example, although they formally work together in a research team, there may be informal group boundaries between academics and technicians that adversely affect their collaboration.

If leaders fail to understand the social reality of organizational members—and more specifically, the social identities that shape their behavior—it is likely that their efforts to create and shape shared social identities will also fail (Haslam et al., 2011). For example, if the words and actions of the leader of a work group imagine the team to be a united group when in reality other social identities are salient for its members (e.g., as academics and technicians) then it is likely that those words and actions will have limited meaning and hence limited impact.

Reflecting Relevant Group Memberships

Understanding social identities in organizational contexts needs to be a *bottom-up* rather than a top-down process (Haslam, Eggins, et al., 2003; Peters et al., 2013). This means that to be able to mobilize social identity as a resource, leaders need to understand both (a) which groups—formal as well as informal—people identify with and what they see as the defining elements of these groups (i.e., norms and goals), and (b) how different groups relate to each other within the organization (Haslam et al., 2017; Peters et al., 2013). Attentive observation and careful listening certainly help in this regard, but the insights leaders take away from these activities will often be limited. Accordingly, there is value in taking a structured approach to this process. With this in mind, researchers recently developed a *social identity mapping* tool (Bentley et al., 2020; Cruwys et al., 2016) to help capture the group memberships and patterns of intergroup relations that inform people's behavior in organizations and the world at large.

In organizational contexts, this mapping process asks respondents to identify personally relevant groups in the organization and then to identify other groups that their group interacts with and to characterize the nature and quality of the relationships with those groups. For example, despite being formally categorized as members of the same department, different groups in a marketing department may perceive themselves to be competition for scarce organizational resources (e.g., money, staff, time) rather than as allies. Understanding this (e.g., through social identity mapping) therefore gives would-be leaders a clearer picture of the nature of the organizational identities that bear upon their organizational behavior. Sensitivity to this then allows leaders to engage in identity entrepreneurship more effectively through rhetoric and actions that help to create and shape (new) group identities that are meaningful to potential followers. Three strategies to do so are discussed next.

The Importance of Respecting Relevant Identities

One strategy commonly applied by those who seek to lead—indeed, the one employed by DM in the BBC Prison Study—is to introduce a superordinate group identity that encompasses multiple (sub)groups. The idea here is for leaders to cultivate a broader, more inclusive "we" category that members of different groups can all identify with. This involves leaders trying to break down subgroup "us versus them" dynamics by redefining group boundaries. In the example above, DM suggests to form a new group that encompasses both, prisoners and guards, that works collectively together (Haslam & Reicher, 2007). In organizational contexts, this could resemble leaders' efforts to promote a sense of superordinate organizational identity (e.g., we are *one* company; Strategy 1a). While this strategy seems appealing—and there is some laboratory evidence that can support it (Dick et al., 2005)—several authors suggest that introducing superordinate groups can threaten a person's beliefs of "who I am" and "where I belong." On a group level, this may result in a backlash on relationships between the subgroups via increased bias and conflict (Hornsey & Hogg, 2000a; Pittinsky & Simon, 2007). One way to prevent this is to pay attention and respect relevant (sub)group identities (cf. Eggins et al., 2003).

This is for three reasons. First, broad and inclusive groups—such as an organization with hundreds or thousands of employees—often do not satisfy individuals' need for in-group distinctiveness (Hornsey & Hogg, 2000a, 2000b). In addition, broad social groups tend to be less meaning-

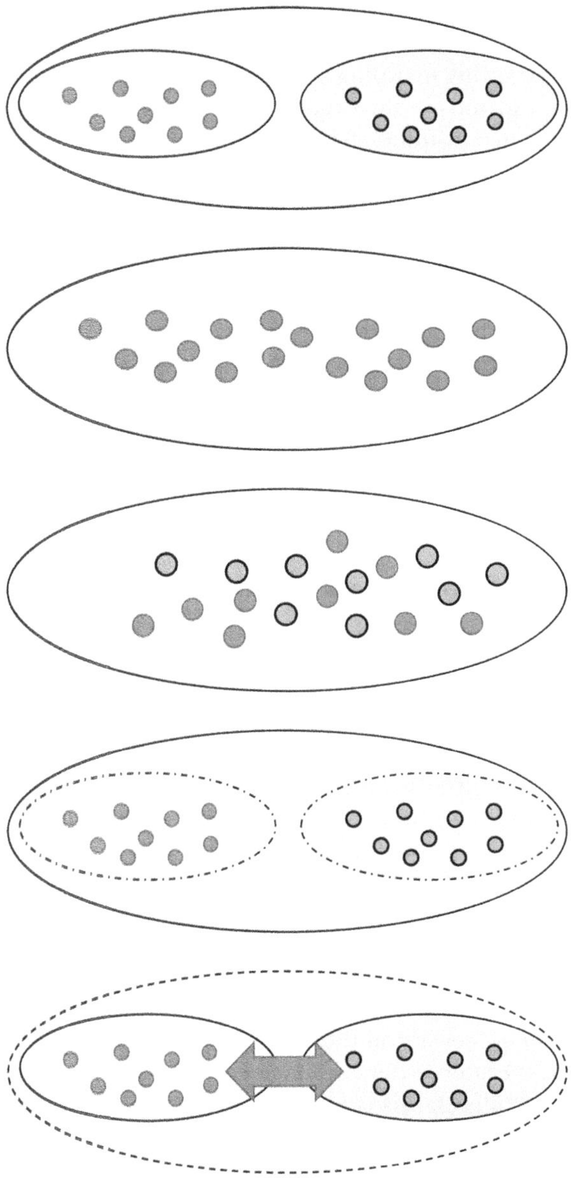

Figure 3.2. Strategies of identity entrepreneurship within organizations.

ful for persons' day-to-day lives. For example, generally organizational members identify more strongly with their work group than with their organization as a whole (Riketta & van Dick, 2005). Second, individuals may perceive groups to be incompatible or even be in conflict which will reduce their willingness to identify with those groups. Third, members of subgroups will resist to be categorized in superordinate categories when the divide is diagnostic of unfavorable real-life differences, such as low status or prestige. The groups individuals are a part of give them a sense of belonging and purpose and they do not want to see them to be marginalized in favor of more inclusive groups.

By way of example, we can turn to an experiment conducted by Eggins and colleagues (2003). In the experiment, male and female participants engaged in a mixed-sex negotiation on strategies to increase university health funding for men and women. In a first phase, participants' social identity as men and women was either acknowledged or ignored. When each group's identity (i.e., as men or women) was recognized appropriately in the second phase of the experiment, participants approached the mixed-sex negotiations with higher expectations of consensus, lower expectations of bias of the other-sex participants and—after the process—reported higher levels of satisfaction with the collaboration (see also Hornsey & Hogg, 2000b).

Thus, ignoring or downplaying relevant (sub)group memberships in the creation of new groups will more likely do more harm than good. Instead, and as shown in Strategy 1b, efforts to create shared understanding are more likely to lead to positive outcomes when relevant group identities are recognized and respected (e.g., Eggins et al., 2003).

Promoting Dual Identifications

A second strategy (Strategy 2), is often referred to as *promoting dual identifications* (Hewstone & Brown, 1986), focuses on promoting identification with both a subjectively important subgroup and a more inclusive, superordinate group (e.g., a professional specialists and a department as a whole). For a leader of a research department, this could mean to acknowledge group members' identifications as technicians or academics whilst also making the superordinate identity as research department salient for all members. This could, for example, happen in team meetings or other internal communications forums by addressing issues (and their effects) on the subgroup and superordinate group level alike. Thereby, leaders can reduce the threat to individuals' valued self-concepts in terms of their group memberships and increase the willingness to engage in cooperative behaviors on the superordinate group level (Eggins et al., 2003; Hornsey & Hogg, 2000a).

Successfully balancing multiple identities is a challenging task that faces many obstacles. A first challenge may be leaders' own subgroup affiliation(s). Even when leaders promote identification with a superordinate identity, they will still be seen as a representative of their subgroup (e.g., as technician or academic). This is likely to limit their influence over members of the other subgroup and thus, hinder their leadership effectiveness (Duck & Fielding, 1999, 2003).

As a demonstration of this, an experimental study by Duck and Fielding (1999) examined individuals' perceptions of leaders in situations in which two subgroups were meant to integrate as part of a superordinate group. Results showed that participants were still aware of the leader's subgroup affiliation which limited their ability to elicit favorable responses from those they sought to lead. When the leader was member of one subgroup (rather than both or neither one), he was perceived to be less fair, less concerned with the interests of the superordinate group and more biased toward their subgroup.

A second challenge for leaders is the compatibility of different groups: While a superordinate identity can bind subgroups together in specific situations—such as competition with an outgroup on the superordinate level (e.g., another organization; Duck & Fielding, 1999)—it will not eradicate conflicts or incompatibilities at the subgroup level. Thus, if subgroup members do not see a common ground that justifies recategorization they will likely resist leaders' efforts to create a superordinate identity (Pittinsky & Simon, 2007).

Shaping Intergroup Relational Identities

The two strategies presented so far focused on creating new and redrawing category boundaries to bring individuals and groups together. A third strategy, advocated by Pittinsky and Simon (2007) as well as Hogg and colleagues (2012), focuses on shaping group norms and values; that is, the category content in terms of "how we relate to another group." Specifically, rather than introducing a new (superordinate) identity, the researchers argue that leaders can define cooperation with a specific other group as norm or core value of the ingroup (Strategy 3). Hogg and colleagues termed this aspect of social identity: *intergroup relational identity*. They define it as "the self defined in terms of the relationship between one's own group and a specific outgroup" (Hogg et al., 2012, p. 239). This encompasses reducing the negative feelings toward the outgroup as well as strengthening positive feelings toward the outgroup ("we like them"; Pittinsky & Simon, 2007). This is a point often misconceived by scholars and practitioners; strongly identifying with one's own group does not necessarily imply derogating or working against other groups (Jetten et al., 1996; Steffens, Haslam, Reicher et al., 2014). Indeed, many groups, such as the Red Cross, put giving to others and other groups at the heart of their identity. Another example can be found in the national value of *manaakitanga* in New Zealand. Rooted in the culture of the Māori people, *manaakitanga* means being hospitable and looking after visitors and caring how others are treated. That is why the violent death of a young backpacker traveling New Zealand in late 2018 evoked nationwide feelings of shame and guilt expressed by prime minister Jacinda Ardern (Ainge Roy, 2018).

A strength of this strategy is its focus on shaping the group's norms and values without the necessity of creating new shared identities. This reduces the risk of group members' resistance to being recategorized into a broader—potentially less meaningful and incompatible—group (Hogg et al., 2012). Applying this to organizations, leaders may seek to shape how we as the human resources department want to interact with members of the legal department. In a hospital, this could mean to define how *we*, the group of doctors, want to interact with *them*, the group of nurses.

As shown in Figure 3.2, leaders can engage in different strategies to create and develop group identities. Based on the chosen strategy, entrepreneurs of identity face different challenges. The three core challenges are (1) to recognize identities that are meaningful to organizational members in addition to groups assigned through the formal structure of the organization and to respect those when developing (new) identities, (2) to align subgroup and superordinate identities in ways that reduce negative and bolster positive attitudes (and behaviors) toward other groups, and (3) to ensure that their verbal efforts that advocate intergroup collaboration are met with congruent actions that create social reality for organizational members.

The ASPIRe Model

Integrating the findings previously described and translating them into a model of practice, researchers developed the ASPIRe—*actualizing social and personal identity resources*—model (e.g., Haslam, Eggins et al., 2003; Peters et al., 2013; Peters et al., 2015). This model offers a structured, bottom-up process for leaders and organizations to form *organically* superordinate identities (e.g., department or organizational identities). The ASPIRe model has two particular strengths: (1) it provides practical methods and tools, and (2) it acknowledges the role followers (i.e., rank-

and-file members) play in this process. That is, rather than assuming followers to be passive consumers of identity, here they are active agents in the process of identity creation and development. In the following, we will outline the model and the activities involved.

The ASPIRe model (e.g., Haslam, Eggins et al., 2003; Peters et al., 2013; Peters et al., 2015) consists of four phases (see Figure 3.3): Two of these take stage at the subgroup level and two on the superordinate level. Specifically, the objective of the first phase, AIRing, is to identify in a bottom-up manner the relevant groups within a superordinate group (e.g., organization or department) and the relationships among these. As described above, the technique of social identity mapping (Bentley et al., 2020; Cruwys et al., 2016) can be applied in this phase.

Once the groups are identified, in the second phase, subcasing, members of each group come together to discuss their groups' key goals and barriers to their achievement. The goal is to allow members to raise shared concerns and achieve a consensual understanding—thereby increasing the likelihood of creating dual identifications (e.g., Eggins et al., 2003).

Moving into the third phase, supercasing, and to the superordinate group level, the subgroups (or representatives of these) present the outcomes of the previous phase to the remaining other groups. Jointly the subgroups then discuss these outcomes before identifying shared higher order goals at the superordinate level that promote organizational functioning. This process should increase shared understanding alignment between groups.

In the final phase, organizing, the subgroups' and higher order goals are translated into a strategy in the form of a formal plan (with deadlines, responsibilities, etc.) by the subgroups (or their representatives).

Peters et al. (2013) present a test of the ASPIRe model in action: The researchers worked with 20 leading members of a military health services organization in the United Kingdom in a 2-day organizational strategy workshop. In line with the models' assumptions, at the end of the first day (after Phase 1 and 2), participants reported positive change in terms of greater goal clarity and identification with their subgroups. At the end of the second day, participants not only reported a positive change in goal clarity, identification and alignment between groups but also a positive change in organizational identification. Furthermore, participants perceived their organizational strategy to be clearer and expressed stronger support for it.

The structure of the program gives all groups members—formal leaders and followers alike—the opportunity to participate in a shared development process—a form of *action-based learning* to create leadership within an organization (Day & Harrison, 2007). Thus, rather than forcing a version

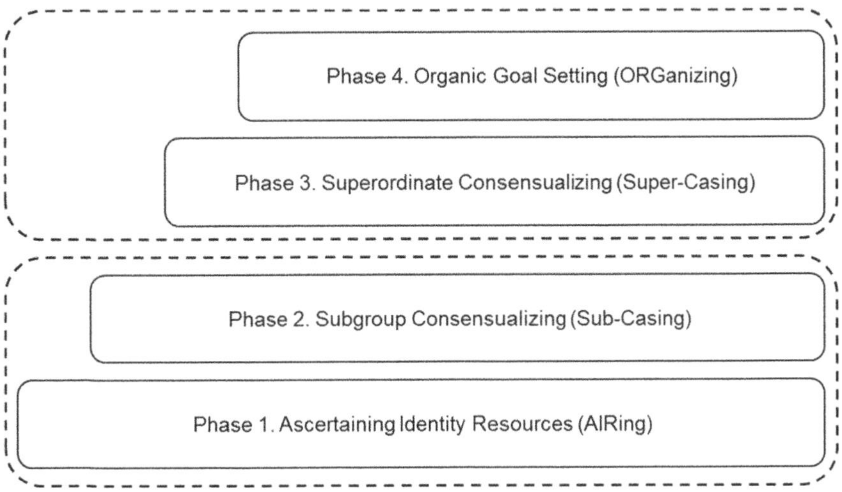

Source: Based on description by Haslam et al. (2003).
Note: Phase 1 and 2 are subgroup phases. Phase 3 and 4 are superordinate phases.

Figure 3.3. The ASPIRe model.

of identity on group members, leaders interact with other members to coproduce a sense of shared collective identity (i.e., a shared sense of us).

CONCLUSION

Today's organizations are differentiated social systems that offer a multitude of formal and informal social identities for organizational members to choose from. These identities are meaningful aspects of people's subjective social reality. Organizational members' identification with specific groups affects their behavior within the organization (Haslam, 2004). On the one hand, a shared social identity facilitates organizational functioning such that members are more willing to cooperate exchange information and contribute to shared goals. At the same time, group boundaries may create obstacles for collaboration (e.g., silo thinking) resulting in conflicts and inefficiencies (Richter et al., 2006).

These findings underscore the importance of organizational leaders acting as entrepreneurs of identity (Reicher & Hopkins, 2001, 2003). As identity entrepreneurs, leaders bring people together by creating a shared sense of we and us (Haslam et al., 2011; Steffens, Haslam, Reicher, et al., 2014). Through their rhetoric and actions, they clarify people's understanding of who belongs to the group (and who does not) and what the group stands for (and what not). However, ultimately, leaders' efforts will be much more likely to be successful if they are also seen to embody the group and champion its interests.

Bringing identity entrepreneurship into practice, leaders can engage in different strategies to bridging the gap between individuals and groups. We discussed two strategies that focus on developing superordinate identities (e.g., Eggins et al., 2003) and a third strategy that puts emphasis on shaping the relational identity between two groups (Hogg et al., 2012). Integrating these strategies and adding the aspect of leader and follower cocreation, we described the ASPIRe Model (Haslam, Eggins, et al., 2003; Peters et al., 2013) as a means to develop organically (as bottom-up process) a shared organizational identity.

To conclude, we would note that identity entrepreneurship is neither a unidirectional, top-down process nor is it a one-shot activity. Instead, it is a continuous process of reflecting, negotiating and cocreating. To bring people together and be effective as leaders, leaders need to listen to those they seek to lead because this puts them in a much better position to understand *who we are* and to be able to shape *who we want to be*.

REFERENCES

Abrams, D., Randsley de Moura, G., & Travaglino, G. A. (2013). A double standard when group members behave badly: Transgression credit to ingroup leaders. *Journal of Personality and Social Psychology, 105*, 799–815. https://doi.org/10.1037/a0033600

Abrams, D., Travaglino, G. A., Marques, J. M., Pinto, I., & Levine, J. M. (2018). Deviance credit: Tolerance of deviant ingroup leaders is mediated by their accrual of prototypicality and conferral of their right to be supported. *Journal of Social Issues, 74*, 36–55. https://doi.org/10.1111/josi.12255

Ainge Roy, E. (2018, December 10). 'Your daughter should have been safe here': NZ's apology to family of Grace Millane. *The Guardian*. Retrieved from https://www.theguardian.com/world/2018/dec/10/grace-millane-accused-appears-in-court-for-the-first-time

Ashforth, B. E., & Johnson, S. A. (2001). Which hat to wear?: The relative salience of multiple identities in organizational contexts. In M. A. Hogg & D. J. Terry (Eds.), *Social identity processes in organizational contexts* (31–48). Psychology Press.

Ashforth, B. E., & Kreiner, G. E. (1999). "How can you do it?": Dirty work and the challenge of constructing a positive identity. *Academy of Management Review, 24*, 413. https://doi.org/10.2307/259134

Augoustinos, M., & de Garis, S. (2012). 'Too Black or not Black enough': Social identity complexity in the political rhetoric of Barack Obama. *European Journal of Social Psychology, 42*, 564–577. https://doi.org/10.1002/ejsp.1868

Barreto, N. B., & Hogg, M. A. (2017). Evaluation of and support for group prototypical leaders: A meta-analysis of twenty years of empirical research. *Social Influence, 12*, 41–55. https://doi.org/10.1080/15534510.2017.1316771

Bentley, S. V., Greenaway, K. H., Haslam, S. A., Cruwys, T., Steffens, N. K., Haslam, C., & Cull, B. (2020). Social identity mapping online. *Journal of Personality and Social Psychology, 118*(2), 213–241. https://doi.org/10.1037/pspa0000174

Cruwys, T., Steffens, N. K., Haslam, S. A., Haslam, C., Jetten, J., & Dingle, G. A. (2016). Social identity mapping: A procedure for visual representation and assessment of subjective multiple group memberships. *British Journal of Social Psychology, 55*, 613–642. https://doi.org/10.1111/bjso.12155

Day, D. V., & Harrison, M. M. (2007). A multilevel, identity-based approach to leadership development. *Human Resource Management Review, 17*, 360–373. https://doi.org/10.1016/j.hrmr.2007.08.007

Dick, R., Wagner, U., Stellmacher, J., & Christ, O. (2005). Category salience and organizational identification. *Journal of Occupational and Organizational Psychology, 78*, 273–285. https://doi.org/10.1348/096317905X25779

Duck, J. M., & Fielding, K. S. (1999). Leaders and subgroups: One of us or one of them? *Group Processes & Intergroup Relations, 2*, 203–230. https://doi.org/10.1177/1368430299023001

Duck, J. M., & Fielding, K. S. (2003). Leaders and their treatment of subgroups: Implications for evaluations of the leader and the superordinate group. *European Journal of Social Psychology, 33*, 387–401. https://doi.org/10.1002/ejsp.153

Eggins, R. A., Haslam, S. A., & Reynolds, K. J. (2003). Social identity and negotiation: Subgroup representation and superordinate consensus. *Personality and Social Psychology Bulletin, 28*, 887–899. https://doi.org/10.1177/014616720202800703

Ellemers, N., & Rink, F. (2005). Identity in work groups: The beneficial and detrimental consequences of multiple identities and group norms for collaboration and group performance. In E. J. Lawler & S. R. Thye (Eds.), *Advances in group processes* (Vol. 22, pp. 1–41). Elsevier JAI.

Fiol, C. M. (2002). Capitalizing on paradox: The role of language in transforming organizational identities. *Organization Science, 13*, 653–666. https://doi.org/10.1287/orsc.13.6.653.502

Fladerer, M. P., Haslam, S. A., Steffens, N. K., & Frey, D. (2020). The value of speaking for "us": The relationship between CEOs' use of I- and we-referencing language and subsequent organizational performance. *Journal of Business and Psychology*. Advance online publication. https://doi.org/10.1007/s10869-019-09677-0

Giessner, S. R., Ullrich, J., & van Dick, R. (2011). Social identity and corporate mergers. *Social and Personality Psychology Compass, 5*, 333–345. https://doi.org/10.1111/j.1751-9004.2011.00357.x

Greenaway, K. H., Wright, R. G., Willingham, J., Reynolds, K. J., & Haslam, S. A. (2015). Shared identity is key to effective communication. *Personality and Social Psychology Bulletin, 41*, 171–182. https://doi.org/10.1177/0146167214559709

Haslam, S. A. (2004). *Psychology in organizations: The social identity approach*. SAGE.

Haslam, S. A., Adarves-Yorno, I., Postmes, T., & Jans, L. (2013). The collective origins of valued originality: A social identity approach to creativity. *Personality and Social Psychology Review*, *17*, 384–401. https://doi.org/10.1177/1088868313498001

Haslam, S. A., Eggins, R. A., & Reynolds, K. J. (2003). The ASPIRe model: Actualizing social and personal identity resources to enhance organizational outcomes. *Journal of Occupational and Organizational Psychology*, *76*, 83–113. https://doi.org/10.1348/096317903321208907

Haslam, S. A., & Platow, M. J. (2001). The link between leadership and followership: How affirming social identity translates vision into action. *Personality and Social Psychology Bulletin*, *27*, 1469–1479. https://doi.org/10.1177/01461672012711008

Haslam, S. A., Postmes, T., & Ellemers, N. (2003). More than a metaphor: Organizational identity makes organizational life possible. *British Journal of Management*, *14*, 357–369. https://doi.org/10.1111/j.1467-8551.2003.00384.x

Haslam, S. A., & Reicher, S. (2007). Identity entrepreneurship and the consequences of identity failure: The dynamics of leadership in the BBC prison study. *Social Psychology Quarterly*, *70*, 125–147. https://doi.org/10.1177/019027250707000204

Haslam, S. A., Reicher, S. D., & Platow, M. J. (2011). *The new psychology of leadership: Identity, influence and power*. Psychology Press.

Haslam, S. A., Steffens, N. K., Peters, K., Boyce, R. A., Mallett, C. J., & Fransen, K. (2017). A social identity approach to leadership development. *Journal of Personnel Psychology*, *16*, 113–124. https://doi.org/10.1027/1866-5888/a000176

Haslam, S. A., & Turner, J. C. (1992). Context-dependent variation in social stereotyping 2: The relationship between frame of reference, self-categorization and accentuation. *European Journal of Social Psychology*, *22*, 251–277. https://doi.org/10.1002/ejsp.2420220305

Haslam, S. A., & Turner, J. C. (1995). Context-dependent variation in social stereotyping 3: Extremism as a self-categorical basis for polarized judgement. *European Journal of Social Psychology*, *25*, 341–371. https://doi.org/10.1002/ejsp.2420250307

Heracleous, L., & Klaering, L. A. (2014). Charismatic leadership and rhetorical competence: An analysis of Steve Jobs's rhetoric. *Group & Organization Management*, *39*, 131–161. https://doi.org/10.1177/1059601114525436

Hewstone, M., & Brown, R. (1986). Contact is not enough: An intergroup perspective on the 'contact hypothesis'. In M. Hewstone & R. Brown (Eds.), *Social psychology and society: Contact and conflict in intergroup encounters* (pp. 1–44). Basil Blackwell.

Hogg, M. A. (2001). A social identity theory of leadership. *Personality and Social Psychology Review*, *5*, 184–200. https://doi.org/10.1207/S15327957PSPR0503_1

Hogg, M. A., & Terry, D. J. (Eds.). (2001). *Social identity processes in organizational contexts*. Psychology Press.

Hogg, M. A., van Knippenberg, D., & Rast, D. E., III. (2012). Intergroup leadership in organizations: Leading across group and organizational boundaries.

Academy of Management Review, *37*, 232–255. https://doi.org/10.5465/amr.2010.0221

Hornsey, M. J., & Hogg, M. A. (2000a). Assimilation and diversity: An integrative model of subgroup relations. *Personality and Social Psychology Review*, *4*, 143–156. https://doi.org/10.1207/s15327957pspr0402_03

Hornsey, M. J., & Hogg, M. A. (2000b). Subgroup relations: A comparison of mutual intergroup differentiation and common ingroup identity Models of prejudice reduction. *Personality and Social Psychology Bulletin*, *26*, 242–256. https://doi.org/10.1177/0146167200264010

Isaacson, W. (2011). *Steve Jobs*. Simon & Schuster.

Jetten, J., Spears, R., & Manstead, A. S. R. (1996). Intergroup norms and intergroup discrimination: Distinctive self-categorization and social identity effects. *Journal of Personality and Social Psychology*, *71*, 1222–1233. https://doi.org/10.1037/0022-3514.71.6.1222

Kreiner, G. E., & Ashforth, B. E. (2004). Evidence toward an expanded model of organizational identification. *Journal of Organizational Behavior*, *25*, 1–27. https://doi.org/10.1002/job.234

Levine, M., Prosser, A., Evans, D., & Reicher, S. (2005). Identity and emergency intervention: How social group membership and inclusiveness of group boundaries shape helping behavior. *Personality and Social Psychology Bulletin*, *31*, 443–453. https://doi.org/10.1177/0146167204271651

Marks, M. L., & Mirvis, P. H. (2001). Making mergers and acquisitions work: Strategic and psychological preparation. *Academy of Management Executive*, *15*, 80–92. https://doi.org/10.5465/AME.2001.4614947

Millward, L. J., & Postmes, T. (2010). Who we are affects how we do: The financial benefits of organizational identification. *British Journal of Management*, *21*, 327–339. https://doi.org/10.1111/j.1467-8551.2009.00667.x

Oakes, P. J., Haslam, S. A., & Turner, J. C. (1994). *Stereotyping and social reality*. Blackwell.

Peters, K., Haslam, S. A., Ryan, M. K., & Fonseca, M. (2013). Working with subgroup identities to build organizational identification and support for organizational strategy: A test of the ASPIRe model. *Group & Organization Management*, *38*, 128–144. https://doi.org/10.1177/1059601112472368

Peters, K., Haslam, S. A., Ryan, M. K., & Steffens, N. K. (2015). To lead, ASPIRe: Building organic organizational identity. In S. Otten, K. I. van der Zee, & M. B. Brewer (Eds.), *Towards inclusive organizations. Determinants of successful diversity management at work* (pp. 87–107). Psychology Press.

Pittinsky, T. L., & Simon, S. (2007). Intergroup leadership. *The Leadership Quarterly*, *18*, 586–605. https://doi.org/10.1016/j.leaqua.2007.09.005

Platow, M. J., van Knippenberg, D., Haslam, S. A., van Knippenberg, B., & Spears, R. (2006). A special gift we bestow on you for being representative of us: Considering leader charisma from a self-categorization perspective. *British Journal of Social Psychology*, *45*, 303–320. https://doi.org/10.1348/014466605X41986

Postmes, T., & Branscombe, N. R. (Eds.). (2010). *Rediscovering social identity*. Psychology Press.

Reicher, S., & Haslam, S. A. (2006). Rethinking the psychology of tyranny: The BBC prison study. *British Journal of Social Psychology, 45*, 1–40. https://doi.org/10.1348/014466605X48998

Reicher, S., & Hopkins, N. (2001). *Self and nation: Categorization, contestation, and mobilization*. SAGE.

Reicher, S., & Hopkins, N. (2003). On the science of the art of leadership. In D. van Knippenberg & M. A. Hogg (Eds.), *Leadership and power: identity processes in groups and organizations* (pp. 197–209). SAGE. https://doi.org/10.4135/9781446216170.n15

Reicher, S. D., Haslam, S. A., & Hopkins, N. (2005). Social identity and the dynamics of leadership: Leaders and followers as collaborative agents in the transformation of social reality. *The Leadership Quarterly, 16*, 547–568. https://doi.org/10.1016/j.leaqua.2005.06.007

Richter, A. W., West, M. A., van Dick, R., & Dawson, J. F. (2006). Boundary spanners' identification, intergroup contact, and effective intergroup relations. *Academy of Management Journal, 49*, 1252–1269. https://doi.org/10.2307/20159831

Riketta, M., & van Dick, R. (2005). Foci of attachment in organizations: A meta-analytic comparison of the strength and correlates of workgroup versus organizational identification and commitment. *Journal of Vocational Behavior, 67*, 490–510. https://doi.org/10.1016/j.jvb.2004.06.001

Schuh, S. C., van Quaquebeke, N., Göritz, A. S., Xin, K. R., Cremer, D. de, & van Dick, R. (2016). Mixed feelings, mixed blessing?: How ambivalence in organizational identification relates to employees' regulatory focus and citizenship behaviors. *Human Relations, 69*, 2224–2249. https://doi.org/10.1177/0018726716639117

Spears, R., & Otten, S. (2012). Discrimination: Revisiting Tajfel's minimal group studies. In J. R. Smith & S. A. Haslam (Eds.), *Social Psychology. Revisiting the Classic Studies* (pp. 160–177). Los Angeles: Sage.

Steffens, N. K., & Haslam, S. A. (2013). Power through 'us': Leaders' use of we-referencing language predicts election victory. *PloS one, 8*, e77952. https://doi.org/10.1371/journal.pone.0077952

Steffens, N. K., Haslam, S. A., Peters, K., & Quiggin, J. (2018). Identity economics meets identity leadership: Exploring the consequences of elevated CEO pay. *The Leadership Quarterly*. https://doi.org/10.1016/j.leaqua.2018.10.001

Steffens, N. K., Haslam, S. A., Peters, K., & Quiggin, J. (2020). Identity economics meets identity leadership: Exploring the consequences of elevated CEO pay. *The Leadership Quarterly, 31*(3), 101269. https://doi.org/10.1016/j.leaqua.2018.10.001

Steffens, N. K., Haslam, S. A., Reicher, S. D., Platow, M. J., Fransen, K., Yang, J., Ryan, M. K., Jetten, J., Peters, K., & Boen, F. (2014). Leadership as social identity management: Introducing the Identity Leadership Inventory (ILI) to assess and validate a four-dimensional model. *The Leadership Quarterly, 25*, 1001–1024. https://doi.org/10.1016/j.leaqua.2014.05.002

Steffens, N. K., Haslam, S. A., Ryan, M. K., & Kessler, T. (2013). Leader performance and prototypicality: Their inter-relationship and impact on leaders' identity entrepreneurship. *European Journal of Social Psychology, 43*, 606–613. https://doi.org/10.1002/ejsp.1985

Tajfel, H. (1970). Experiments in intergroup discrimination. *Scientific American, 223*(5), 96–103.

Tajfel, H. (1972). Social categorization. English manuscript of 'La catégorisation sociale.' In S. Moscovici (Ed.), *Introduction à la psychologie sociale* (Vol. 1, pp. 272–302). Larousse.

Tajfel, H., Billig, M. G., Bundy, R. P., & Flament, C. (1971). Social categorization and intergroup behaviour. *European Journal of Social Psychology, 1*, 149–178. https://doi.org/10.1002/ejsp.2420010202

Tajfel, H., & Turner, J. C. (1979). An integrative theory of intergroup conflict. In W. G. Austin (Ed.), *The social psychology of intergroup relations* (pp. 33–47). Brooks/Cole.

Terry, D. J. (2003). A social identity perspective on organizational mergers: The role of group status, permeability, and similarity. In S. A. Haslam, D. van Knippenberg, M. J. Platow, & N. Ellemers (Eds.), *Social identity at work: Developing theory for organizational practice* (pp. 223–240). Psychology Press.

Turner, J. C. (1982). Towards a redefinition of the social group. In H. Tajfel (Ed.), *Social identity and intergroup relations* (pp. 15–40). Cambridge University Press.

Turner, J. C. (1985). Social categorization and the self-concept: A social cognitive theory of group behavior. In E. J. Lawler (Ed.), *Advances in group processes* (Vol. 2, pp. 77–122). JAI Press.

Turner, J. C. (1991). *Social influence*. Open University Press.

Turner, J. C., & Haslam, S. A. (2001). Social identity, organizations and leadership. In M. E. Turner (Ed.), *Groups at work: Advances in theory and practice* (pp. 25–65). Erlbaum.

Turner, J. C., Hogg, M. A., Oakes, P. J., Reicher, S. D., & Wetherell, M. S. (Eds.). (1987). *Rediscovering the social group: A self-categorization theory*. Blackwell.

Turner, J. C., Oakes, P. J., Haslam, S. A., & McGarty, C. (1994). Self and collective: Cognition and social context. *Personality and Social Psychology Bulletin, 20*, 454–463. https://doi.org/10.1177/0146167294205002

van Dick, R., Lemoine, J. E., Steffens, N. K., Kerschreiter, R., Akfirat, S. A., Avanzi, L., Dumont, K., Epitropaki, O., Fransen, K., Giessner, S., González, R., Kark, R., Lipponen, J., Markovits, Y., Monzani, L., Orosz, G., Pandey, D., Roland-Lévy, C., Schuh, S., … Haslam, S. A. (2018). Identity leadership going global: Validation of the identity leadership inventory across 20 countries. *Journal of Occupational and Organizational Psychology, 91*(4), 697–728. https://doi.org/10.1111/joop.12223

van Knippenberg, B., & van Knippenberg, D. (2005). Leader self-sacrifice and leadership effectiveness: The moderating role of leader prototypicality. *Journal of Applied Psychology, 90*, 25–37. https://doi.org/10.1037/0021-9010.90.1.25

van Knippenberg, D. (2011). Embodying who we are: Leader group prototypicality and leadership effectiveness. *The Leadership Quarterly, 22*, 1078–1091. https://doi.org/10.1016/j.leaqua.2011.09.004

van Knippenberg, D., & Hogg, M. A. (2003a). A social identity model of leadership effectiveness in organizations. *Research in Organizational Behavior, 25*, 243–295. https://doi.org/10.1016/S0191-3085(03)25006-1

van Knippenberg, D., & Hogg, M. A. (Eds.). (2003b). *Leadership and power: Identity processes in groups and organizations*. SAGE.

PART 2

JANUSIAN TENSIONS

CHAPTER 4

PARADOX, LEADERSHIP, AND THE CONNECTING LEADER

Camille Pradies
EDHEC Business School

Marieke Delanghe
EDHEC Business School

Marianne W. Lewis
Lindner College of Business, University of Cincinnati

ABSTRACT

Paradoxes pervade organizations, challenging leaders to manage a barrage of conflicting yet interwoven and persistent demands. As both leaders to some and followers to others, these tensions compound for connecting leaders. They are charged with making sense of competing demands imposed by upper management and rising from subordinates and daily operations. They need to interpret, communicate and execute responses in both directions but also to motivate people to embrace and work through paradoxes. With these challenges in mind, this chapter presents an integrative framework for understanding the interplay between paradox and leadership so pertinent to the connecting leader. We first provide a systematic literature review that highlights the breadth and depth of the study of leadership in the face of paradoxes. It surfaces *different loci of paradox:* paradoxes inherent

The Connecting Leader: Serving Concurrently as a Leader and a Follower
pp. 99–129

to leadership and paradoxes stemming from the leader's work environment. It puts forth *leadership as a means to engage paradoxes*. It also stresses that *paradoxes can be used as a leadership resource* to develop others or bring about changes. We then illustrate insights from this framework in the case of the connecting leader. Our conclusion poses implications for research and practice that could deepen understandings of leadership and paradoxes.

INTRODUCTION

Connecting leaders face intense and interwoven paradoxes as tensions swirl around their competing demands as both leaders and followers. Arguably, all leaders report to someone; even chief executive officers report to a governing board and midlevel leaders must effectively follow, translate and implement directives of upper leadership (Farrell, 2018). Effective leaders also glean value from their followers' front-line expertise, learning from and with them. Scholars depict these tensions as the "leader/follower paradox":

> [Leaders] work with followers in such a way as they will become leaders and develop an ability to make the right decisions on their own. Under this kind of leadership it is not always clear just who is leading whom. (Cronin & Genovese, 2012, p. 20)
>
> Followers can point the way and provide insights from their vantage point that may not be evident to a leader. Leading while following and following while leading becomes more of an "ebb and flow" rather than an "either or" technique for effective leaders. (Farrell, 2018, p. 168)

As these quotes emphasize, connecting leaders uniquely embody the interplay between paradox and leadership. Paradoxes pervade organizations, challenging leaders to manage a barrage of conflicting yet interwoven and persistent demands (Lavine, 2014; Smith, 2014; Smith & Lewis, 2011). Leaders strive to build supportive teams, foster subordinates' learning and fuel exploration and more radical innovation, while also seeking to fight daily operational fires, hold their subordinates accountable for high performance, and exploit greater efficiency and value from existing capabilities. While the list can seem endless, imagine how such tensions compound for connecting leaders. Simultaneously leader and follower, connecting leaders are charged with making sense of competing demands imposed by upper management and rising from subordinates and daily operations, needing to interpret, communicate and execute responses in both directions (Jaser, 2017).

Locked in a tug-of-war, connecting leaders are pulled in opposing directions: asked to follow the strategic imperatives stated by their leaders on the one hand and attentive to the operational demands advanced by their followers on the other. These demands are interrelated: being attentive to input from the field or to operational constraints may trigger new strategic conversations, surfacing future opportunities or dangers. And understanding strategic demands may help prioritize operational activities. Finally, these demands persist over time; structurally embedded in the connecting leaders' role. Because of this paradoxical nature, Jaser (2017) notes that the coenactment of the juxtaposed roles of leader and follower can be facilitated by embracing the inherent paradoxes of leadership and organizations.

As the experience of tensions intensifies so do calls for more paradoxical leaders, those adept at embracing and helping others embrace and thrive through tensions (Knight & Paroutis, 2017; Smith, 2014; Zhang et al., 2015). Researchers have sought to contribute by developing an array of new concepts to study this capacity, such as "paradoxical leader behaviors" (Zhang et al., 2015), "paradox-savvy leader" (Waldman & Bowen, 2016), "blended leadership" (Collinson & Collinson, 2009), or "hybrid leadership" (Townsend, 2015). Yet as often the case when concepts such as leadership and paradox are combined, conceptual boundaries can blur, inhibiting fruitful dialogue between scholars and the impact of resulting research. As such, although rich studies document tensions of leaders caught in-between (e.g., Balogun & Johnson, 2004; Gioia & Chittipeddi, 1991; Isabella, 1990), few fully explore the intersection of leadership and paradoxes and potential insights for the connecting leader.

In response, this chapter presents an integrative framework for understanding the interplay between paradox and leadership so pertinent to the connecting leader. We first provide a systematic literature review, contributing a synthesis of both literatures that highlights the breadth and depth of their intersection. We then illustrate insights from this framework using the special case of the connecting leader. Our conclusion poses implications for research and practice that could deepen understandings of leadership in the face of paradoxes, particularly as relates to the tenuous challenges and integral role of the connecting leader.

PARADOX AND LEADERSHIP: METHOD FOR OUR LITERATURE REVIEW

To glean insights for connecting leadership research and practice, we sought to examine the intersection of paradox and leadership literature. We followed a multistage process to develop our literature sample (Krippendorff, 2013) as adopted in other recent reviews (e.g., Schad et al., 2016). To explore when and how scholars have examined the paradox-leadership intersection, we surveyed studies over the past 30 years that adopted a paradox lens and applied it to leadership. We conducted the initial search in Business Source Complete. We included publications that explicitly used three types of keywords. The first keyword was *leadership*. As many articles used the word leadership. To better target our search, the second keyword pertained to leadership figures: *chief executive officer, top management team(s)* (TMT), *top executive(s), manager(s), managerial, top leadership team(s).* Finally, the last type encompassed keywords often used by paradox scholars in review articles (see Smith & Lewis, 2011): *paradox(es), ambivalence(s), ambidexterity(ies), tension(s), contradiction(s).*

To ensure that we captured the diversity of scholarship at the intersection of leadership and paradox we performed our keyword search in title, abstract and/or keywords given by the authors. We limited our search to articles published in peer-reviewed journals written in English.[1] However, we did not limit our search to top journals in management studies. On the contrary, we purposefully included papers from a wide range of outlets as the research area at the intersection of leadership and paradoxes is emergent.

The search terms were selected to ensure inclusivity while enable focus on leadership and paradoxes. Combining these searches and deleting multiple references to the same article across database, the search generated more than 300 articles. From this initial set, a more detailed analysis of titles, abstracts and full articles resulted in a sample of 53 papers. Two of the authors conducted this screening process separately and then met to discuss all articles and reach an agreement on those articles in which their opinion diverged. The main inclusion criteria were whether the primary focus was paradoxes and tensions experienced by leaders that could be understood as paradoxical even if the authors did not use the term explicitly and whether the article addressed a process of influence as understood by leadership scholars.

Finally, as we read these articles, we carefully reviewed the references to make sure that our keyword search had not prevented us from identifying any prominent articles referenced across studies. This allowed us to reach a total number of 64 articles in this review. The complete list of papers is presented in the appendix.

The sample spreads across 44 journals and includes articles from *The Leadership Quarterly* (9.38%); *Leadership* (6.25%); *Academy of Management Journal* (4.69%), *Human Relations* (4.69%), *Organization Science* (4.69%), and *The Journal of Applied Behavioral Science* (4.69%). The literature review is dominated by empirical studies (71%) with 32 articles using qualitative and 14 articles drawing on quantitative methods.

Second, we coded all 64 articles, developing a codebook through iterative discussions between the authors until achieving consistency and stability across the codes (Krippendorff, 2013). We proceeded inductively.

Two authors independently reread all short-listed papers and formed a set of key themes. Any points of disagreement between authors were solved through extensive discussions. We now discuss the findings from our review.

PARADOX AND LEADERSHIP: THREE THEMES AT THE HEART OF PARADOXICAL LEADERSHIP

Research at the intersection of paradox and leadership has often been initiated by scholars who seek to move away from models that propose leaders adopt one path fitting their contextual demands to leaders adaptively engaging complexities and tensions in their environment (T. Keller & Weibler, 2015; Smith & Lewis, 2012). As Murphy and colleagues (2017, p. 1) explain: "leadership scholars are expressing growing concerns that existing models of leadership may not fully capture the leadership dynamics operating in today's environment." Similarly, Uhl-Bien and Arena (2018, p. 1) write:

> Leadership for organizational adaptability [i.e., an organizational strategy particularly suited to face paradoxical demands] differs from leader change in that, rather than focusing on those should be, leaders can drive change top down e.g., through vision and inspiration ... it addresses how leaders can position organizations and the people within them to be adaptive in the face of complex challenges.

Beyond rethinking the dynamics of leadership, our review of articles at the intersection of paradox and leadership revealed three themes: the *locus of paradoxes* (98.43% of articles), *leadership as means to engage paradoxes* (60.94% of articles), *paradoxes as a leadership resource* to develop oneself or the organization in the face of paradoxes (26.56% of articles). The locus of paradoxes refers to the fact that some articles pointed to tensions that were stemming from the (organizational) context while others identified tensions that were inherent to a leadership position. Leadership as means to engage paradoxes addresses articles that examine specific leadership behaviors or leadership skills that leaders can use to navigate paradoxical demands. Finally, some articles explained how paradoxes can be used as a leadership resource for self-development or for organizational development. The appendix offers a literature review summary, providing an overview of each article included with the corresponding theme(s) noted. Taken together, our review reveals how connecting leaders are surrounded by paradoxes. As illustrated in the figure below, the connecting leader not only responds to these tensions, but may also proactively use paradox as a resource.

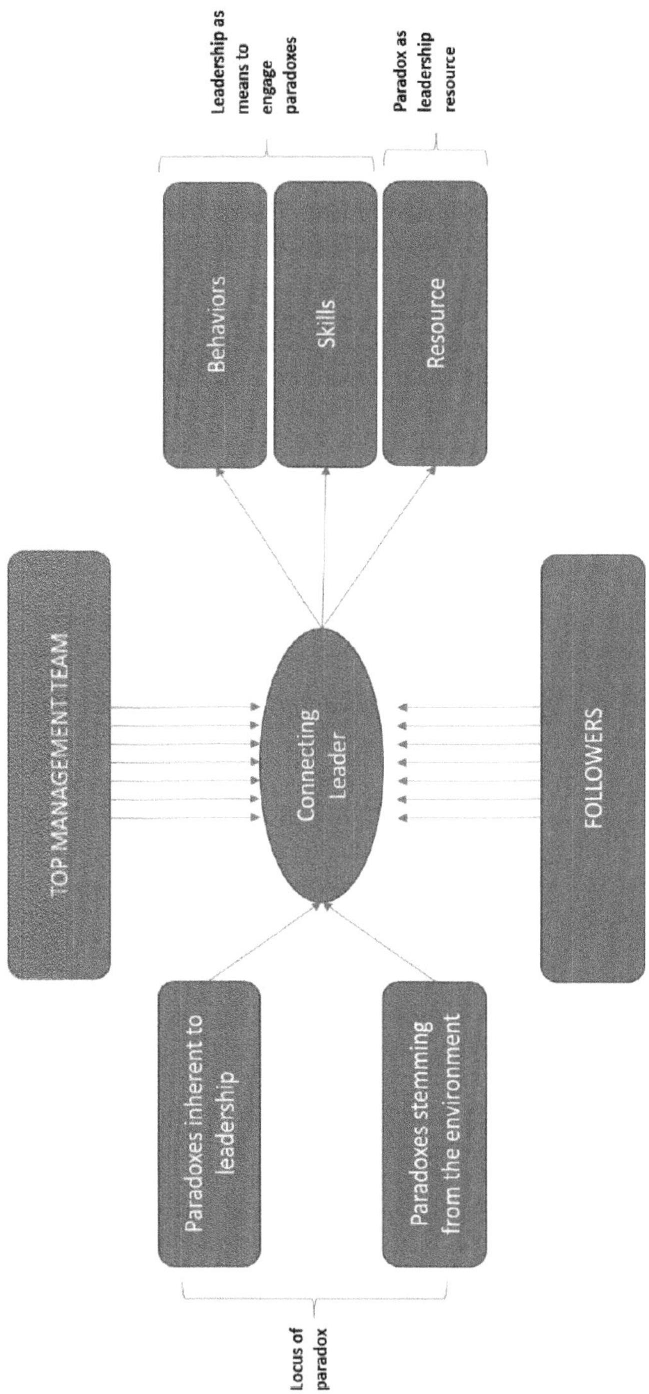

Figure 4.1. Paradox, leadership, and the connecting leader.

Locus of Paradox: Inherent or External to Leadership

At the heart of leadership lies the interplay between the context, the leader and the followers. Acknowledging this interplay implies recognizing that a leader's skills and behaviors are contextualized and that they are not only embedded in an (organizational) context but also in interactions with followers (Northouse, 2010). Thus, our review surfaces two loci of paradoxes: paradoxes tied to the interactional nature of leadership, that is, paradoxes inherent to leadership; and paradoxes that arise from competing organizational or field level goals, that is, external paradoxes.

Paradoxes Inherent to Leadership

The first category of literature identifies the inherently paradoxical nature of leadership. Core to the connecting leader, inherent paradoxes are particularly visible in leader-follower relationships and more broadly through tensions created through social interactions (see, for example, Collinson, 2005). Questions of empowerment and control are embedded within leadership and abound in the literature. For example, leaders have to both retain control and let go of it (Waldman & Bowen, 2016), or need to monitor and control as well as to empower and trust others (Bartunek et al., 2000). Such paradoxes often stem from cultural understandings of leadership as centralization of power and of the leader as one who imposes her/his vision on others, countering calls for leaders to empower and serve others (Johnson, 2016). Similarly, Mink and colleagues (1989) suggest that, in the face of change, leaders (in their case public school superintendents) are required to take actions to innovate but such actions are risky and may threaten their position, simultaneously preventing change.

Other leadership scholars stress questions of authenticity and politics. Nyberg and Sveningsson (2014) note this as a paradox central to authentic leadership. They state the double bind: leaders often claim that authenticity is key to what makes them a good leader, yet they cannot be fully authentic and be perceived as a good leader by followers. Rhodes and Badham (2018) explore the paradoxical nature of ethical relational leadership as leaders strive to engage in honest and trusting relationships. Yet such leaders become caught "between an infinitely demanding ethics and the finite possibilities of a response to those demands" (Brower et al., 2000, p. 1). The authors posit how this paradox is enabled and constrained by the hierarchical discourses and power dynamics that construct leadership relationships.

Leaders are also confronted with the need to navigate high self-esteem and humble demeanor. Indeed, leaders need to maintain a strong sense of self while cultivating humility (Waldman & Bowen, 2016). Scholars tie this paradox to ethical leadership (Liu & Baker, 2016; Rhodes & Badham, 2018). For example, in their qualitative study of philanthropic leaders in Australia, Liu and Baker (2016) advance that philanthropy—a key demonstration of ethical leadership—is constructed as highly paradoxical by the media. Philanthropic leaders must navigate competing yet interrelated identities such as aristocratic battlers, caring controllers, and publicity-shy celebrities.

Paradoxes External to Leadership

An alternative locus of paradox is external, arising from the environment and organizational context. External tensions impact leaders at all levels, yet may particularly challenge connecting leaders who must respond to related imperatives imposed by their top management, while communicating and enabling their chosen responses to their own followers. Perhaps because of its strategic relevance, ambidextrous contexts—in which leaders seek to leverage exploitation and exploration—have attracted much of the scholarly attention. While exploitation (such as applying existing knowledge to enhance efficiency and productivity) is demanded to hit current results, exploration (e.g., generating new knowledge via experimentation and innovation) is needed to sustain future success and viability (Andriopoulos & Lewis, 2009). As organizations seek to both explore and exploit, leadership teams are pushed to engage paradoxical demands (Smith, 2014).

Other strategic paradoxes similarly challenge organizational leaders, such as pursuing a social and for-profit mission (Sharma & Good, 2013; Smith & Besharov, 2019; Smith et al., 2012; Waldman & Bowen, 2016); the intricate demands of global strategy and local needs (Fredberg, 2014); or questions pertaining to organizational structure with formal and informal systems (Gurd & Helliar, 2016). For example, Murphy and colleagues (2017) explain how leaders in the public sector need to balance formal, top-down, administrative functions (e.g., routine focused practices centered on efficiency) and informal, emergent, adaptive functions (e.g., adaptive practices required to respond to dynamic circumstances). Their work explores how leadership is enacted over six urban regeneration projects representing high, medium, and low levels of project complexity. The article suggests that in complex environments involving both adaptive and administrative practices, leaders must balance opposing behaviors. Pointing to another paradox-ripe context, Fredberg (2014) studies chief executive officer practices in global organizations to manage seven paradoxes such as the tensions between the "creation of economic and social value" (p. 175).

Researchers have investigated specific fields or industries that require leaders to embrace paradoxical demands such as healthcare (Pascuci et al., 2017; Scott & Timmons, 2017) and education (D. Keller, 2015; Thornton et al., 2018). Scott and Timmons (2017) portray the paradoxical demands experienced by ward leaders in a United Kingdom hospital, challenged to deliver high-quality care and hit profit-oriented performance indicators.

Others note how paradoxical tensions are intensified by leaders' structural positions, such as top managers' focus on competing stakeholders' expectations (Alfes & Langner, 2017) and myriad tug-of-wars faced by middle management (Lüscher & Lewis, 2008; Thornton et al., 2018) or, as will be discussed at the end of this chapter, by connecting leaders. Alfes and Langner (2017, p. 97) demonstrate

> how volunteer managers can achieve this aim [finding the right balance between giving freedom to enhance volunteers' sense of work meaning and providing structure to ensure effective services delivery and coordination] by using a paradoxical leadership style … to meet competing follower demands simultaneously and over time.

Leadership as Means to Engage Paradox

Leadership Behaviors for Paradox Engagement

To answer competing yet interrelated paradoxical demands, leaders combine seemingly opposing approaches. Such behaviors are often directly connected to the specificity of the context (i.e., engaging external paradoxes) or the stakeholders involved (i.e., navigating paradoxes inherent to the nature leadership). For example, Smith (2014) finds that TMT leaders who engage exploratory and exploitative demands adopt differentiating approaches (i.e., allocating exploration or exploitation roles) and integrating approaches (i.e., stressing overarching goals and integrating roles). Uhl-Bien and Arena (2018) explore leadership behaviors that foster organizational adaptability, such as the capacity to embrace exploration and exploitation. They posit that adaptable leaders should both foster conflict and integration. To Baškarada and colleagues (2016), approaches to engage exploration-exploitation tensions can be mapped to transformational and transactional leadership behaviors from top to connecting to lower level leaders.

To offer a more holistic view, some scholars focus on behaviors pertaining the inherently paradoxical nature of leadership (Kodish, 2006). For instance, Collinson and Collinson (2009) examine blended leadership, describing the need to combine heroic and post heroic leadership behaviors. Drawing on the example of delegating and controlling behaviors, they suggest that opposing leadership behaviors are conducive of leadership effectiveness. Zhang and colleagues (2015, p. 538) offer a definition of what they called "paradoxical leader behavior" which denotes "seemingly competing yet interrelated behaviors to simultaneously and over time meet structural and follower demands." This leadership behavior relies on five dimensions: self-centeredness and other-centeredness, managing distance and closeness, treating subordinates uniformly while fostering individualization, enforcing work requirements while allowing flexibility, and maintaining decision control while allowing autonomy.

Thus, no matter the type of paradoxes faced, scholars converge toward the idea that leaders need to be adept at seemingly opposite yet interrelated behaviors. However, effectively demonstrating such behaviors challenges even the most skilled connecting leaders. As such, Lawrence et al. (2009, p. 88) suggest that behavioral complexity is a robust predictor of leadership effectiveness. Consider the following claims.

> A behaviorally complex leader is someone who has the ability to "perform the multiple roles and behaviors that circumscribe the requisite variety implied by an organizational or environmental context" (Denison, Hooijberg, & Quinn, 1995, p. 526), such as stakeholders and competitive demands. (Brower et al., 2000)

Denison and colleagues (1995, p. 526) further state:

> The test of a first-rate leader may be the ability to exhibit contrary or opposing behaviors (as appropriate or necessary) while still retaining some measure of integrity, credibility, and direction. Thus, effective leaders are those who have the cognitive and behavioral complexity to respond appropriately to a wide range of situations that may in fact require contrary or opposing behaviors.

Leadership Skills for Paradox Engagement

Behavioral complexity and resulting leadership effectiveness may be seen as the behavioral manifestation of a series of leadership skills to know *when and how* to develop these seemingly contradictory behaviors. For some scholars, mastering behavioral complexity starts with *acceptance and awareness* of paradoxical demands, that is, the cognitive capacity for leaders to ignite and accept paradoxical demands. As Farrell (2018) wrote:

> How does a leader balance the need for organizational stability while also being daring to seize opportunities? ... Effective leaders are aware of this paradox and with experience may develop a sense where and how risks might be taken. (Farrell, 2018, p. 170)

In this vein, Smith and her colleagues (2012) suggest that acceptance in the form of embracing an abundance mentality and paradoxical thinking is a skill vital to leading through paradoxes of social enterprises. Likewise, Lewis et al. (2014) note that leaders who develop agility across paradoxical poles need to proactively identify and raise tensions, while Miron-Spektor and colleagues (2018, p. 12) conceptualize a paradox mindset as "a tendency to value, accept and feel comfortable with tensions."

Thus, acceptance belongs to a body of leadership skills involving paradoxical cognition in terms of mindset or sensemaking capabilities. For example, Keller (2015) portrays the dualities of international schools and suggests that leaders need to make sense of these tensions (e.g., realizing coexisting needs to promote local pride and international mindedness) and reframe them to lead. Similarly, Smith and Tushman (2005) show how leaders must manage contradictions stemming from the need to explore new products and exploit existing ones by developing paradoxical cognition. Zhang and colleagues (2015) also found two cognitive and individual antecedents (holistic thinking and integrative complexity) linked to paradoxical leadership behaviors. Holistic thinking refers to the cognitive capability to see that everything is interconnected, including contradictory demands (Peng & Nisbett, 1999). Integrative complexity refers to a greater capacity to differentiate and integrate different perspectives (Miron-Spektor et al., 2018). Smith and Lewis (2012, p. 229) stress the role of cognitive complexity at the heart of paradoxical leadership "to juxtapose seeming contradictions, explore potential synergies, and question oversimplified either/or assumptions."

Some studies explore the leadership skill of reflexivity (Lüscher & Lewis, 2008; Rhodes & Badham, 2018) or critical thinking (Mink et al., 1989). Mink and colleagues (1989) suggest that leaders need to identify and reflect on the dilemmas they face to engage paradoxical demands inherent to the nature of leadership and display leadership behaviors and bring about change. To them, critical reflection is a vital skill and the very process of interviewing allowed the superintendents stuck between the necessity to innovate and the risks that innovating poses for their career, to reflect and realize the paradoxical demands imposed on them and have a more open mind. Yet they warn, "to be able to do this and to facilitate such critical thinking in others requires a long process of learning to reflect on action, to identify and challenge assumptions, and to explore and imagine alternatives" (Mink et al., 1989, p. 238). Smith and Lewis (2012) advance a related skill of confidence. "Managing paradox demands confidence, an inner strength to take risks, to act on uncertainty and ambiguity rather than become anxious and defensive" (p. 229).

Finally, some scholars explore behavioral skills that aid in building confidence and enabling acceptance of seemingly opposite yet interrelated behaviors: namely communication and conflict management skills. In this context, Smith and Lewis (2012, p. 229) note that: "Attending to paradox requires leaders who can manage conflict, actively eliciting tensions and using such information to seek creative solutions." They advance that communication skills are critical as: "Leaders who can articulate their logic and justify their decisions can more effectively involve others in paradox management" (2012, p. 229). In this line, Kuna (2017) advances that public managers need conflict management skills and communication skills to engage paradoxical demands. Kuna (2017, p. 200) notes:

> Conflict management capabilities enable public managers to address the tensions underlying change processes as well as their negative consequences, including organizational disputes and rivalry among employees and between units. At the same time, public managers utilize their newly acquired communication skills to engage their staff more positively in the demanding process of implementing reform. Thus, both sets of skills may enlarge the capacity of public managers to handle paradox effectively instead of regressing to an ambivalent stance toward it.

Finally, some authors point to team specific skills. For example. Lubatkin and colleagues (2006) suggest that behavioral integration or transactive memory are key for teams that want to weather paradoxical demands. As they propose (2006, p. 647):

> Our thesis is that a TMT's level of behavioral integration directly influences how its members deal with the contradictory knowledge processes that underpin the attainment of an exploitative and exploratory orientation, such that greater integration enhances the likelihood of jointly pursuing both.

Similarly, Heavy and Simsek (2017) argue that transactive memory provides a top management team with a system for generating, distributing, and integrating knowledge based on members' specific areas of expertise in ways that increase its ability to both differentiate and integrate strategic agendas for ambidexterity.

Paradox as Leadership Resource

Our review reveals that not only do effective leaders manage paradoxes, but they can also put their underlying tensions to use, leveraging paradox as a resource. Most of the research at the intersection of leadership and paradox has focused on leading *from* paradoxes, that is, leading once paradoxical demands arise from the organizational context or from the competing yet interrelated demands inherent to leadership. However, an emerging body of work views—often times implicitly—paradox as a resource for enhancing leadership, others and the organization. As such, these scholars stress that leading may also occur *through* paradoxes. These works recognize how paradoxes can be raised to gain new insights (Farrell, 2018), as actors actively seek to provoke tensions and create new ways of seeing among followers. Viewed as a leadership resource recognizes the generative and transformative power of paradox:

> Yet, in today's complex organizations, models based on linear and rational problem-solving do managers a tremendous disservice. Managers need to recognize, become comfortable with, and even profit from tensions and the anxieties they provoke, for "the contribution of paradox to management thinking is the recognition of its power to generate creative insight and change." (Lewis, 2000, p. 764)

Some studies focus on paradoxes as a resource for developing leaders themselves. For example, Lavine (2014) suggests that tools that help make paradoxes visible—such as the competing value framework—can be used in leadership training. As tensions are mapped, leaders can better understand that their role is not one that can be framed in terms of making either/or decisions but rather that their responsibilities and actions occur "along a much more nuanced continuum" (p. 200). Kark and colleagues (2016) show how paradox studies themselves can be utilized for leadership development, particularly to foster paradoxical thinking. They stress that exploring tensions fosters leaders' learning (see also Jarvis et al., 2013) and illustrate how paradoxes guided the design of a leadership seminar within a gender studies program in Israel. As their conflicting identities come to the surface, seminar participants moved away from viewing their situation in terms of dilemmas to acknowledging paradoxes. Similarly, in their qualitative study of nursing leadership, Kan and Parry (2004) note that making the tensions explicit and shedding light on paradoxes stemming from the coexistence of multiple realities between three hospital subcultures (nurses, managers, and doctors) helped make the nurses leadership more effective and bring about changes and acceptation from various stakeholders.

Other literature identifies how leaders can use paradox to develop others and the organization more broadly. A few scholars suggests that leaders need to simplify the paradoxical demands to prevent followers' resistance and motivate them to engage (Fredberg, 2014; Sundgren & Styhre, 2006). In this vein, Sundgren and Styhre (2006) propose that the role of a leader is to deparadoxify. The leader needs to show herself and others that one should not be paralyzed by paradoxical demands, but rather should engage them. In their study of creativity and paradoxes in pharmaceutical research, they write (2006, p. 47):

> In many cases, the role of leader is to 'deparadoxify' what seems to be a paradox in order to enable action, that is to point out and explicate the intricate relationship between a number of different resources, activities, and actors enlisted in the course of progress toward a new, registered drug, the favored and ultimate outcome of all new drug development processes.

Pushing this idea further, Fredberg (2014) stresses that the role of a leader is to simplify the followers' experience of paradoxes. Yet others call for leaders to communicate and instill a both/and vision in order to build commitment to paradoxical goals (Lewis et al., 2014; Smith et al., 2010). Given their positioning at the nexus of numerous, interwoven tensions, such skills are at a premium for connecting leaders.

Some scholars stress that fostering awareness of paradox is a valued leadership practice whereby leaders help followers identify their paradoxes. Sparr (2018) advances that leaders engage in sense-giving activities to communicate paradoxes in times of change. She explains how leaders' paradoxical sense-giving help followers make sense of the paradoxes inherent to organizational change. A leader could for example ask followers to define rules, but also deviations from the rules to help followers make sense of the need to be both stable and flexible in a change effort (Sparr, 2018). Knight and Paroutis (2017) suggest that the TMT leaders need to give sense on the competing yet interrelated exploration and exploitation strategic imperatives to help middle managers see the paradox. They see this action as engaging in "paradoxical leadership" that they define as "a 'nonindividualized phenomenon' (Schatzki, 2005), in which leaders create the structural conditions for salience for lower level managers by creating interpretive contexts" (Knight & Paroutis, 2017, pp. 426–427).

For Havermans, Keegan, and Den Hartog (2015) the way in which the manager frames the paradoxes has a direct impact on how followers navigate paradoxical demands. They write (Havermans, Keegan, et al., 2015, p. 8):

> As leader's narratives play an important role in the development of collective sensemaking, the storylines that are developed by leaders can have a major impact on the ways in which complex emergent problems are constructed and resolved, and thus potentially the success of the project and program

For example, when leaders emphasize the value of conflicting perspectives as well as the advantages of aligned perspectives, they foster team members' iteration "between enabling different perspectives and aligning perspectives" (Havermans, Keegan, et al., 2015, p. 9). This way of framing effective complex emergent problem resolution involves iterating between enabling different perspectives and aligning perspectives, which makes it possible for the team to work both flexibly and efficiently.

Beyond stressing the importance of 'seeing' paradoxical demands, some studies suggest that leaders may leverage paradox to help followers to better manage tensions and develop ambidextrous behaviors (Kauppila & Tempelaar, 2016; Li, 2016). For example, the work of Havermans and colleagues (2015) and Jansen and colleagues (2016) suggests that leaders may leverage tensions to foster ambidexterity among employees by displaying organizational level supportive leadership behaviors (e.g., encouragement of initiative, provide clear performance feedback, emphasize task orientation) (Jansen et al., 2016) or by adopting practices that stimulate a higher complexity of responses (e.g., encouraging group conversations, involving others, being available) and practices that stimulate a lower complexity of responses (e.g., sticking to plans and agreements, stopping discussions) (Havermans, Den Hartog, et al., 2015).

Others further argue that leaders need to share their thoughts and feelings to initiate paradox management practices among followers. Guarana and Hernandez (2015) advance that leaders and followers need to jointly experience and communicate about their ambivalence in the face of paradoxical demands, engaging in shared contextual interpretation to reap benefits of their collaboration. They note that when only one experiences ambivalence then the other strives to offer a simpler understanding of the situation to diminish the discomfort. It is thus important for leaders to openly and collaboratively engage paradoxes. In this vein, Bartunek et al. (2000) conducted a 6-year, longitudinal study of leadership succession in a group designed to empower women. Their findings suggest the necessity for those in leadership positions to voice their ambivalence about paradoxes of empowerment and control inherent to leadership (being simultaneously directive and facilitative) so that the team can learn to expect and work through the tensions.

DEEP DIVE INSIGHTS FOR THE CONNECTING LEADER

To further explore paradox and leadership insights for the connecting leader, we now draw on two studies by one of the authors that examine this interplay among middle managers during an organizational change effort (Lüscher & Lewis, 2008) and through the role of deans as university middle management (Lewis, 2017). Leveraging this work and the themes surfaced through our review, we discuss how paradoxical leadership can enrich our understanding of connecting leaders.

Case 1: Lüscher and Lewis (2008)

Lüscher and Lewis (2008) conducted an action research study at LEGO, helping middle managers navigate paradoxical demands surfaced by organizational change. Jaser (2017) reflects on this study and the insights of these exemplary connecting leaders:

> "How can I follow executive mandates, when I have been told to make my own decisions?" (manager at the LEGO Company, Lüscher and Lewis, 2008, p. 231), this is the voice of an individual stuck in the middle, a follower to some, and a leader to others.

The organizational change at LEGO unleashed a myriad of tensions reflecting both the external paradoxes and paradoxes inherent to leadership. On one side, the managers were prey to external pressures created by opposing yet interrelated environmental demands. For example, managers wrestled with seeking change and stability, highlighted by the question managers asked themselves in the study: "Should I implement teams now or should I wait until things stabilize?" (Lüscher & Lewis, 2008, p. 231). Yet the LEGO middle managers were also attuned to the paradoxical nature of leadership itself. These managers pondered issues of empowerment and control, for example: "Should I lead the way or recede into the background? Should I talk or should I wait for them to take the initiative? Should I manage or should I let my employees manage?" (Lüscher & Lewis, 2008, p. 231).

While this study did not seek to identify definitive leadership behaviors, it does explore cognitive leadership skills needed to engage paradox and thereby identify paths for actions. Indeed, the action research conducted by Lüscher and Lewis (2008) allowed the managers to develop an awareness and an acceptance of leadership tensions. Applying "reflexive questioning" helped mangers make sense of the tensions and work through the knotted "mess" of contradictions they faced. The result was a state of "workable certainty," enabling insights into how to both empower and control, while developing flexible teams to weather change and stability.

This study also demonstrates paradox as a leadership resource. Leading through paradox proved not only a means to manage the "mess," but these connecting leaders at LEGO also found value in proactively provoking paradox. Acting as an external consultant or "sparring partner" one of the authors helped the managers surface tensions and learn to benefit from their creative friction. By the study's conclusion, the managers expressed eagerness to integrate paradoxes in their leadership and in their organization's routine, pushing Lüscher and Lewis to question whether paradoxical thinking could become an institutionalized leadership resource.

Case 2: Lewis (2017)

In a reflection on the paradoxes of deanship, Lewis (2017) positions deans as connecting leaders who must answer to and engage faculty members and students as well as senior university leaders. As Thornton and colleagues (2018, p. 3) acknowledge:

> Heads of school are middle managers in their institutions and therefore need to manage expectations from above (senior leadership in faculties and the wider university) and below (academic and professional staff in the school) (Bolden, Petrov, & Gosling, 2009; Branson et al., 2015; Degn, 2015; Preston & Price, 2012; Whitchurch & Gordon, 2017) which may be in conflict.

As in the case of the LEGO middle managers and indeed of any such connecting leader, deans find themselves at the nexus of numerous, intersecting tensions. For example, deans must:

> Build an academic institution that creates knowledge, inspires learning and impacts practice and grow revenue to meet rising costs, support university ambitions and enable reinvestment. Nurture and reward world-leading research and engage faculty in enhancing the student experience, collegiate community and external partnerships. Fuel innovation to confront digital, workplace and macroeconomic disruptions and ensure offerings and systems align to current national, accreditation and university requirements. (Lewis, 2017)

Lewis further argues:

> Deans know too well public criticisms of academic publications lacking relevance while regulatory and institutional demands for faculty teaching and impact rise. Yet the external faculty market—and hence salaries—remains driven by their publications as also, ironically, do research assessments by the same national and institutional regulators.

Lewis (2017) presents mainly the variety of external paradoxes that deans face. Our review, however, orients our attention to the inherent paradoxical nature of their leadership. Thornton and colleagues (2018, pp. 3–4) study this missing piece. They explore the tenuous relationships that deans entertain because they are both colleague and supervisor to academic professionals and thereby must learn to be close yet distant:

> They need to maintain collegial relationships in their discipline and department and at the same time undertake managerial tasks that may be in conflict with notions of collegiality, academic freedom and scholarship (Bolden et al.; Branson et al.). The situation is exacerbated because heads are drawn from their scholarly community and in many universities will return to the ranks of their peers after their term (Branson et al., 2015; Degn, 2015; Floyd, 2016; Whitchurch & Gordon, 2017). Often heads are selected because they are excellent academics not because they have previous leadership or management experience or capabilities (Bryman, 2007; Floyd & Dimmock, 2011; Parrish, 2015). Once in the role, heads need to sustain their scholarly activity to maintain ongoing credibility with their peers and to meet institutional research requirements. This can be a challenge when duties do not leave sufficient time for research (Preston & Price, 2012; Wolverhamptonetal, 2007) and can result in the erosion of academic identity and ultimately affect career progression including promotion (Floyd & Dimmock, 2011; Youngs, 2017).

To Lewis (2017), deans should adopt seemingly opposing behaviors. While she mentions communication as a leadership skill in passing, she stresses relevant separating and integrating behaviors in detail (see also Smith, 2014; Smith & Lewis, 2011). For example, business school deans must meet pressures for higher teaching impact and business relevance and enter the race for academic publications that often lack relevance. Separating teaching and research faculty roles with research and teaching profiles can accentuate their distinct value. While integrating these roles may "foster development and recognition of one's accumulating thought leadership."

Perhaps because of the succinct nature of the article, Lewis (2017) does not dwell on paradox as a leadership resource. Rather it stresses need to foster a "culture of feedback and continuous improvement, as well as celebration of success" that "nurtures collective ambition, humility and resilience." Building from these insights, our review would further encourage deans to lead through paradoxes, while using the creative friction enabled by their tensions to develop and energize all stakeholders involved.

CONCLUDING THOUGHTS: CONNECTING LEADERS, PARADOX AND LEADERSHIP

To conclude, connecting leaders are in a structural position that exposes them to at least one (i.e., being a leader and a follower) but more likely to a plethora of external paradoxes. The inherent nature of leadership adds a further layer of complexity. As a result, connecting leaders face multiplying and intensifying tensions, making their ability to grasp and lead through paradoxes all the more critical. Their position requires that they enact seemingly opposite behaviors (integration and differentiation) and rely on paradoxical cognitive skills to sustain these behaviors (Jaser, 2017). What our review reveals, however, is that paradoxes can also be used as a resource to lead. By pointing to the transformative potential of paradoxes as a leadership resource, that is, leading through paradoxes, this review suggests that connecting leaders may capitalize on their crossroads position. Thus, while being stuck in-between could feel paralyzing, our work stresses that the paradoxes experienced by the connecting leader may also prove generative and empowering.

NOTE

1. Or French but no article written in French has been selected in the final list.

REFERENCES

Alfes, K., & Langner, N. (2017). Paradoxical leadership. *Organizational Dynamics, 46*(2), 96–103.

Andriopoulos, C., & Lewis, M. W. (2009). Exploitation-exploration tensions and organizational ambidexterity: Managing paradoxes of innovation. *Organization Science, 20*(4), 696–717.

Balogun, J., & Johnson, G. (2004). Organizational restructuring and middle manager sensemaking. *Academy of Management Journal, 47*(4), 523–549.

Bartunek, J. M., Walsh, K., & Lacey, C. A. (2000). Dynamics and dilemmas of women leading women. *Organization Science, 11*(6), 589–610.

Baškarada, S., Watson, J., & Cromarty, J. (2016). Leadership and organizational ambidexterity. *Journal of Management Development, 35*(6), 778–788.

Brower, H. H., Schoorman, F. D., & Tan, H. H. (2000). A model of relational leadership: The integration of trust and leader–member exchange. *The Leadership Quarterly, 11*(2), 227–250.

Collinson, D. (2005). Dialectics of leadership. *Human Relations, 58*(11), 1419–1442.

Collinson, D., & Collinson, M. (2009). 'Blended leadership': Employee perspectives on effective leadership in the UK further education sector. *Leadership, 5*(3), 365–380.

Cronin, T. E., & Genovese, M. A. (2012). *Leadership matters: Unleashing the power of paradox*. Paradigm.

Denison, D. R., Hooijberg, R., & Quinn, R. E. (1995). Paradox and performance: Toward a theory of behavioral complexity in managerial leadership. *Organization Science, 6*(5), 524–540.

Farrell, M. (2018). Leadership reflections: Leadership paradoxes. *Journal of Library Administration, 58*(2), 166–173.

Fredberg, T. (2014). If I say it's complex, it bloody well will be CEO strategies for managing paradox. *The Journal of Applied Behavioral Science, 50*(2), 171–188.

Gioia, D. A., & Chittipeddi, K. (1991). Sensemaking and sensegiving in strategic change initiation. *Strategic Management Journal, 12*(6), 433–448.

Guarana, C., & Hernandez, M. (2015). Building sense out of situational complexity: The role of ambivalence in creating functional leadership processes. *Organizational Psychology Review, 5*(1), 50–73.

Gurd, B., & Helliar, C. (2017). Looking for leaders: 'Balancing' innovation, risk and management control systems. *The British Accounting Review, 49*(1), 91–102. https://doi.org/10.1016/j.bar.2016.10.008

Havermans, L. A., Den Hartog, D. N., Keegan, A., & Uhl-Bien, M. (2015). Exploring the role of leadership in enabling contextual ambidexterity. *Human Resource Management, 54*(1), 179–200.

Havermans, L. A., Keegan, A., & Den Hartog, D. N. (2015). Choosing your words carefully: Leaders' narratives of complex emergent problem resolution. *International Journal of Project Management, 33*(5), 973–984.

Heavey, C., & Simsek, Z. (2017). Distributed cognition in top management teams and organizational ambidexterity: The influence of transactive memory systems. *Journal of Management, 43*(3), 919–945.

Isabella, L. (1990). Evolving interpretations as change unfolds: How managers construe key organizational events. *Academy of Management Journal, 33*, 7–41.

Jansen, J. J., Kostopoulos, K. C., Mihalache, O. R., & Papalexandris, A. (2016). A Socio-psychological perspective on team ambidexterity: The contingency role of supportive leadership behaviours. *Journal of Management Studies, 53*(6), 939–965.

Jarvis, C., Gulati, A., McCririck, V., & Simpson, P. (2013). Leadership matters: Tensions in evaluating leadership development. *Advances in Developing Human Resources, 15*(1), 27–45.

Jaser, Z. (2017). Pulled in two directions. Being in concert a leader to some and a follower to others. *Academy of Management Proceedings, 2017*(1), 16660.

Johnson, J. D. (2016). Tensions between teams and their leaders. *Journal of Technology Management & Innovation, 11*(3), 117–126.

Kan, M. M., & Parry, K. W. (2004). Identifying paradox: A grounded theory of leadership in overcoming resistance to change. *The Leadership Quarterly, 15*(4), 467–491.

Kark, R., Preser, R., & Zion-Waldoks, T. (2016). From a politics of dilemmas to a politics of paradoxes: Feminism, pedagogy, and women's leadership for social change. *Journal of Management Education, 40*(3), 293–320.

Kauppila, O. P., & Tempelaar, M. P. (2016). The social-cognitive underpinnings of employees' ambidextrous behaviour and the supportive role of group managers' leadership. *Journal of Management Studies, 53*(6), 1019–1044.

Keller, D. (2015). Leadership of international schools: Understanding and managing dualities. *Educational Management Administration & Leadership, 43*(6), 900–918.

Keller, T., & Weibler, J. (2015). What it takes and costs to be an ambidextrous manager: Linking leadership and cognitive strain to balancing exploration and exploitation. *Journal of Leadership and Organizational Studies, 22*(1), 54–71.

Knight, E., & Paroutis, S. (2017). Becoming salient: The TMT leader's role in shaping the interpretive context of paradoxical tensions. *Organization Studies, 38*(3/4), 403–432.

Kodish, S. (2006). The paradoxes of leadership: The contribution of Aristotle. *Leadership, 2*(4), 451–468.

Krippendorff, K. (2013). *Content analysis: An introduction to its methodology* (3rd ed.). SAGE.

Kuna, S. (2017). Paradoxical processes impeding public management reform implementation: Perspectives of management consultants. *Public Personnel Management, 46*(2), 188–207.

Lavine, M. (2014). Paradoxical leadership and the competing values framework. *The Journal of Applied Behavioral Scince, 50*(2), 189–205.

Lawrence, K. A., Lenk, P., & Quinn, R. E. (2009). Behavioral complexity in leadership: The psychometric properties of a new instrument to measure behavioral repertoire. *The Leadership Quarterly, 20*(2), 87–102.

Lewis, M. W. (2017). Paradoxes of business schools. *Global Focus,* https://globalfocusmagazine.com/paradoxes-business-schools/

Lewis, M. W. (2000). Exploring paradox: Toward a more comprehensive guide. *Academy of Management Review, 25*(4), 760–776.

Lewis, M. W., Andriopoulos, C., & Smith, W. K. (2014). Paradoxical leadership to enable strategic agility. *California Management Review, 56*(3), 58–77.

Li, C. R. (2016). The role of top-team diversity and perspective taking in mastering organizational ambidexterity. *Management and Organization Review, 12*(4), 769–794.

Liu, H., & Baker, C. (2016). Ordinary aristocrats: The discursive construction of philanthropists as ethical leaders. *Journal of Business Ethics, 133*(2), 261–277.

Lubatkin, M. H., Simsek, Z., Ling, Y., & Veiga, J. F. (2006). Ambidexterity and performance in small- to medium-sized firms: The pivotal role of top management team behavioral integration. *Journal of Management, 32*(5), 646–672.

Lüscher, L. S., & Lewis, M. W. (2008). Organizational change and managerial sensemaking: Working through paradox. *Academy of Management Journal, 51*(2), 221–240. https://doi.org/10.5465/amj.2008.31767217

Mink, O., Rogers, R., & Watkins, K. (1989). Creative leadership: Discovering paradoxes of innovation and risk. *Contemporary Educational Psychology, 14*(3), 228–240.

Miron-Spektor, E., Ingram, A., Keller, J., Smith, W. K., & Lewis, M. (2018). Microfoundations of organizational paradox: The problem is how we think about the problem. *Academy of Management Journal, 61*(1), 26–45.

Murphy, J., Rhodes, M. L., Meek, J. W., & Denyer, D. (2017). Managing the entanglement: Complexity leadership in public sector systems. *Public Administration Review, 77*(5), 692–704.

Northouse, P. G. (2010). *Leadership: Theory and practice* (5th ed.). SAGE.

Nyberg, D., & Sveningsson, S. (2014). Paradoxes of authentic leadership: Leader identity struggles. *Leadership, 10*(4), 437–455.

Pascuci, L. M., Meyer Júnior, V., & Crubellate, J. M. (2017). Strategic management in hospitals: Tensions between the managerial and institutional lens. *Brazilian Administration Review, 14*(2), e160092. https://doi.org/10.1590/1807-7692bar2017160092

Peng, K., & Nisbett, R. E. (1999). Culture, dialectics, and reasoning about contradiction. *American Psychologist, 54*(9), 741.

Rhodes, C., & Badham, R. (2018). Ethical irony and the relational leader: grappling with the infinity of ethics and the finitude of practice. *Business Ethics Quarterly, 28*(1), 71–98.

Schad, J., Lewis, M. W., Raisch, S., & Smith, W. K. (2016). Paradox research in management science: Looking back to move forward. *Academy of Management Annals, 10*(1), 5–64.

Scott, A., & Timmons, S. (2017). Tensions within management roles in healthcare organisations. *Nursing Management, 24*(1), 31–37.

Sharma, G., & Good, D. (2013). The work of middle managers: Sensemaking and sensegiving for creating positive social change. *The Journal of Applied Behavioral Science, 49*(1), 95–122.

Smith, W. K. (2014). Dynamic decision making: A model of senior leaders managing strategic paradoxes. *Academy of Management Journal, 1015*(1), 58–89.

Smith, W. K., & Besharov, M. L. (2019). Bowing before dual gods: How structured flexibility sustains organizational hybridity. *Administrative Science Quarterly, 64*(1), 1–44.

Smith, W. K., Besharov, M. L., Wessels, A. K., & Chertok, M. (2012). A paradoxical leadership model for social entrepreneurs: Challenges, leadership skills, and pedagogical tools for managing social and commercial demands. *Academy of Management Learning & Education, 11*(3), 463–478.

Smith, W. K., Binns, A., & Tushman, M. L. (2010). Complex business models: Managing strategic paradoxes simultaneously. *Long Range Planning, 43*(2/3), 448–461.

Smith, W. K., & Lewis, M. W. (2011). Toward a theory of paradox: A dynamic equilibrium model of organizing. *Academy of Management Review, 36*(2), 381–403.

Smith, W. K., & Lewis, M. W. (2012). Leadership skills for managing paradoxes. *Industrial and Organizational Psychology*, 227–231.

Smith, W. K., & Tushman, M. L. (2005). Managing strategic contradictions: A top management model for managing innovation streams. *Organization Science*, 522–536.

Sparr, J. L. (2018). Paradoxes in organizational change: The crucial role of leaders' sensegiving. *Journal of Change Management, 18*(2), 162–180.

Sundgren, M., & Styhre, A. (2006). Leadership as de-paradoxification: Leading new drug development work at three pharmaceutical companies. *Leadership, 2*(1), 31–52.

Thornton, K., Walton, J., Wilson, M., & Jones, L. (2018). Middle leadership roles in universities: Holy Grail or poisoned chalice. *Journal of Higher Education Policy and Management, 40*(3), 208–223.

Townsend, A. (2015). Leading school networks: Hybrid leadership in action? *Educational Management Administration & Leadership*, 1–19.

Uhl-Bien, M., & Arena, M. (2018). Leadership for organizational adaptability: A theoretical synthesis and integrative framework. *The Leadership Quarterly, 29*(1), 89–104.

Waldman, D. A., & Bowen, D. E. (2016). Learning to be a paradox-savvy leader. *Academy of Management Perspectives, 30*(3), 316–327.

Zhang, Y., Waldman, D. A., Han, Y., & Li, X. (2015). Paradoxical leader behaviors in people management: Antecedents and consequences. *Academy of Management Journal, 58*(2), 538–566.

APPENDIX BEGINS ON NEXT PAGE

Appendix: Literature Review Summary

			Locus of Paradoxes		*Paradoxical Leadership*		
Author(s)	*Title*	*Journal*	*Paradoxes as Stemming From the Environment*	*Paradoxes as Inherent to Leadership*	*Behaviors*	*Skills*	*Resource*
Mink et al. (1989)	Creative Leadership: Discovering Paradoxes of Innovation and Risk	*Contemporary Educational Psychology*		X		X	
Denison et al. (1995)	Paradox and Performance: Toward a Theory of Behavioral Complexity in managerial Leadership	*Organization Science*				X	
Bartunek et al. (2000)	Dynamics and Dilemmas of Women Leading Women	*Organization Science*		X			X
Beech et al. (2004)	Paradox as Invitation to Act in Problematic Change Situations	*Human Relations*	X		X		
Kan & Parry (2004)	Identifying Paradox: A Grounded Theory of Leadership in Overcoming Resistance to Change	*The Leadership Quarterly*	X				X
Collinson (2005)	Dialectics of Leadership	*Human Relations*		X			
Smith & Tushman (2005)	Managing Strategic Contradictions: A Top Management Model for Managing Innovation Streams	*Organization Science*	X			X	
Kodish (2006)	The Paradoxes of Leadership: The Contribution of Aristotle	*Leadership*		X			
Lubatkin et al. (2006)	Ambidexterity and Performance in Small- to Medium-Sized Firms: The Pivotal Role of Top Management Team Behavioral Integration	*Journal of Management*	X			X	
Sundgren & Styhre (2006)	Leadership as De-Paradoxification: Leading New Drug Development Work at Three Pharmaceutical Companies	*Leadership*	X				X

Carmeli & Halevi (2009)	How Top Management Team Behavioral Integration and Behavioral Complexity Enable Organizational Ambidexterity: The Moderating Role of Contextual Ambidexterity	*The Leadership Quarterly*	X		X	X
Collinson & Collinson (2009)	'Blended Leadership': Employee Perspectives on Effective Leadership in the UK Further Education Sector	*Leadership*		X		
Gibbs (2009)	Dialectics in a Global Software Team: Negotiating Tensions Across Time, Space, and culture	*Human Relations*	X		X	
Lawrence et al. (2009)	Behavioral Complexity in Leadership: The Psychometric Properties of a New Instrument to Measure Behavioral Repertoire	*The Leadership Quarterly*	X		X	
Nemanich & Vera (2009)	Transformational Leadership and Ambidexterity in the Context of an Acquisition	*The Leadership Quarterly*	X		X	X
Ospina & Saz-Carranza (2010)	Paradox and Collaboration in Network Management	*Administration & Society*	X		X	
Smith et al. (2010)	Complex Business Models: Managing Strategic Paradoxes Simultaneously	*Long Range Planning*	X			X
O'Reilly (2011)	Organizational Ambidexterity in Action: How Managers Explore and Exploit	*California Management Review*	X		X	X
Rosing et al. (2011)	Explaining the Heterogeneity of the Leadership-Innovation Relationship: Ambidextrous Leadership	*The Leadership Quarterly*	X		X	

(Appendix continues on next page)

Appendix (Continued)

			Locus of Paradoxes		Paradoxical Leadership		
Author(s)	*Title*	*Journal*	*Paradoxes as Stemming From the Environment*	*Paradoxes as Inherent to Leadership*	*Behaviors*	*Skills*	*Resource*
Tushman et al. (2011)	The Ambidextruous CEO	*Harvard Business Review*	X		X		
Peters (2012)	The Rhythm of Leading Change: Living With Paradox	*Journal of Management Inquiry*	X				X
Smith & Lewis (2012)	Leadership Skills for Managing Paradoxes	*Industrial and Organizational Psychology*	X		X	X	
Smith et al. (2012)	A Paradoxical Leadership Model for Social Entrepreneurs: Challenges, Leadership Skills, and Pedagogical Tools for Managing Social and Commercial Demands	*Academy of Management Learning and Education*	X		X	X	
Sharma & Good (2013)	The Work of Middle Managers: Sensemaking and Sensegiving for Creating Positive Social Change	*The Journal of Applied Behavioral Science*	X			X	X
Collinson (2014)	Dichotomies, Dialectics and Dilemmas: New Directions for Critical Leadership Studies?	*Leadership*		X			
Fredberg (2014)	If I Say It's Complex, it Bloody Well Will Be: CEO Strategies for Managing Paradox	*The Journal of Applied Behavioral Science*	X				X
Heavey & Simsek (2014)	Distributed Cognition in Top Management Teams and Organizational Ambidexterity: The influence Of Transactive Memory Systems	*Journal of Management*	X			X	
Lavine (2014)	Paradoxical Leadership and The Competing Values Framework	*The Journal of Applied Behavioral Science*		X	X	X	X

Lewis et al. (2014)	Paradoxical Leadership to enable Strategic Agility	*California Management Review*	X		X	X	
O'Kane & Cunningham (2014)	Turnaround Leadership Core Tensions During the Company Turnaround Process	*European Management Journal*	X			X	
Smith (2014)	Dynamic Decision Making: a Model of Senior Leaders Managing Strategic Paradoxes	*Academy of Management Journal*	X		X		
Zacher & Wilden (2014)	A Daily Diary Study on Ambidextrous Leadership and Self-Reported Employee Innovation	*Journal of Occupational & Organizational Psychology*	X		X		
Guarana & Hernandez (2015)	Building Sense Out of Situational Complexity: The Role of Ambivalence in Creating Functional Leadership Processes	*Organizational Psychology Review*	X				X
Havermans, Den Hartog et al. (2015)	Exploring the Role of Leadership in Enabling Contextual Ambidexterity	*Human Resource Management*	X				X
Havermans, Keegan, & Den Hartog (2015)	Choosing Your Words Carefully: Leaders' Narratives of Complex Emergent Problem Resolution	*International Journal of Project Management*	X				X
Keller & Weibler (2015)	What It Takes and Costs to Be an Ambidextrous Manager: Linking Leadership and Cognitive Strain to Balancing Exploration and Exploitation	*Journal of Leadership & Organizational Studies*	X		X		
Keller (2015)	Leadership of International Schools	*Educational Management Administration & Leadership*	X		X		X

(Appendix continues on next page)

Appendix (Continued)

			Locus of Paradoxes		Paradoxical Leadership		
Author(s)	*Title*	*Journal*	*Paradoxes as Stemming From the Environment*	*Paradoxes as Inherent to Leadership*	*Behaviors*	*Skills*	*Resource*
Onyemah & Pesquera (2015)	Cognitive Ambidexterity in Entrepreneurial Leadership: A Four Country Exploratory Study of Women Entrepreneurs' Early Customer Acquisition Strategies	*Organizations & Markets in Emerging Economies*	X			X	
Townsend (2015)	Leading School Networks: Hybrid Leadership in Action?	*Educational Management Administration & Leadership*	X				
Zhang et al. (2015)	Paradoxical Leader Behaviors in People Management: Antecedents and Consequences	*Academy of Management Journal*		X	X	X	
Liu & Baker (2016)	Ordinary Aristocrats: The Discursive Construction of Philanthropists as Ethical Leaders	*Journal of Business Ethics*		X			
Baškarada et al. (2016)	Leadership and Organizational Ambidexterity	*Journal of Management Development*	X		X		
Jansen et al. (2016)	A Socio-Psychological Perspective on Team Ambidexterity: The Contingency Role of Supportive Leadership Behaviours	*Journal of Management Studies*	X				X
Johnson (2016)	Tensions Between Teams and Their Leaders	*Journal of Technology Management & Innovation*		X			
Kark et al. (2016)	From a Politics of Dilemmas to a Politics of Paradoxes	*Journal of Management Education*	X	X			X

Kauppila & Tempelaar (2016)	The Social-Cognitive Underpinnings of Employees' Ambidextrous Behaviour and the Supportive Role of Group Managers' Leadership	*Journal of Management Studies*	X		X		X
Li (2016)	The Role of Top-Team Diversity and Perspective Taking in Mastering Organizational Ambidexterity	*Management & Organization Review*	X	X		X	
Waldman & Bowen (2016)	Learning to Be a Paradox-Savvy Leader	*Academy of Management Perspectives*	X	X			
Alfes & Langner (2017)	Paradoxical Leadership: Understanding and Managing Conflicting Tensions to Foster Volunteer Engagement	*Organizational Dynamics*	X		X		
Gurd & Helliar (2017)	Looking for Leaders: 'Balancing' Innovation, Risk and Management Control Systems	*British Accounting Review*	X				
Knight & Paroutis (2017)	Becoming Salient: The TMT Leader's Role in Shaping the Interpretive Context of Paradoxical Tensions	*Organization Studies*	X				X
Kuna (2017)	Paradoxical Processes Impeding Public Management Reform Implementation: Perspectives of Management Consultants	*Public Personnel Management*	X			X	
Murphy et al. (2017)	Managing the Entanglement: Complexity Leadership in Public Sector systems	*Public Administration Review*	X				
Pascuci et al. (2017)	Strategic Management in Hospitals: Tensions Between the Managerial and Institutional Lens	*Brazilian Administration Review*	X				
Scott & Timmon (2017)	Tensions Within Management Roles in Healthcare Organisations	*Nursing Management - UK*	X				

(Appendix continues on next page)

Appendix (Continued)

			Locus of Paradoxes		*Paradoxical Leadership*		
Author(s)	*Title*	*Journal*	*Paradoxes as Stemming From the Environment*	*Paradoxes as Inherent to Leadership*	*Behaviors*	*Skills*	*Resource*
Farrell (2018)	Leadership Reflections: Leadership Paradoxes	*Journal of Library Administration*		X	X	X	X
Lee & Reade (2018)	The Role of Yin-Yang Leadership and Cosmopolitan Followership in Fostering Employee Commitment in China	*Cross Cultural & Strategic Management*	X		X		
Miron-Spektor et al. (2018)	Microfoundations of Organizational Paradox: The problem Is How We Think About the Problem	*Academy of Management Journal*	X			X	
Morais et al. (2018)	The Chairperson and CEO Roles Interaction and Responses to Strategic Tensions	*Corporate Governance: The International Journal of Effective Board Performance*	X		X		
Rhodes & Badham (2018)	Ethical Irony and the Relational Leader: Grappling With the Infinity of Ethics and the Finitude of Practice	*Business Ethics Quarterly*		X	X		
Sparr (2018)	Paradoxes in Organizational Change: The Crucial Role of leaders' Sensegiving	*Journal of Change Management*	X				X
Thornton et al. (2018)	Middle Leadership Roles in Universities: Holy Grail or poisoned Chalice	*Journal of Higher Education Policy & Management*	X		X		
Uhl-Bien & Arena (2018)	Leadership for Organizational Adaptability: a Theoretical Synthesis and Integrative Framework	*The Leadership Quarterly*	X				

Smith & Besharov (2019)	Bowing Before Dual Gods: How structured Flexibility Sustains Organizational Hybridity	*Administrative Science Quarterly*	X	X

CHAPTER 5

MEDDLING IN THE MIDDLE

The Middle Manager Yo-Yo on a Constant Move

Mats Alvesson
University of Queensland Business School, Australia and Cass Business School, City University of London

Susann Gjerde
BI Norwegian Business School, Norway and Lund University, Sweden

ABSTRACT

Management and leadership studies are not well known for a dynamic or processual thinking. So much of the understanding, including that of middle managers (MM), is highly static and circles around fixed categories like traits, types, styles, values, relations, roles, et cetera. Sometimes, more dynamic concepts such as negotiations, sense-making, identity work and role-making surface, but these are fairly marginal compared to a more static terminology of role-sets in the literature where one is either a leader or a follower. In reality, the MM is expected to be *both-and*, and will engage with dynamic and shifting roles and identities. This chapter presents a theorizing of life in the middle, which takes these dynamic shifts seriously. We make use of the yo-yo as a metaphor to elucidate inherent tensions between the

The Connecting Leader: Serving Concurrently as a Leader and a Follower
pp. 131–151

MM's tasks, identity, and relationality (TIR) and address what is characteristically *middle* about these three elements. The yo-yo image draws our attention to fluctuating movements up and down, back and forth, suddenly and repeatedly, and creates awareness around different pulls on TIR that may easily turn life in the genuine middle into a knotted experience.

INTRODUCTION

Middle manager (MM) refers to all those below top management—and in large companies, the board of directors (Dopson & Stewart, 1990, p. 12). It is of course misleading to paint all MMs as a "single, univocal, homogenous entity" (Thomas & Linstead, 2002, p. 73). Still, organizational members that adhere to this category tend to share a common challenge: their position in the "sandwiched" middle (Bryman & Lilley, 2009) means they have to engage with a particular form of middle levelness that can be strenuous. Relationality is key as a middle only exist in the context of *others* above and below.

All people are no doubt in the "middle" of something: between following the expectations of formal rules and requirements and showing flexibility and judgment, between being a loyal organizational or family member and an autonomous subject, and between fulfilling social scripts and behaving authentically, to name a few. But for the MM these middle aspects may be particularly pronounced. And so, although this middle experience tends to be downplayed in the literature which often portrays the MM simply as a superior manager with subordinates, their reality is a paradoxical one: MMs are seniors, but are not at the top, and they have some autonomy and authority, but may easily be challenged from above and below (Sims, 2003). MMs also have many reporting relationships and "overlapping territories" (Kanter, 1982, p. 161) which requires them to sell their ideas not only to formal superiors and subordinates, but also to individuals who are more or less on the same status and hierarchical level as themselves, including peers and external business partners in the market and/or network relations. Thus, much like Janus, the two-faced Roman god who could face two directions at once, MMs face at least two directions if not simultaneously, then consecutively throughout the day (Laurent, 1978). This double relationality where the MM has to operate as superior *and* subordinate is an important aspect of the role that makes it a particularly dynamic one.

Although the Januslike feature is characteristic of the MM role, few studies have explored what it means to *be* genuinely middle and *engage* in the middle levelness that this role implies (Gjerde & Alvesson, 2020). In this chapter we address this lack and attend to what is uniquely middle about the MM's doings (tasks), self-understanding (identities) and ways of relating to significant others in the organization (relationality). We argue that pulls from above and below that relate to these TIR domains implies that the MM has to work on being flexible and move between task orientations; engage in identity work in terms of superior/subordinate; and manage within complicated relationalities which includes dealing with different notions of *we* and *them*. This constant TIR-work creates a particularly dynamic MM role and identity.

Through our theorizing, we add to the literature of management and leadership that challenges static dichotomies of superior/leader and subordinate/follower and suggest a messier and more dynamic understanding of life in the middle. The chapter also contributes to practice and may be of value to MMs who wish to reflect more deeply on what it means to be and engage with middle-levelness for a more reflective and reflexive management and leadership practice, that is, to act with awareness of how assumptions, identifications, choices and actions impact self, others and emerging roles (Cunliffe, 2016).

We start by briefly describing views on MMs in the literature, before we identify task, identity and relationality as three key domains of the MM role which are sometimes in harmony and sometimes inconsistent or even in conflict. We go on to discuss harmony and inconsistency and how the MM moves back and forth between being upward- or downward-orientated in relation to work tasks, identification and relatedness. We talk about MM moves between superiority and subordinateship as a smooth ride or a knotted mess. We continue by addressing issues of MM processuality, before we end on some themes for reflection encouraged by the yo-yo metaphor.

MIDDLE MANAGEMENT

MMs hold important functions in the organizations. They have been described as "lieutenants" who execute top management's orders, "lynchpins" that hold complex organizations together (Huy et al., 2014, p. 1651), and "umbrella carriers" who protect subordinates from "shit" and "stupidities" that top management pass down the hierarchy (Gjerde & Alvesson, 2020). Since Burns (1957) first suggested that the MM role consisted of a large bulk of conversation, micropolitics, and human relationships (Tengblad & Vie, 2012), an extensive stream of research has taught us *who* the MM is, *how* they work, *why* they matter and whether or not this role has *changed* over the years (e.g., Dopson & Stewart, 1990; Heyden et al., 2017; Huy et al., 2014; Osterman, 2008).

The MM role spans many organizational levels, from top executives running large divisions to small team leaders responsible for only a few subordinates, and a wide range of contexts. It is therefore no surprise that the research has been fairly inconclusive. For example, while McCann et al. (2008) argue that information technology, massive restructuring of organizations (e.g., delayering, downsizing and lean production), and international competition has led to heightened intensity in work hours and harsh terms of engagement for the MM, Hales (2005, p. 501) suggests that MM roles have not changed much but "exhibit remarkable stability over time and across organizations."

Without claiming or attempting to present any absolute truths, several MM studies suggest that inhabiting this middle position can be a confusing. Thomas and Linstead (2002) found an outspread insecurity, ambiguity and confusion among 150 managers in 50 organizations under restructuring. The MMs in this study felt pressure to work hard and legitimize their work, while an unclear managerial identity was eroded. Down and Reveley (2009) reveal discourse confusion among managers who face "conflicting managerial discourses" in their organization, and Musson and Duberley (2007) underline variety and complexity of responses experienced by MMs to these discourses. Still, Clarke et al. (2009, p. 324) on the other hand, found that rather than being confused by conflicting discourses, the managers they studied drew on "mutually antagonistic discursive resources in authoring conceptions of their selves". Thus, while some researchers find that MMs struggle with a variety of discourses which produces a variety of experiences and some "losing the plot" (Thomas & Linstead, 2002), other MMs seem to integrate these discourses.

Despite a growing literature on the what, why and how of MMs and their experiences, we are still lacking in studies that offer an in-depth understanding of what it means to *be* middle and engage in the *middle-levelness* that is characteristic of this role (Gjerde & Alvesson, 2020). MM studies tend to present fairly general themes that are not necessarily characteristics of life in the middle, such as value-related struggles and issues of subjectivity in relation to discourses that concern strategy, change or participation (Down & Reveley, 2009; Musson & Duberley, 2007; Sveningsson & Alvesson, 2016; Thomas & Linstead, 2002). These are themes that any organizational member may be faced with.

In addition, there is a frequent downplaying of the subordinate aspects of the MM role. From the literature, one may easily get the impression that organizations are full of generals who lead privates, rather than sergeants and corporals which would be a more fitting military-based description (Laurent, 1978). But MMs are with few exceptions in large organizations *also* subordinate managers. A growing infatuation with leadership over management in research and society at large (Alvesson et al., 2017; Mintzberg, 2004) may perhaps explain why researchers rarely study MMs as subordinate managers or followers, but rather (only) as superiors and leaders. This may perhaps also explain why MMs themselves are very willing to describe themselves as leaders, even though contradictory organizational situations challenge them in their doings of leadership (Alvesson & Sveningsson, 2003). No matter the reason, a consequence is that we still do not really grasp the *middle*-level experience of how MMs navigate levels above and below and oscillate between somewhat opposing ideals such as compliance and authority. But there are some exceptions in the literature.

Sims' (2003) study is among the few that does address what it is like to be and work from the middle. He emphasizes the MM's challenging experience "between millstones" where both superiors and subordinates can undermine their positionings. According to Sims (2003, p. 1201), MMs face both ways and have to put together a convincing story about what they are doing both for the benefit of their seniors and for their juniors. The two different audiences are not necessarily convinced by the MMs' often conflicting stories and behaviors which may be perceived as inconsistent across levels. The MMs experience tensions and anxiety as they try to protect those who work for them from "meaninglessness" through storytelling, only to experience that their sensible stories may be turned into "nonsense" by their own superiors (Sims, 2003, p. 1196).

Another exception is an in-depth study of a group of MM professionals (business school deans and institute managers in higher education) (Gjerde & Alvesson, 2020). In this study they find that the MMs take on one of three main subject positions that are influenced by a general identification (or lack thereof) with the level above or below, and with heroic leadership ideas. Among these studied MMs some take the position as "*performance driver,*" a superior position where the aim is to not only pass on but accentuate performance pressures from above; others take an "*impotent*" low-energy position where the MM experiences a lack of agency; while others again take on the position of *protector* or "*umbrella carrier.*" This latter position is subordinate-energized, and the aim is—counter to more general expectations to implement pressures from above—to protect colleagues, professional work and culture from what is perceived to be unnecessary and/or disturbing initiatives and communication from superiors. The study suggests that these three positions help the MMs make sense of their own role and identity while navigating up and down the organizational hierarchy across opposing logics and values. In this chapter we bring additional dynamics to the picture that Sims (2003), Gjerde and Alvesson (2020) paint in their studies as we explore middle-level aspects of task, identity and relationality and how these three interact. This suggests an even messier and more dynamic picture of life in the genuine middle.

ON TASK, IDENTITY, AND RELATIONALITY OF THE MM ROLE

When managerial *role* is used as a term in the organization and management literature, it is often to point to the tasks, activities and duties that are linked to a managerial job (Katz & Kahn, 1966; Stewart, 1982; Tsui, 1984). One may easily mistake role simply for tasks (e.g., to motivate subordinates), but role spans a wider array of behaviors and may also include "standardized patterns of behavior" associated with such organizational tasks (Katz & Kahn, 1966, p. 37). In other words, behavioral expectations that concern *how* tasks should be addressed are also part of role (e.g., to motivate subordinates through individualized consideration).

In the forming of MM roles there is an indirect, even loose relationship between tasks, identity, and relational behavior. The MM operates in a "crossfire of pressures" (Gallos, 2002). From this crossfire MMs engage with task and behavioral expectations, life history, overall identity issues and a supply of identity prescriptions (e.g., to be a transformative leader, an authentic person or something similar). Sometimes the MM will use "impression management" to make their social image come across as real while they conform to prototypic characteristic behaviors of their role almost like actors follow "scripts" in the theatre (Goffman, 1959). Other times they will challenge behavioral and task expectations that do not fit their sense of self or their own role definition (Gjerde & Ladegård, 2019; Sveningsson & Alvesson, 2003).

Social interaction between the MM and their role-set (superior, subordinate and peer) will stir up a dynamic interplay of task, identity, and relationality (TIR) expectations that sometimes draw in opposite directions and other times align. The three TIR elements are *within* themselves varied. This means there may be different, sometimes inconsistent, even contradictory sets of tasks, identities and relations that pull in different directions at once, while other times they align within and pull in the same direction. There may also be variations of conflict and alignment *between* tasks, identities and relations. For space and pedagogical reasons, we will concentrate only on the dynamics between TIR elements. It is this interplay that we address in this chapter with the use of the yo-yo metaphor. We are open for the idea of a triple yo-yo in use, but here for the sake of simplification we address TIR as discrete themes, that move up and down in different ways.

There is a wide set of themes which relate to TIR that managers, entrepreneurs and professionals in nonroutinized work, who are supposed to take responsibility, plan ahead, use autonomy, work with colleagues and judgment at work, share. Many of these are not characteristic of the *middle* manager role, even if they are relevant for people who are formally and substantively in such a middle position. These will not receive our attention, as we will only address the typical middle aspects of these within hierarchical relations.

Task

Task here is what the MM *does* in terms of work tasks that relate to engagements with people who are superior and subordinate. Thus, task relates to functions and practices that come from dealing with work that are more or less contingent upon senior and/or junior levels. MM tasks may be passed down and up the organizational hierarchy, and the task ratios of above to below and below to above will result in different dynamics and fleeting MM roles.

Sometimes when the MM experiences a strong link to *superior* levels and is predominately occupied with tasks from above, s/he may be governed by strategies, policies, bureaucratic requirements, careful monitoring, and the use of performance indicators. For example, tasks may be to "translate" expectations of senior management "into actual operational activities by a process of specification and/or amplification" (Hales & Nightingale, 1986: 11), "design the systems, carry out the plans and redirect their staffs' activities accordingly" (Kanter, 1982, p. 151), "whip up excitement over a vision" (Kanter, 1982, p. 158), or "ensure junior staff fulfill organizational requirements" (Harding et al., 2014, p. 1230). The ratio of tasks above to below creates a Sm role, that is, *Subordinate* manager, where the MM attends to implementation and deliveries with a compliant attitude and behavior. The formal MM may thus taskwise be more of a Subordinate than a Manager, as the latter is typically seen as a superior position, which implies controlling more than being controlled by task requirements.

The task situation may at other times be much more open and *decoupled* from the superior level. Focus may be on issues outside the radar of top management, since these may be too complicated and long-term oriented to monitor in the short-term perspective and difficult to assess for outsiders or even insiders (like much of the work we find in higher education, research and development, and complicated engineering). MMs "have their fingers on the pulse of operations" and can therefore "conceive, suggest, and set in motion new ideas that top managers have not thought of" (Kanter, 1982, p. 151). For example, during strategic change processes MMs may see it as their main task to "read the wind" (Dutton et al., 1997, p. 407) and "sell issues to top management" (Dutton & Ashford, 1993, p. 397) rather than the other way around. The ratio of tasks below to above may during these instances create a sM role, that is, subordinate *manager*, where the subordinate element in relation to top levels is marginal while a more authoritative attitude is emphasized.

The MM will also relate to *subordinates* and their task requirements through stronger and weaker links. Sometimes, subordinates may be inclined to work autonomously or in groups which only invokes the superior manager to a limited extent (Blom & Alvesson, 2014). During other instances, the MM may experience strong requirements and demands from subordinates who call upon their involvement as advisor or decision-maker or as general support to reduce uncertainty or anxiety or even take on the risk for blame if things should go wrong. Subordinates may see it as the MM's task to challenge and resist radical organizational change (Huy et al., 2014), attend to their emotions during such challenging times (Huy, 2002), explain and make sense of what goes on in the organization (Sims, 2003), and protect their time, peace of mind and professional culture (Gjerde & Alvesson, 2020). Initiatives, requests, and problems from subordinates may be put on the MM's agenda, and operational problems which are more or less handled by subordinates may beg the MM's attention.

Depending upon how strong an imprint the subordinates and superiors put on the role through their task requirements, the MM may be pulled into a Ms role, that is, expected to *manage* subordinates (e.g., to decide, give advice, support etc.) or into a mS role, that is, *"managed by"* subordinates (e.g., to follow their wishes). The mS is not necessarily a "servant leader" (Greenleaf, 1977), but may reflect organizational complexities and contingencies or simply issues around organizational power. In many organizations the managerial prerogative is quite weak (e.g., in the higher education or in professional service firms, Parker, 2004), and resourceful subordinates may give feedback, come up with requests, engage in resistance, et cetera, in a way that creates an mS role. Thus, MM roles are not given but emerge as external forces, and as we will soon see "internal" forces, trigger the creation of new MM identities and relational interactions.

Identity

We define identity as "a reflexively organized understanding of one's distinctiveness and valued key characteristics" (Alvesson & Robertson, 2016, p. 9) and see MM-identity as a response to questions such as "who am I" in relation to the MM role, "what should I do" in this middle, and "who am I becoming" as a consequence of my doings? According to social identity theory, social identification with a group, such as, managers,

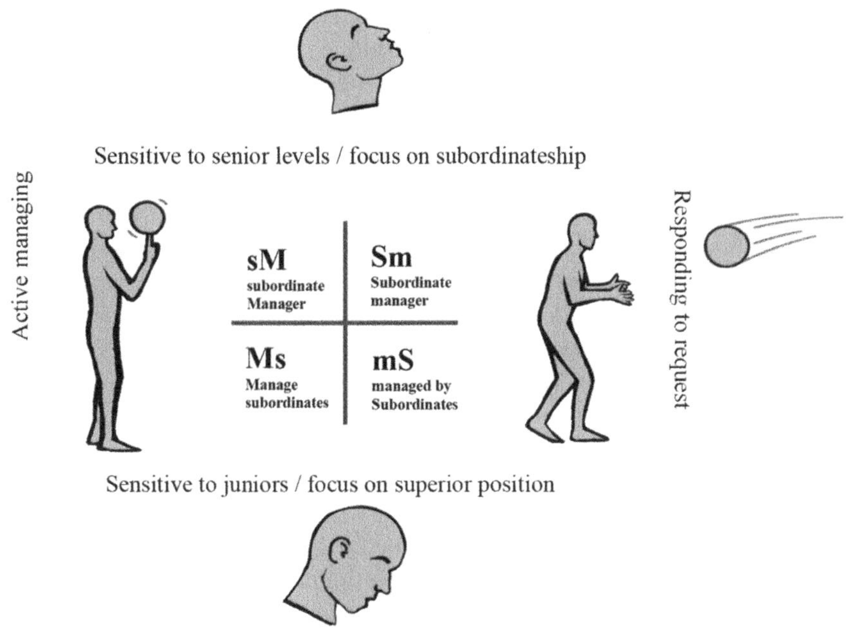

Figure 5.1. Four MM roles.

results in taking on activities that are congruent with the identity and stereotypical perceptions of self (Ashforth & Mael, 1989). One could imagine that for the MMs their task activities are prescribed, and their identities grow as they incorporate "the distinctiveness and prestige of the group" into their sense of self (Alveson & Robertson, 2016, p. 20). However, neither task requirements nor identity is a straightforward matter for the MM. There is a vagueness surrounding what "management" is and a lack of agreement of what "middle" is, which makes it challenging to secure a meaningful identity from this role (Thomas & Linstead, 2002, p. 77).

Furthermore, the Januslike feature of the MM role means it comes with dual identities: to be a "leader" to some and "follower" to others (Caughron & Mumford, 2012; Chun et al., 2009; Jaser, 2017). This implies incorporating somewhat opposing attitudes (e.g., authoritative and compliant) and contradictory subject positions as "controller" and "controlled," "resister" and "resisted" (Harding et al., 2014, p. 1213) into one's self-in-role understanding. The need to see oneself both as a superior "leader" and a subordinate "follower" may create a volatile sense of being and result in fluctuating identity work, that is, attempting to form, repair, maintain, strengthen or revise "the constructions that are productive of a sense of coherence and distinctiveness" (Sveningsson & Alvesson, 2003, p. 1165).

To add to this complexity, the MM's story "is one in which they are always at risk of losing the self" (Sims, 2003, p. 1208). The MM is "under the eye" of superior levels and therefore never able to tell narratives as freely as they could earlier in their career. They have to come up with plausible and meaningful stories to explain what goes on even when they do not understand it themselves, and present compelling stories about decisions and visions they may disagree with or for which they have little concern. If they fail to tell a compelling story, their identity may quickly be turned into a passionless or impotent one by self and others (Sims, 2003).

To counteract passionless and impotent identities and make meaning out of tasks that may easily be described as "just stuff" (Sims, 2003, p. 1205), the MM (and the MM literature) construct identities with a hint of heroism: such as, to be a "performance driver" (Gjerde & Alvesson, 2020, p. 18), "path-finder," "problem-solver" (Leavitt, 1986, as cited in Beatty & Lee, 1992, p. 961), or "therapist" who alleviates pain and attends to deflated moral, depression and paralysis during change (Huy, 2001). Other semiheroic MM identities are linked to change: such as, to be a status quo challenger (Kanter, 1981), an "influencer" of change (Taylor & Helfat, 2009), change initiator and executioner (Heyden et al., 2017), "change agent" and "resistor" (Huy et al., 2014). Some identities form in relation to creative tasks: such as, to be an "innovator" (Kanter, 1982) and "idea entrepreneur" (Kanter, 1986, p. 19). Others revolve around communication from the middle: such as, to be a "liaison" and "information disseminator" (Jacobsen, 2019), or "organizational linking pin" (Glaser et al., 2016). While others again link to how the MM feels obliged to enable subordinates to do their work: such as, to be a creator of "workarounds" for smooth day-to-day accomplishments (Caughron & Mumford, 2012: 352), or an "umbrella carrier" that is, a protector of subordinates' time, mental states and culture (Gjerde & Alvesson, 2020).

What people do when enacting roles feeds into their self-understanding and identity creation. But roles will also be enlarged, modified, marginalized and rejected during "identity work" (Sveningsson & Alvesson, 2003: 1178). This mutual interaction between doing and being is described in an in-depth study of a senior manager where the "heroine" had a strong preference for dealing with strategy, visions and culture—tasks that align with a leadership discourse—while she disliked and distanced herself from the "janitor issues" tied to her MM role. As a consequence, she was more prone to act upon her convictions and ideal leader identity, while putting off the janitor-related task expectations, much to the dismay of her subordinates and colleagues. This resulted in tensions as the Heroine attempted to change overall role by challenging task priorities, while engaging in identity work to maintain her self-in-role under-

Table 5.1. Heroic and Semiheroic MM-Identities

Fixer	*Change-Agent*	*Creator*	*Communicator*	*Enabler/Protector*
• Performance driver" • Path-finder • Problem-solver • Therapist	• Status quo challenger • Influencer of change • Change initiator and executioner • Resistor	• Innovator • Idea entrepreneur	• Liaison and information disseminator • Organizational linking pin	• Creator of workarounds • Umbrella carrier, that is, a protector of subordinates' time, mental states, and culture

standing, including referring to vital work tasks as "janitor work" to emphasize that this was *not* her.

MM identity constructions may be strongly fueled by the want to progress along the organizational hierarchy, which means that a key reference point is an imagined future position as a top manager. However, upward orientation may vary. Youth, signs of promise, a particular elite class and school background tend to support upward identifications. Others may have less ambition, or personal or social qualities that support upward mobility and/or may at a certain age be adapted to a MM position. People with a strong anchoring in a profession may identify more with this and other professionals and thus share identification with subordinates rather than with senior people. In such instances they may see the superiors more like administrators than professionals, even if they in one sense or another also belong to or used to belong to the profession (such as, universities, see Parker, 2014; or professional service firms see Empson & Langley, 2015).

Relationality

Relationality, our third and final theme, is a complicated one and we mainly focus on aspects that deal with group belongingness and valued interactions: Who is (are) the significant other(s) and if there is more than one which is common, how does the subject relate to these? How does the MM engage with the in-group/out-group theme? Who are "we" (if any) and who are "they"?

Of course, people have many versions of we and they within an organization. In some cases, there is the big happy family where everyone in the organization is united and forms an overall whole. but you cannot have close and strong relations with all. Time, energy, and emotions are limited and the better relations you have with some, the more other relations tend to be weakened, even though it is not a simple zero-sum game. In most cases, there are differentiations along several dimensions. In- and outgroups call for each other and they often shift (Ashforth & Mael, 1989). With every we there is a they. Sometimes this indicates not only being different but may be actively used in negative ways for disidentification in order to strengthen self against another group (e.g., as the previously mentioned heroine did when she made it clear she was one of the leaders and not a janitor). Or as we saw in the study of MMs in the professions where several heads of departments in United Kingdom universities were sure to underline that they, unlike management (above), cared for their subordinates and professional work (Gjerde & Alvesson, 2020).

The MM is a "pivotal role in liaising between senior management and junior staff" (Harding et al., 2014, p. 1215) which implies shifting between we and them. To be good issue sellers, MMs have to engage in interpersonal processes that involve individuals with different status levels (Dutton et al., 1997). However, for the MM wishing to influence, this can prove to be particularly challenging. According to social identity theory, the more a person is seen as embodying group prototypical characteristics and perceived to be a representative of a group, the more leaderlike and influential s/he will be in the group. If s/he is able to craft a sense of us and is seen as someone who promote our interest, s/he will be more accepted and influential (Ibarra et al., 2014). This is to some degree an identity issue for the MM, but very much also a relational one since *signaling* group belongingness is a way to deal with credibility in the eyes of the subordinates. The key point is to be seen as "one of us" more than actually experiencing oneself as a prototypical group member. However, to be perceived as one of us may be difficult for the MM with dual identities, since prototypicality in one group (followers/subordinates) may be mutually exclusive of another (leaders/superiors). Thus, to gain credibility the MM needs to navigate through relations and group affiliations that point both upwards and downwards.

Relating Task, Identity and Relationality—Smooth Ride or Knotted Mess?

How then do MMs handle this interplay of TIR that pull them up and down the organizational hierarchy much like a yo-yo? Is it all a smooth ride or more of a knotted mess?

One possibility is of course full harmony: when TIR mutually define each other and form a coherent whole. We can refer to this as *TIR coherence*. This may be a stable condition, with only minor variation and occasional frictions between elements, which calls for some modest flexibility now and then. However, since we find the stable coherence to be less likely due to the complexities inherent in most organizations, and since a stable coherent ride is less of a problem in need of attention, we only touch marginally upon this here. We turn instead to variation and complications in terms of incoherence and dynamics. This leaves us with three main categories: stable incoherence, dynamic incoherence, and dynamic coherence. The latter implies a number of balancing acts that may give the impression of a static coherence due to quick but disguised and fairly effortless position shifting. Let us develop these ideas in turn.

Stable incoherence is characterized by an ongoing, more or less permanent tension between TIR at least within a specific time period. The MM may be caught in a problematic relationship between superiors and subordinates and perhaps feel that task priority expectations pull their attention in opposite directions. Or they may perhaps feel that identity and tasks are not aligned much like the previously mentioned Heroine who identified with being a leader (Sveningsson & Alvesson, 2003). This Heroine felt very strongly she was a Ms, but she was expected to deal with tasks of a "janitorial" kind, that is, managing hands-on issues like dealing with gardening, cleaning, the archive et cetera. For the MM heroine many work tasks were despised as they clashed with her preferred identity. Her tasks indicated she was Sm (subordinate manager) while she identified with being a Ms (managing subordinates). Thus, her identity and the tasks she was expected to perform were in a constant state of tension. As a consequence, she would spin off into identity work to form, repair, strengthen or revise a sense of identity coherence. The strong disidentification with certain tasks allowed for a positive identity construction (I am a leader, not a janitor). But the contradiction between material work and expectations of what to work with, on the one hand, and identity, on the other, added to the tension and the frustration and locked her into a stable and painful incoherence, that ended with her leaving the job.

Dynamic incoherence is characterized by different types of incoherencies over time. An example of this is a manager who emphasized his authenticity, reliability and trustful relationship with subordinates who generally appreciated his friendly and considerate style (Sveningsson & Alvesson, 2016). But every time the owners of the company he worked for intervened and ran over his decisions, the subordinates found him weak and unreliable and were doubtful of how sincere his appreciative style was. Thus, his self-image and the way he was viewed by others did not always align. In this case, the manager was in fact a chief executive office and thus not formally a MM. Still, the MM-label described him well as he clearly became subordinated to the owners from time to time. Whenever those above took a strong and dominant operational role he was pulled into a Sm (Subordinate manager) role, while he tried to enact the role of sM (subordinate Manager) in line with his considerate identity, seeing himself as the good leader over faithful coworkers.

Dynamic coherence is characterized by contradictions and dilemmas at work which are handled through the processing of TIR and many balancing acts which create an overall, well-functioning and smooth MM existence. The TIR elements may be quite diverse. Still the MM is not too conflicted but jumps fairly effortlessly between different tasks and relationships. Identity work is done flexibly or may even be downplayed, much like we find in a study of senior employees in the investment banking sector who engaged in teflonic identity maneuvering. This is a form of identity minimalism where identity-related issues are deflected away from themselves (Alvesson & Robertson, 2016). Other examples of dynamic coherence may be found in a study with experienced managers who had recently changed jobs (Gjerde & Ladegard, 2018). In this study, we learn how new role-sets require the managers' attention to new tasks and behaviors (e.g., to enable and support subordinates with expert knowledge rather than direct them), and how engaging in new tasks led to new self-in-role understanding (e.g., I am a facilitator) without too much tension for some.

But dynamic coherence may also take the form of a MM moving up and down between different types of positionings without much friction. Over time the MM may shift between being a Subordinate manager (Sm) who takes on a follower position in relation to superiors; a subordinate Manager (sM) where subordinates are managed according to requirements; a Manager of subordinates (Ms) where the MM takes a clear superior position; and managed by Subordinates (mS) responding to initiatives and requests by people who formally are subordinates. Different identities may change without problems, and various types of work tasks may be carried out without much emphasis on being one or the other. The MM may engage in a variety of relations, agreeing with different people and groups despite of their different values and priorities, without being too bothered or feeling a need to show integrity, consistency and authenticity.

Dynamic coherence may for advocates of authentic leadership and believers that people have an "essential" identity or even a coherent narrative about themselves (e.g., George et al., 2007) sound peculiar. Nevertheless, studies indicate that people may be quite adaptive at work. Jackall (1988) writes: "adeptness at inconsistency, without moral uneasiness, is essential for executive success." He cites a senior manager saying that "people up high ... are able to speak out of both sides of their mouth without missing one step" (p. 160). And it is suggested that although it may feel artificial and political to try to get buy-in with different groups, learning to pitch one's ideas to diverse stakeholders may be a sign of "growth." Operating in dynamic coherence and learning to perform smooth yo-yo work, means dealing with the motion of moving up and down the organizational hierarchy, between opposing attitudes, tasks, identities and relational interactions without too much friction.

We believe all four above-mentioned forms of dynamic/stable and coherence/incoherence TIR relations will be more or less salient in the work lives of MMs. There are arguably a variety of stabilizing processes and dynamics of a more or less harmonious kind that characterize many people's work lives. But the dynamics are perhaps especially noticeable for the MMs. Even when faced with stabilizing forces such as explicitly formulated leadership principles, incentive systems and developed organizational cultures, the MM may still be pulled up and down in processual ways and forced to adapt.

THE PROCESSUAL YO-YO RIDE OF MMS

We believe that acknowledging the dynamics inherent in the MM role due to the many contradictory aspects of TIR, is key to understanding the characteristic "middle-levelness" of this role. The yo-yo metaphor is an image that aids us to better see this dynamic process. The metaphor suggests that the MM rarely is a stable position but consists of an ongoing movement between different positionings.

While most work on MM—and other topics—assume that we address stable phenomena, or phenomena that can be captured in stabilized ways (leadership style, managerial tasks, functions, organizational forms, positions, subordinate, etc.) we think the yo-yo image illuminates certain aspects that tend to go undetected under the research radar. For example, during a workday, or even in one's overall storytelling of oneself, the *middle*-M-part may not be that central. Some people in MM positions probably think of themselves mainly as *superiors*, like the "performance driver" who sees it as their main role to wake up sleepy subordinates (Gjerde & Alvesson, 2020). Others will mainly think of themselves as *subordinate* managers (Sm), where their main task is to implement demands from top management. Still others may experience themselves as having mainly collegian relations to fellow coworkers, such as, other professionals or people in the department/function seen as peers. Many issues at work, including doing administration, dealing with customers and suppliers, reading policy documents, feeling overworked, experiencing health problems, doubts about the meaningfulness of what one is doing et cetera are not necessarily connected to being middle managers but are part of (working-)life. And so, the middle aspects may be (temporarily) forgotten.

But then when the MM is called upon to be a leader one minute, and a follower the next due to a meeting, a spontaneous interaction or an incoming email, the middle aspects may become particularly visible as they feel themselves forced to jump between being authoritative and compliant, implementing change and challenging it. Thus, the yo-yo idea suggests that the MM is more or less constantly on the move. There are moments where a mix of TIR pulls the MM toward a strong subordinateship, and other instances where the MM is pulled into becoming a manager and leader in control while subordinate aspects of the MM role fade away into the background. And so, the MM yo-yo moves from these positioned experiences from one moment to the next.

The yo-yo processuality of MM roles means that TIR may hang together in coherent ways, while other times TIR expectations from above, below and within may create a messy and tangled up situation for the MM. Still, contradictory expectations may not necessarily create too many problems: tasks and identity may go in opposite directions, but the role and identity may still feel coherently aligned. And the MM may carry out an instruction from senior management, but still see him- or self as a leader, if s/he frames the tasks that imply carrying instructions from above such as informing about a vision or writing up a budget, in a "leaderly" way. The MM may perhaps also emphasize the in-group relation with top management and feel like a leader and in turn experience that friction between TIR elements is minimized.

REFLEX, REFLECTION, AND REFLEXIVITY FOR THE YO-YO MM

Our theorizing of the yo-yo MM contributes not only to the middle management literature, but we believe it may be of value for the practicing manager who wishes to reflect more closely on his or her own role. Rather than simply reacting out of *reflex* in the moment, and responding based upon our instincts, habits and routines (Cunliffe, 2016), the MM may use the yo-yo framework to better understand these reflexes more deeply. The MM may engage in *reflective* analysis, that is, stop for a moment and look for patterns, logic, and order, to make connections and sense of what s/he sees. The TIR framework and yo-yo metaphor may help the MM conduct *retrospective* analysis, that is, make sense of how they have previously responded to task requirement, own identities and relational aspects tied to being in the middle, and how well it turned out. They may also use the framework in *anticipatory* ways to plan for future ways of responding and perhaps avoid that unconscious identifications upwards or downwards lead to biased attention that may come in the way of what they wish to accomplish, and be detrimental for the organization, the subordinates et cetera.

The MM may also go one step deeper and engage in *reflexivity*. This means thinking critically about one's own assumptions, values and actions and how they construct realities and identities in relational ways (Cunliffe, 2016). As the MM questions taken for granted assumptions about how to perceive tasks, identities and relationality, he or she may be able to expose contradictions, doubts and dilemmas and come to discover and create new possibilities for their role. To be clearer about one's own loyalties and aware of tendencies to respond strongly to expectations and requirements from some groups and demands over others, may perhaps also aid the MM to occasionally take a clearer stance. This way they may perhaps become less a puppet on a string pulled in different directions. Clarification efforts may perhaps also help the MM in his/her yo-yo-acts so they do not go too far in their moves and overidentify with either senior or junior levels, as this may be problematic. And so, a more reflexive approach to yo-yo rides may perhaps reduce the risk of being tied up in knots.

ON MM IN "POSTINDUSTRIAL" CONTEXTS AND CONCLUDING REMARKS

Before concluding, we need to remind ourselves that MMs of course exist in many, very diverse contexts. Some are less in line with traditional, hierarchical organizations with strict demarcations between levels and top-down management. Many organizations may not look like pyramids, but resemble balloons, open fields, clouds or networks or even upside-down pyramids. In this chapter we try to make a broader argument—sacrificing precision—and thus will not go in detail into different types of organizations or MM situations. We will here remind the reader that a MM may be in a decentralized context with much discretion or in a work context that is tightly coupled and constrained by various contingencies. Thus, within specific organizations there will be much variation in terms of MM.

Alternative beliefs about a role, such as the MM, reflect the fact that roles are not purely objective, but rather socially constructed (Parker, 2007). An interesting aspect here is how people involved think in terms of hierarchies, levels, superior/subordinate-ship. It is important to recognize the variation and be careful about attributing too much essential meaning to notions such as top, senior, superior as well as low level, junior, subordinate et cetera. We should avoid the problem of "dead metaphors" where we mistake expressions such as higher and lower levels for mirrors of reality, rather than see them as the metaphors they are, which tends to freeze them. Even though notions such as the postbureaucratic organization, flat, network-based firm seldom offer good representations of organizations, we need to be aware that the metaphorical representations along a top-bottom or superior-subordinate may be only partially helpful and need to be used with caution. MM is an experience which reflects social constructions around tasks, identity and relationality which sometimes make the MM see him/herself as the top manager's assistant and sometimes as the top dog in a specific habitat. The phenomenology of MM is here to be emphasized, and as we have seen, this is seldom straightforward, but may be both a joyful and a knotted and chaotic ride.

Seeing the MM's experience in the middle through a yo-yo lens encourages us to think in processual terms. The MM moves up and down and tries to steer clear of being caught in contradictory and knotted situations. Sometimes this moving around a variety of tasks, identity positions and dealings with relations (including us and we-definitions) works smoothly, but few MMs can entirely avoid becoming caught up in knots. Tasks, identities and relations will from time to time push and pull the MM in different directions, as will demands and expectations of loyalties from superiors and subordinates. While some MMs master a yo-yo existence, others may feel tied up and be perceived as not of the true grit by their key reference groups. The MM may be experienced as a "Judas" or "management poodle" by subordinates if the responsiveness to top managerial is perceived as exaggerated, difficult or not entirely trustworthy if subordinates' viewpoints are emphasized (Gjerde & Alvesson, 2020). A good, appreciated MM is at the same time seen as a servant of top management *and* a spokesperson for the unit and the subordinates' interests, an implementer of top management strategy *and* a leader over appreciative followers. This calls for balancing acts, some camouflaging and a constant processing of MM work life, and so learning to master the yo-yo is a key skill.

REFERENCES

Alvesson, M., Blom, M., & Sveningsson, S. (2017). *Reflexive leadership: Organising in an imperfect world.* SAGE.

Alvesson, M., & Robertson, M. (2016). Money matters: Teflonic identity manoeuvring in the investment banking sector. *Organization Studies, 37*(1), 7–34.

Alvesson, M., & Sveningsson, S. (2003). The great disappearing act: difficulties in doing "leadership" *The Leadership Quarterly, 14*(3), 359–381.

Ashforth, B. E., & Mael, F. (1989). Social identity theory and the organization. *Academy of Management Review, 14*(1), 20–39.

Beatty, C. A., & Lee, G. L. (1992). Leadership among middle managers—An exploration in the context of technological change. *Human Relations, 45*(9), 957–989.

Blom, M., & Alvesson, M. (2014). Leadership on demand: Followers as initiators and inhibitors of managerial leadership. *Scandinavian Journal of Management, 30*(3), 344–357.

Bryman, A., & Lilley, S. (2009). Leadership researchers on leadership in higher education. *Leadership, 5*(3), 331–346.

Burns, T. (1957) Management in action. *Operational Research Quarterly, 8*(2), 45–60.

Caughron, J. J., & Mumford, M. D. (2012). Embedded leadership: How do a leader's superiors impact middle-management performance? *The Leadership Quarterly, 23*(3), 342–353.

Chun, J. U., Yammarino, F. J., Dionne, S. D., Sosik, J. J., & Moon, H. K. (2009). Leadership across hierarchical levels: Multiple levels of management and multiple levels of analysis. *The Leadership Quarterly, 20*(5), 689–707.

Clarke, C, Brown, A., & Hope Hailey, V. (2009). Working identities? Antagonistic discursive resources and managerial identity. *Human Relations, 62*(3), 323–352

Cunliffe, A. L. (2016). Republication of "on becoming a critically reflexive practitioner." *Journal of Management Education, 40*(6), 747–768.

Dopson, S., & Stewart, R. (1990). What is happening to middle management? *British Journal of Management, 1*(1), 3–16.

Down, S., & Reveley, J. (2009). Between narration and interaction: Situating first-line supervisor identity work. *Human Relations, 62*(3), 379–401.

Dutton, J. E., & Ashford, S. J. (1993). Selling issues to top management. *Academy of Management Review, 18*(3), 397–428.

Dutton, J. E., Ashford, S. J., O'neill, R. M., Hayes, E., & Wierba, E. E. (1997). Reading the wind: How middle managers assess the context for selling issues to top managers. *Strategic Management Journal, 18*(5), 407–423.

Empson, L., & Langley, A. (2015) Leadership and professionals: Multiple manifestations of influence in professional service firms. In L. Empson, D. Muzio, & J. Broschak (Eds.), *The Oxford handbook of professional service firms* (pp. 163–189). Oxford University Press.

Gallos, J. V. (2002). The dean's squeeze: The myths and realities of academic leadership in the middle. *Academy of Management Learning & Education, 1*(2), 174–184.

George, B., Sims, P., McLean, A. N., & Mayer, D. (2007). Discovering your authentic leadership. *Harvard Business Review, 85*(2), 129–138.

Gjerde, S., & Alvesson, M. (2020). Sandwiched: Exploring role and identity of middle managers in the genuine middle. *Human Relations, 73*(1), 124–151

Gjerde, S., & Ladegård, G. (2019). Leader role crafting and the functions of leader role identities. *Journal of Leadership & Organizational Studies, 26*(1), 44–59.

Glaser, L., Stam, W., & Takeuchi, R. (2016). Managing the risks of proactivity: A multilevel study of initiative and performance in the middle management context. *Academy of Management Journal, 59*(4), 1339–1360.

Goffman, E. (1959). *The presentation of self in everyday life*. Penguin Books.

Greenleaf, R. K. (1977). Servant leadership in business. In G. R. Hickman (Ed.), *Leading organizations: Perspectives for a new era*, 87–95. SAGE.

Hales, C. (2005). Rooted in supervision, branching into management: Continuity and change in the role of first-line manager. *Journal of Management Studies*, *42*(3), 471–506.

Hales, C., & Nightingale, M. (1986). What are unit managers supposed to do? A contingent methodology for investigating managerial role requirements. *International Journal of Hospitality Management*, *5*(1), 3–11.

Harding, N., Lee, H., & Ford, J. (2014). Who is 'the middle manager'? *Human Relations*, *67*(10), 1213–1237.

Heyden, M. L., Fourné, S. P., Koene, B. A., Werkman, R., & Ansari, S. (2017). Rethinking 'top-down' and 'bottom-up' roles of top and middle managers in organizational change: Implications for employee support. *Journal of Management Studies*, *54*(7), 961–985.

Huy, Q. N. (2001). In praise of middle managers. *Harvard Business Review*, *79*(8), 72–79.

Huy, Q. N. (2002). Emotional balancing of organizational continuity and radical change: The contribution of middle managers. *Administrative Science Quarterly*, *47*(1), 31–69.

Huy, Q. N., Corley, K. G., & Kraatz, M. S. (2014). From support to mutiny: Shifting legitimacy judgments and emotional reactions impacting the implementation of radical change. *Academy of Management Journal*, *57*(6), 1650–1680.

Ibarra, H., Wittman, S., Petriglieri, G., & Day, D. V. (2014). Leadership and identity: An examination of three theories and new research directions. In D. V. Day (Ed.), *The Oxford handbook of leadership and organizations* (pp. 285–301). Oxford University Press.

Jackall, R. (1988). *Moral mazes: The world of corporate managers*. Oxford University Press.

Jacobsen, D. I. (2019). Mellomledelse—En spesiell form for ledelse? *Magma*, *2*(2019), 46–54.

Jaser, Z. (2017). Pulled in two directions: Being in concert a leader to some and a follower to others. *Academy of Management Proceedings, 1,* 16660.

Kanter, R. M. (1981). Power, leadership, and participatory management. *Theory into Practice*, *20*(4), 219–224.

Kanter, R. M. (1982, July–August). The middle manager as innovator (Reprint). *Best of Harvard Business Review*, 150–161.

Kanter, R. M. (1986). The reshaping of middle management. *Management Review*, *75*(1), 19–20.

Katz, D., & Kahn, R. L. (1966). *The social psychology of organizations*. Wiley.

Laurent, A. (1978). Managerial subordinacy: A neglected aspect of organizational hierarchies. *Academy of Management Review*, 3(2), 220–230.

McCann, L., Morris, J., & Hassard, J. (2008). Normalized intensity: The new labour process of middle management. *Journal of Management Studies, 45*(2), 343–371.

Mintzberg, H. (2004). Enough leadership. *Harvard Business Review*, *82*(11), 20–22.

Musson, G., & Duberley, J. (2007). Change, change or be exchanged: the discourse of participation and the manufacture of identity. *Journal of Management Studies, 44*(1), 143–164.

Osterman, P. (2008). *The truth about middle managers: Who they are, how they work, why they matter.* Harvard Business School.

Parker, M. (2004). Becoming manager: Or, the werewolf looks anxiously in the mirror, checking for unusual facial hair. *Management Learning, 35*(1), 45–59.

Parker, M. (2014) University, Ltd: Changing a business school. *Organization, 21,* 281–292.

Parker, S. K. (2007). That is my job: How employees' role orientation affects their job performance. *Human Relations, 60*(3), 403–434.

Sims, D. (2003). Between the milestones: A narrative account of the vulnerability of middle managers' storytelling. *Human Relations, 56,* 1195–211.

Stewart, R. (1982). A model for understanding managerial jobs and behavior. *Academy of Management Review,* 7(1), 7–13.

Sveningsson, S., & Alvesson, M. (2003). Managing managerial identities: Organizational fragmentation, discourse and identity struggle. *Human Relations, 56,* 1163–1193

Sveningsson, S., & Alvesson, M. (2016). *Managerial lives.* Cambridge University Press.

Taylor, A., & Helfat, C. E. (2009). Organizational linkages for surviving technological change: Complementary assets, middle management, and ambidexterity. *Organization Science, 20*(4), 718–739.

Tengblad, S., & Vie, O. E. (2012). Management in practice: Overview of classic studies on managerial work. In S. Tengblad (Eds.), *The work of managers.* (pp. 18–47). Oxford University Press.

Thomas, R., & Linstead, A. (2002). Losing the plot? Middle managers and identity. *Organization, 9*(1), 71–93.

Tsui, A. S. (1984). A role set analysis of managerial reputation. *Organizational Behavior & Human Performance, 34*(1), 64–96.

PART 3

THE CONNECTING LEADER IN PRACTICE

CHAPTER 6

FROM CONNECTING LEADER TO CONNECTING LEADERSHIP

A Study of Interaction

Christian Dyrlund Wåhlin-Jacobsen
Department of Organization, Copenhagen Business School and the National Research Centre for the Working Environment, Denmark

Magnus Larsson
Department of Organization, Copenhagen Business School

ABSTRACT

The recognition that leaders do not only engage in dyadic relationships with their followers, but are also sometimes led by others has received some attention in the literature, especially from a role perspective. However, previous studies have tended to see roles, their features, and the organizational structure in which they are embedded, as static, easily understood and uncontroversial. In this chapter, we present an alternative perspective inspired by ethnomethodology and conversation analysis which sees roles and their meaning in the organizational context as continuously enacted and negotiated during organization members' daily interactions. From this perspective, leadership is not only performed by invoking one's role-based authority as a leader, but also through the management of meaning. We

The Connecting Leader: Serving Concurrently as a Leader and a Follower
pp. 155–190

then present analyses of data from meetings in 2 work settings, demonstrating that by constructing their roles and the organizational context in certain ways, managers (and other organization members) may influence the situation—a process we call connecting leadership. Organization members sometimes hold many different roles that can be invoked to this effect, suggesting that future work on the topic of connecting leaders should be careful not to only focus on these leaders' relationships with their immediate superiors and subordinates.

INTRODUCTION

Although leadership research has tended to focus on how persons in a managerial position exercise influence over subordinates in dyadic relationships (Drath et al., 2008; Graen & Uhl-Bien, 1995; Uhl-Bien et al., 2014), there is a growing recognition that most managers also have superiors and thus occasionally take a subordinate role themselves[1] (DeRue & Ashford, 2010; Jaser, 2017). Furthermore, managers typically also hold other roles, such as being peers to other managers or participating in project and work groups based on collaboration across organizational units and levels, at least in organizations of some size. The circumstance that managers hold multiple roles within the organization has previously received some attention in the literature: Likert (1961), for example, described managers as *linking pins* performing the function of bridging different parts of the organization based on their various roles. But the multiple roles also place demands on the manager, who is subjected to a diverse set of expectations and obligations, as well as the tensions and ambiguities that arise between their roles. As a result, managers face the challenge of handling potential role conflicts (Kahn et al., 1964) by juggling and balancing the different (and sometimes opposing) expectations they are met with.

However, it is noteworthy that many classical role studies, such as those mentioned above, tend to conceptualize the organizational context as a structural network characterized by the organization members' interrelated roles, and thus as being fixed. As a result, the specific rights, expectations and obligations that managers face in relation to their various roles are more or less taken as given. This realist understanding of organizations as structures of roles is also found in more recent studies: for example, although the leader-member-exchange literature is diverse, many studies within this field tend to see leadership as a question of developing high quality interpersonal relationships within a context of formal organizational roles that is typically taken for granted (Graen & Uhl-Bien, 1995). The same could be said of the followership literature, where a number of studies have focused on how followership is enacted from a fixed, formal subordinate role (Uhl-Bien et al., 2014).

In contrast, it can be argued from a constructionist position that the organization and its role structure are at least partly negotiated in situ, so that organization members effectively "talk organizations into being" (Boden, 1994, p. 202). Thus, the organization is not simply an overall container within which daily work situations are embedded, but rather something that is actively coconstructed and enacted by organization members in their interactions (as in Uhl-Bien and Carsten's coconstruction model of leader-follower relations, 2018). As a consequence, role features such as rights and obligations are not given beforehand, but are somewhat malleable and negotiable by the participants in the setting. Similarly, it cannot be known in advance exactly which of their various roles organization members will invoke in a given situation, how they will enact them, and how their situated negotiation of roles and role features will influence the trajectory of the interaction. For example, managers may within a single encounter speak as a manager, a subordinate, a peer, a "dotted-line" report, a committee member, et cetera, and those they are interacting with may draw upon a similarly broad set of role-based positions.

In this chapter, we present an interactional perspective on leadership and roles that is rooted in ethnomethodology and conversation analysis. Keeping with the theme of this anthology, the chapter highlights how managers actively embody their various organizational roles. We are also inspired by recent developments in the literature where leadership is viewed as a social influence process produced in interaction (Crevani et al., 2010; Larsson, 2017), rather than a reference for certain behaviors that organization members in a formal leadership position exercise toward subordinates.[2] Specifically, we attend to how managers invoke their various roles within the organization in their interactions with others, thereby simultaneously constructing the organizational context in a particular way and shaping the trajectory (and thus potentially the outcomes) of the situation. We wish to emphasize three points:

1. roles are an important aspect of the constructed context because of how roles ascribe certain rights or obligations to the parties involved, thereby shaping the horizon of possible future actions they can or should take;
2. managers (and other organization members) may influence situations by constructing their roles and the wider organizational context in a specific way—a process we call connecting leadership; and

3. managers do not only act as managers or subordinates, but also draw on various other organizational roles in order to influence the local situation.

In this chapter, we briefly review approaches to conceptualizing leadership in light of roles, focusing on two important perspectives that have been central in the literature: realist models of how role relationships develop in vertical dyads (Dansereau et al., 1975; Graen & Scandura, 1987) and DeRue and Ashford's (2010) more recent identity construction model. We focus on these theoretical perspectives not just because of their tremendous impact on the leadership field, but also because they are helpful for highlighting the distinguishing features of our position in the subsequent section of the manuscript. After accounting for our perspective on roles, we will describe our methodological approach and provide a detailed analysis of work interaction in two settings, exemplifying different forms of connecting leadership. Finally, the results of the analysis are discussed in relation to the conceptualization of roles within the leadership literature and the concept of *the connecting leader*.

LEADER'S ROLES IN THE LITERATURE

While a number of different perspectives can now be found within the literature on organizational roles, many classical studies adopted what has been called a "structural functionalist" understanding of roles, seeing these as "a basic building block of organizations" (Sluss & Ashforth, 2007, p. 10). From this perspective, roles are understood realistically, focusing on formal role requirements and how the fulfilment of these (or the lack thereof) contributes to organizational performance. What constitutes role requirements and satisfactory performance are taken as largely uncontroversial.

In contrast, studies which adopt a more psychologically oriented understanding of roles have instead emphasized that the meaning attributed to a given role depends on the overall network of other roles within which it is located (e.g., Katz & Kahn, 1978). For example, to speak of a person occupying a team-member role presumes other team members, and what "counts" as in-role team-member behavior depends on whether the role is performed in relation to other team members or to a team leader. As a result, organization members are understood as enacting positions in *role relationships*, rather than roles in and by themselves; as noted by Stryker and Statham (1985, p. 323): "To use the term role is necessarily to refer to interaction." This relational understanding of roles is central to both the vertical dyad and the identity construction perspective, to which we will now turn.

Roles in the Vertical Dyad Perspective

The psychological perspective on organizational roles has been both a point of departure and a subject of theoretical development within the broad literature focusing on manager-subordinate dyads. While earlier leadership studies tended to focus on what can be called managers' average leadership style (Graen & Uhl-Bien, 1995), the dyadic perspective criticized the failure to discriminate between the different qualities that characterize manager-subordinate relationships in the work unit. Dansereau and colleagues, for example, claimed that: "the vertical dyad is the appropriate unit of analysis for examining leadership processes because the vertical dyad reflects the processes linking member and superior" (1975, p. 47).

Within the vertical dyad perspective, a movement can be traced over the years in relation to how roles are understood. In Dansereau and colleagues' classic study, roles are organized or "made" (see also Graen, 1976) in a social exchange process between superior and subordinate (or "member"), while still primarily being defined by the tasks that the role incumbent must perform—that is, as *job* roles rather than *relational* roles. A key area of focus for the study is whether the subordinate's behavior is congruent or discrepant with their role, and the techniques that managers employ in order to shape subordinates' role performance. Over time, subordinates' roles are understood to become increasingly fixed and differentiated within the work unit. Thus, the study could be said to represent a gradual shift of attention away from functionalism toward the dynamic and symbolic aspects of roles, while maintaining a realist attitude.

Later developments, such as the work by Graen and Scandura (1987), further elaborated on the process of negotiating roles between managers and subordinates over time by describing the role making phase as preceded by a role taking phase and succeeded by a role routinization phase. Furthermore, within each of these three phases, the importance of communication, observation of the other part's behavior, and consideration of social norms and mutual adjustment was emphasized, further underscoring the social and symbolic aspects of the role development process. The dyadic perspective has in recent years been developed within the growing literature of leader-member exchange theory, or *LMX*, where a central tenet is that managers enact their supervisory role based on their stance toward the specific subordinate they are interacting with (Graen & Uhl-

Bien, 1995; Liden et al., 1997), thus further attending to relational roles rather than job roles.

The question of how manager-subordinate dyads are influenced by and become connected to the wider organizational settings has been addressed, for example, through what Graen and Uhl-Bien (1995) call the *leadership structure*, that is, the network of relationships existing in any organization through which tasks are accomplished. The leadership structure is not the formal hierarchical structure; instead, drawing on the concepts of role sets and role conflicts (Katz & Kahn, 1978), the leadership structure is thought to represent a field in which the manager faces a range of different expectations that he or she must handle. Different parts of the field are interconnected, and, as argued by Graen and Uhl-Bien (1995), "relationship quality in some parts of the leadership structure will likely influence relationship development in other parts of the structure" (p. 234). However, more precisely how this influence occurs is not fully explicated, and the actual processes whereby dyads are connected with the surroundings are left unexplored. Instead, the organizational context is seen as fixed, working in the background to enable and constrain the development of particular relationships.

DeRue and Ashford's Identity Construction Perspective

Compared to the development within the vertical dyad literature, DeRue and Ashford's identity construction perspective (2010) draws even further on symbolic interactionism and social constructionism (Stryker & Statham, 1985; Weick, 1995) in focusing on how the meanings associated with roles and role relationships are shaped through organization members' interactions. Thus, the emphasis is not just on individuals' private reflections and personal dispositions, but also on the importance of various social influences on the role enactment of managers and subordinates. According to DeRue and Ashford, well-functioning leadership relationships and clear leader and follower identities are developed through relational recognition in a process called *identity work*. This process comprises iterative claims and grants from both parties in the developing leadership relationship, as well as from other organization members toward these parties. Specifically, claiming an identity is understood as "the actions people take to assert their identity as either a leader or follower", while granting an identity "refers to the actions that a person takes to bestow a leader or follower identity onto another person" (DeRue & Ashford, 2010, p. 631). Over time, these reciprocal claims and grants can escalate what starts out as individually internalized role identities toward wider recognition in the organization. Therefore, leader and follower identities should not be understood in isolation, but as *reciprocal role identities*: the role(s) that a given organization member is recognized as enacting by others, viewed in relation to the roles that these are recognized as enacting (such as how recognizing a person as a leader implies that they have followers).

The negotiation of reciprocal role identities is shaped by various contextual contingencies which can influence both the individual's tendency to claim certain identities and to grant them to others. For example, a more visible claim, as well as a prior history of having negotiated leader and follower identities, are claimed to make for a more smooth and constructive process. Furthermore, according to DeRue and Ashford, leader and follower identities are not determined by, but influenced by the various formal and informal roles that organization members occupy. For example, the process of negotiating identities in specific relationships can reflect the collectives that the parties are identified as being part of, so that being seen as part of the collective of "leaders" in an organization influences more local, relational identity negotiation processes. The effect of collective identities on the negotiation of bilateral and reciprocal role identities is called *collective endorsement*. In addition, *institutional structures* also shape the identity construction process through how people in an authority position, for example, are socially positioned as leaders. According to DeRue and Ashford, the formal hierarchy thus leads to certain members of the organization being more likely to both claim and be granted leadership identities. Thus, their model can be said to acknowledge, but also reinterpret, the significance given to formal roles within the functionalist perspective.

Still, in spite of DeRue and Ashford's claim to present a perspective where leader and follower identities are not tied to formal positions (2010, p. 627), but instead negotiated in an interpersonal relation, the identity negotiation process they describe is thought to occur in a situation that is presented as preexisting and given. For example, while relational recognition of leader identities might facilitate later collective endorsement, the institutional structures within which the negotiation takes place is seen as unaffected by the negotiation itself. In light of our similar criticism of the vertical dyad perspective above, both of the two perspectives can be said to subscribe to a "bucket theory of context" (Drew & Heritage, 1992, p. 19): the understanding that the organizational context is a container for interaction, presenting constraints and opportunities for the participants in the interaction while in itself remaining stable. That is, both perspectives subscribe to the conventional conceptualization of social structures (such as a structure of formal roles in an organizational hierarchy) as being external to specific settings, yet still shaping the actions of people.

In relation to the concept of the connecting leader, we suggest moving away from the idea that managers are already positioned within a given context (such as Graen and Uhl-Bien's leadership structure or DeRue and Ashford's institutional structure), to instead seeing this context as constructed and negotiated. In doing so, we align with Grint's (2005) proposal that influence is exercised in how the context and the situation in which the actors find themselves is constructed:

> leadership involves the social construction of the context that both legitimates a particular form of action and constitutes the world in the process. If that rendering of the context is successful—for there are usually contending and competing renditions—the newly constituted context then limits the alternatives available such that those involved begin to act differently. (pp. 1470–1471)

Grint's conceptualization of the context as constructed is relevant to our study for several reasons: for one, it suggests how the constructed organizational context may shape local interactions between managers and subordinates, instead of simply assuming the context to be fixed and exterior. Second, it highlights how context constructions are often partial because of how they promote certain future courses of action over others. Thus, the parties to the interaction may hold certain context constructions as more favorable than others and work to promote these constructions. Third, it points to how constructing the context in certain ways rather than others can amount to a form of leadership, understood as an asymmetrical influence relationship in the here and now (Uhl-Bien & Carsten, 2018). Thus, when an actor connects a salient role within the current setting to other, thus far dormant, roles in the organization in a way that influences the current interaction so as to make people "act differently" (Grint, 2005, p. 1471), we observe what we term connecting leadership. In the following section, we will further explicate our approach, which draws on the perspective of ethnomethodology and conversation analysis (EM/CA).

Connecting Leadership: An Interactional Perspective

The ethnomethodological perspective attends to how interaction and other orderly forms of social conduct are products of people's active efforts: even for relatively mundane social phenomena, the participants draw upon cultural knowledge and common-sense reasoning procedures to achieve coordinated understandings (which can also be referred to as a shared reality, intersubjectivity, or mutual intelligibility) and thereby coordinated action (Whittle et al., 2014). As a result, what are typically considered "social facts" and taken for granted actually constitute practical accomplishments, actively enacted by the participants in the situation (Garfinkel, 2002; Weick, 1995).[3]

From the ethnomethodological perspective, formal organizational structures are not considered to be stable and unambiguous, but can instead be thought of as "schemes of interpretation" (Bittner, 1974, p. 76). As argued by Whittle and colleagues:

> Formal structures, then, do not determine organizational processes or outcomes, and organizational behavior cannot be 'read off' from the formal structure chart … competent and sanctioned members use such structural categories as part of their common-sense organizational reasoning, such as reasoning about who should do what (i.e. functional division of labor) or who has the power to authorize action (i.e. hierarchical chain of command). (2015, pp. 381–382)

Understanding organizational structures as interpretational schemes does not deny that the structures are treated by organization members as real and existing independently of their ongoing enactment (Heritage, 1984). However, a general understanding of the organizational structure (for example in the form of an organizational chart) still leaves the participants to determine which understandings and which aspects of this structure are relevant in the here and now. As pointed out by Grint (2005), this leads to the possibility of different versions of how to understand and describe the structure, with the ethnomethodological perspective attending to how the particular meaning of the structure for the situation at hand is negotiated and determined by the participants in their interactions—how organizational structures are talked into being. In this regard, considering conversation analysis (often referred to together with ethnomethodology as EM/CA; e.g., Llewellyn & Hindmarsh, 2010) can further focus our approach and provide analytical resources to unpack roles in interaction.

While conversation analysis is a broad field covering many aspects of the social organization of interactions (e.g., Stivers & Sidnell, 2012), an important line of research has concerned how role categories and other types of *membership categories* are claimed, ascribed and resisted in interaction, as well as the social actions achieved through this *category work* (Housley, 2000; Whittle et al., 2015). Within the EM/CA tradition, identities are treated as interactional phenomena and often talked about as "identity-in-interaction." From this perspective, "for a person to 'have an identity'—whether he or she is the person speaking, being spoken to, or being spoken about—is to be cast into a *category with associated characteristics or features*" (Antaki & Widdicombe, 1998, p. 3; italics in original). Among these associated characteristics and features or *predicates* (Whittle et al., 2015) are actions associated with members of the focal category, as well as the rights and obligations that these members are thought to hold, both of a formal and an informal kind.

As noted already by Goffman (1961), some of a person's roles are enacted in a given setting, while others remain dormant. Besides the formal managerial and subordinate roles of those involved in the interaction, various other role categories within the organization may be brought up in the interaction (Clifton, 2014; Larsson & Lundholm, 2013), and the invocation or ascription of these other role categories might also shape the interaction through the additional rights and obligations that are thereby made relevant to the interaction. That is, organization members who act in a number of different roles at various times can invoke these roles strategically in the interaction, "changing hats" (Goffman, 1981, as cited in Halkowski, 1990) in order to further certain interactional goals.

Because the use of categories and predicates in interaction is often taken by the interlocutors as having moral implications, they play an important role in the normative regulation of social life (Jayyusi, 1984). However, it should be stressed that while role categories and their associated predicates carry cultural meaning that may reach beyond the immediate situation, their use in interaction is occasioned and should be studied as such (Antaki & Widdicombe, 1998). Consequentially, from an interactional approach, the point is to attend to whatever work the categories and predicates are used to do in the setting: for example, Samra-Fredericks (2010) presented data of how a senior manager brought up the strategical obligations of his managerial group as a way of substantiating criticism of one his senior management colleagues. And Whittle and colleagues (2015) provided an example of how the members of a marketing team were mobilized to raise criticism and suggest a change of approach to the board of directors based on the way a consultant described the obligations of a nonpresent sales manager and that manager's inability to meet the obligations. Such studies illustrate that in practice, the content of roles in the workplace is not stable and unequivocal, but rather a subject of ongoing negotiation among organization members with potentially important organizational consequences (Housley, 1999; Whittle et al., 2015). In addition, the study by Whittle and colleagues is particularly illustrative of how influencing can be done without formal authority (in their study, from the role as a consultant or as a subordinate), corresponding to what has been called the "balanced view" of the leadership process (Shamir, 2007; Uhl-Bien & Carsten, 2018). In other words, when understood as a social influence process, exercising leadership is not reserved for organization members who are usually recognized *as* leaders. This conceptualization of leadership represents a clear and significant difference compared to the realist and constructionist role-based conceptualizations of leadership discussed earlier. Furthermore, exercising leadership is not predicated on the actors thinking about themselves in terms of "leaders" or "followers"—we reserve the notion of leadership as an analytical concept, leaving the actors to use whatever labels and categories they find most appropriate (Larsson & Nielsen, 2017).

It is on the basis of the EM/CA literature that we argue that the way certain versions of role categories are invoked, constructed and presented in interaction constitutes an important resource for performing *connecting leadership*. By connecting leadership, we refer to a type of leadership process where influence is accomplished through constructing a context of roles beyond the current interaction. While the classical, realist view of linking pins sees managers as promoting coordination and cooperation between different parts of the organizational structure, the point of connecting leadership is how a particular version of role features which are typically only salient in another setting is actively constructed and presented as a resource in the here and now to mobilize and influence the present parties. In contrast to other influence tactics, such as rational persuasion, inspirational appeal, or ingratiation (Yukl et al., 2008), that directly target the influenced party, connecting leadership produces a more indirect influence effect by rendering certain actions understandable and "natural," while framing others as problematic.

Thus, in this chapter, we attend to the following research questions: (1) how are particular versions of leaders' roles, the features of these roles, and the wider organizational context constructed in situated interactions, and (2) how can such constructions entail influence effects, both when the focal manager is primarily enacting a role *as* a manager (that is, toward their own subordinates) or as a subordinate (toward their own superior)? To pursue this interest, we analyze illustrative recordings of real interactions in the workplace.

METHODS

Case Background and Data Sources

This chapter draws on data from two long-term field research projects in organizations. The data were reopened for use here due to their relevance for the topic of connecting leadership. One project followed the implementation of a researcher-designed intervention in a pharmaceutical company over a 12-month period and featured comprehensive data collection, involving interviews, documents and audio recordings of the intervention activities. From this project, we focus especially on an audio recorded workshop meeting with an overall agenda of developing action plans to improving the workplace health and safety (Case 1). The other project focused on work in a local branch of a large bank in Sweden, lasting 18 months and following the method of discursively sensitive ethnography, involving the collection of interviews, documents, shadowing of a range of managers, field notes and audio recordings of interactions (planned and unplanned) throughout the work day. From this project, we focus on an audio recorded meeting for the managerial team of the branch (Case 2). In both settings, one of the authors was directly involved in the data collection and acted as an observer to the events analyzed in this chapter.

Data Analysis

Within the EM/CA approach, the focus is on analyzing *naturally occurring talk* (Peräkylä, 2011) as it develops on a turn-by-turn basis. Informants' talk is not considered a resource by which the analyst can access underlying phenomena, as it is treated in most interview and observational studies—instead, talk as it plays out in perhaps mundane everyday interactions, is the topic itself (Wieder, 1988). Thus, instead of treating talk as a medium for transmitting information, studies within the conversation analytic tradition are oriented toward how sequences of talk are organized and which actions are accomplished in the talk.

Another special characteristic of EM/CA work is how data is approached in the analytical process. A fundamental insight within this tradition is that if interaction is to be at least somewhat orderly, an intersubjective understanding must be created and maintained between the parties. While the common-sense lexical understanding of language suggests that meaning is inherent to the words and phrases used, pragmatic studies of interaction instead reveal that meaning is highly context-dependent, and thus that order in interaction is an ongoing joint achievement between speakers and recipients. Creating and maintaining order is based on both speakers' context-sensitive turn design and word choice, as well as on the recipients' active displays of understanding. Specifically, when responding to an utterance, recipients display their understanding of the utterance, allowing speakers to see whether their utterance has been understood as intended. If this is not the case, various *repair* strategies are available to attempt to correct the recipients' understanding (Kitzinger, 2012; Schegloff & Sacks, 1973). Interaction is fundamentally based on the availability of this "next-turn proof procedure" to the interlocutors (Hutchby & Wooffitt, 2008, p. 13). In addition, it is the visibility of this procedure for the analyst that is exploited in conversation analytical studies of interaction in order to understand and explain the social machinery that drives the participants' actions in the interaction—the "member's methods" (Garfinkel, 1967, p. 34). Besides attending to the so-called *sequence organization* as structural backbone of interaction, analyses within the EM/CA tradition also draw on literature about other aspects of the organization of interactions when relevant in relation to the data at hand.

Our analysis takes a single-case approach (Hutchby & Wooffitt, 2008; ten Have, 2007) for each of the two cases. Among the advantages of this approach is that it enables the analyst to highlight how complex social events are made sense of and handled in the course of longer stretches of interaction, as opposed to studies focusing on shorter extracts, which often focus on simpler actions. The single-case approach also allows for the demonstration of the diverse practices interlocutors draw upon in relation to a given phenomenon, rather than focusing only on one type of practice, and it makes it possible for the researcher to provide more information about the institutional and interactional context of the presented data. However, the single-case approach also means that examples are chosen based on their illustrative nature, rather than attempting to show the variation in how a phenomenon occurs across one's data set. Thus, our aim is not to provide generalizable knowledge about which types of interactions or interactional practices can be found in the studied settings, but rather to provide examples of how connecting leadership occurs in practice. These examples may or may not reflect how connecting leadership is performed in other settings; however, previous research suggests that the principles of interaction that have been described within the EM/CA tradition are quite universal, both across cultures (e.g., national and linguistic contexts; Stivers et al., 2009) and domains of interaction (e.g., mundane conversations versus work-related interactions; Drew & Heritage, 1992).

While the analysis has been performed on the original data, the excerpts are featured here in a version that has been translated into idiomatic English while staying as close to the word choice and turn structure of the original as possible. Thereby, we have attempted to balance maintaining the details of the original spoken data with the readability of the excerpts. The data are presented in a Jefferson-style transcription (Jefferson, 2004) which enables us to convey various details about how things are said and responded to, such as pauses, overlaps and words uttered with emphasis. A transcription legend is included in the appendix.

ANALYSIS

Case 1: "A Walk During Work Hours"

The next two extracts are taken from a participatory workshop meeting where a group of employees, together with their two team leaders (Anita and Nick) and a facilitator (Frank), discussed potential projects for improving the health, safety and wellbeing of the employees. The meeting was part of a series of meetings where potential problems had been identified on a previous occasion, and relevant initiatives were to be planned at this second meeting. Here, we focus on a discussion about a specific suggested improvement. In the excerpt, one employee (Rod) raises the question of being able to take walks during work hours at times where the production process runs automatically. Besides the participants already mentioned, the employees Dennis, Elvin and Eve also participate in the discussion.

Many things occur in this and the other extracts, which present an abundance of interactional detail. Here, we will focus on how Anita and Nick exercise connecting leadership through constructing the expectable stances of other organization members toward Rod's proposal as relevant for the decision at hand. In doing so, Anita and Nick both enact role relationships which were otherwise dormant in the immediate setting, constructing particular versions of these that are fitted to their current interactional projects[4] (Schegloff, 2007). See Excerpt 1.

In Excerpt 1, first, Rod proposes "try(ing) to challenge the one called eh a walk during work hours." The term "the one" is indexical, but can be heard as a reference to the fact that the idea had come up earlier in the group's discussions. In addition, Rod's suggestion to "challenge" this idea can be taken as a reference to a point that was made earlier about how a previous decision had ruled out a similar proposal, thus setting up the prospects of having the suggestion accepted as slim. This decision is seemingly referenced also by Dennis in line 6, who states that the idea has been "shelved forever." Although Dennis does not mention who actually rejected the idea, the definitive formulation suggests that the decision was made by somebody in an authority position, that is, a manager higher up in the organizational hierarchy. Frank attends to this implied meaning in line 7 ("you won't be allowed to do that or how"), and while Dennis' affirmative response (lines 8–9) still does not cite who made the original decision, Frank infers that Dennis' assessment could be based on having observed discussions in the joint consultation committee (lines 10-11). Nick confirms that Dennis was a member of the joint consultation committee (line 12), thereby indicating the relevance of this role category as a warrant for his claims, and seemingly confirming Frank's inference. Based on our ethnographic knowledge, we note that the joint consultation committee is chaired by the department manager, Anita and Nick's superior, and that decisions made in this committee would thus normally hold priority over more local decisions.

However, from line 13 on the interaction takes a new turn with Anita's introduction of other parts of the organizational context and another, thus far dormant, role. This change works to reframe Rod's suggestion

Excerpt 1

Rod: you know what, we could try to challenge the one that is called eh a
walk during work hours
Frank: a walk during work hours
Rod: yes
((some lines omitted))
Dennis: °that has° that has been shelved forever, we've discussed that before
Frank: we've tried that or you won't be allowed to do that or how
Dennis: well you still have to do all of your work, the last time we were
told you can use your lunch break for that
Frank: mhmm (.) is that like a ((joint consultation committee)) thing, eh
you were in that right hmmh
Nick: Dennis was in [((the joint consultation committee))]
Anita: [well] an opportunity
has arisen in the ((overall project)), where ((the health and safety
coordinator at the site manager level)) is sitting in her ((steering
group)), that we can't go back and say the whole shift can now walk
or run, but but yes (.) you who are here around the table, you could
make a draft, how can this work out eh doing this, then we can try it
out I mean for a for a short period, but of course we have to (.) the
((production)) process has to run [I mean (.)]=

and opens up the possibility of it being feasible after all. First, Anita does subtle disagreement with Dennis (line 13: "well," see Pomerantz, 1984), reporting that the steering group overseeing the workshop meetings has decided that employees can try out proposals under certain conditions. Several aspects of Anita's long turn are interesting: for one, she references a high-level health and safety coordinator who is a direct report to the overall site manager (lines 14–15). Because the project is sanctioned at a higher level in the organization, promoting the project and the employees' engagement with it would thus be likely to take priority over decisions made further down in the organizational hierarchy, such as in the local joint consultation committee that Dennis was a member of. Second, Anita claims privileged access to knowledge about the project. Although it is not made explicit here, Anita is the designated health and safety manager for her area of the production site, thus holding special access to the health and safety coordinator, and this is of course known to the employees. Thus, implicitly invoking this role category provides a way of vindicating

Rod's proposal by redefining it as being aligned with the concerns of site health and safety manager. Anita thus engages in connecting leadership in the sense of invoking a particular version of a role from another part of the organization in a way that has consequences for the current interaction, and more precisely, for the legitimacy and viability of the suggestion being discussed. For the influence to be accomplished, however, the other participants need to align with Anita's suggestion and implied framing of the suggestion. We will return to this point later.

A third point can be made about the remainder of Anita's long turn, since she also orients to managing potential conflicts between her role as health and safety manager and her more production-oriented role as the team leader. Specifically, Anita can be seen to invoke the latter role category through the various conditions she mentions (only some of the employees being allowed to try out the proposed initiative, requiring a draft, setting a short trial period) and her emphasis on keeping the work process running (lines 16–20). Thus, although she implicitly refers to the suggestion of a walk during work hours as being relevant for health and safety, she also constructs an organizational context where performance expectations are resting on the group. Thereby, she can be seen to address the risk of being seen as too optimistic toward Rod's proposal and overlooking its potential consequences for the team's performance. In other words, she orients to the potential moral implications of how she managers her dual roles. This matter is central to Excerpt 2 as well.

Returning to the matter of whether Anita's connecting leadership was successful, the participants did indeed continue their discussion of the suggestion in spite of Dennis' critical comments. However, as Excerpt 2 indicates, the suggestion was still seen as potentially problematic by some participants, including Nick, the other team leader. After Anita's turn, both employees and managers offered various arguments, with some supporting the proposal and others challenging it. Excerpt 2 begins with Rod offering an alternative proposal which would allow the employees to stay in the production area, thus addressing a criticism that had been brought up that the employees' absence could cause problems if unforeseen events occurred.

In this excerpt, we first see Frank acknowledge Rod's updated proposal (lines 1–3). However, Nick's next turn does not respond to Rod's turn as a new proposal. Instead, Nick first acknowledges Anita's suggestion that the group could write up a "decent proposal" but goes on to argue against the idea being "implemented generally." This is of course a fundamental criticism, since there is little point in trying out the proposal if it is not possible to implement it after the trial period. Nick's argument against the proposal invokes the role category of being the manager who has to resolve problems caused by the proposal in a future situation. Specifically,

Excerpt 2

```
Rod:     it doesn't have to be a run, it could be that we had some exercises
         for the lumbar region and shoulders and=
Frank:   =okay=
Nick:    =of course you could put it up there and deliver a decent proposal,
         but from there to it being enacted generally, because I have to damn
         well say, if I am a manager of the shift at that time, you will damn
         well not be running around on the running trail when you have to
         ((perform a certain physical task)) cause then it'll be ( )
         [but you know that it will take NEXT to nothing]=
Elvin:   [no no no no, but it's not like that, no no    ]
         ((more employees indicate agreement with Elvin))
Nick:    =like Eve says it takes NEXT to nothing=
Dennis:  =no:=
Nick:    =you know that you here around [the table]=
Eve:                                    [hehehehe ]
Dennis:  =yes
Nick:    it takes NOTHING, then it'll be said, Anita and Nick, Dennis Johnson
         is scurrying about on the running trail
         ((participants laugh))
Elvin:   okay, that was a silly example
Nick:    that will damn well be over my dead body, I promise you that
```

Nick refers to Rod's original proposal (running as opposed to taking a walk) to describe a potential scenario where the workers are failing to do their job (lines 7-8), thus making Nick's responsibility toward the production and his obligation to ensure adequate manning of tasks relevant. This responsibility is indexed in how Nick can be seen to format his turn as a threat ("you will damn well not be … cause then it'll be …"; see Hepburn & Potter, 2011), although this line is aborted before the consequence is formulated.

Nick's responsibility as a team leader is also a topic of the remainder of the excerpt. In overlap with Elvin (who has indicated support for Rod's proposal in parts of the sequence not featured here) and some other employees who seem to express agreement with Elvin (lines 10–11), Nick goes on to describe another consequence of the proposal. Because of the subtle category work involved, this description requires close examination: First, before describing the consequence itself, Nick describes its likelihood as very high (line 12: "it takes NEXT to nothing"; line 17: "it takes NOTHING"). Next, through (hypothetical) referred speech, Nick references another potential scenario where he and Anita are informed by an unnamed person that "Dennis Johnson" (line 17: this is the full name of the employee Dennis who is participating in the workshop) is out running. Dennis' running is formulated as "scurrying about," which implies a negative evaluation from the would-be speaker. In addition, the referred speech is formatted as a minimal report from a knowing speaker to a non-knowing recipient, implying that the would-be speaker expects Nick and Anita to be unaware of Dennis taking a run during work hours. It can thus also be inferred that the would-be speaker is not a part of the team and does not know of any agreement which would actually allow Dennis to go running, although Nick does not refer to the would-be speaker as having any particular role. Nick's turn thus implies that people outside of the team will see Dennis' running as inapposite and infer that Nick and Anita have failed to notice Dennis' absence. As a result, he and Anita will have failed their managerial obligations of keeping a check on how their employees spend their time at work. The organizational environment that Nick constructs is one where he has to be observant of how others in the organization perceive his role performance, and focus less on promoting employee health. An upshot of trying out Rod's proposal, according to Nick, is thus that he and Anita will be held accountable, and that their reputations as managers may suffer.

Nick's resistance toward the suggestion is further underscored in line 21 ("that will damn well be over my dead body"), which falls after the other participants have laughed at Nick's previous turn—possibly because of the irony of casting Dennis, who took a skeptical stance toward the proposal, as the runner in the hypothetical scenario. And while the discussion of Rod's proposal continued for some time after the sequence in the extract, the proposal was dropped later in the meeting after more critical comments from Nick.

Overall, we thus see Nick engaging in connecting leadership here by invoking a particular version of the organizational context that is of relevance for his role performance. He offers a description of the context where other (not currently present) organization members hold expectations toward his role performance in a way that is presented as highly consequential for his stance toward Rod's proposal. This version introduces a new moral dimension to the issue: if the other participants try to pursue the suggestion, they put him in a problematic position. In contrast to Anita in Excerpt 1, Nick thus reframes the issue from a question of health and safety to one of role expectations and reputation among team leaders in the organization.

It should be noted that Nick also emphasizes a particular version of team leader's role expectations in the organization through how he enacts his role more generally in the excerpt. Specifically, Nick does not explicitly contradict Anita's previously offered description of her role as a health and safety manager, but his construction of the team leader role has very different implications: while Anita took a somewhat facilitative stance toward the employees in Excerpt 1, Nick here enacts a more directive version of the role. Thus, it is clearly possible for the participants to the interaction to construct particular versions of the complex organizational context, emphasize certain aspects of the context over others and enact their roles in a variety of ways. The need to continuously talk the organization into being essentially provides the participants with opportunities to exercise connecting leadership as a sort of influence attempt in the here and now.

Case 2: "It Was a Free Kick"

The second case is taken from a management team meeting in a branch of a bank. The branch has some 35 employees, divided into a group managing private customers and a smaller group for handling companies. Each group has a group manager, Mary and Ronald respectively. In the meeting, four persons are present: the branch manager (Arthur), the two group managers (Ronald and Mary), and an administrative manager (Charles).

We enter the meeting when the four are discussing current challenges and problems. Ronald here raises a problem of losing customers due to how these customers have been handled by the bank. Because of the complexity, the construction of securities and the level of credit involved, another division of the bank is also involved in these cases, and the employee Melanie (who is not present) is that division's main contact to the customer. However, the responsibility for the contracts with the companies, as well as the financial profit from these contracts, resides with this branch and thus with Ronald. Thus, while the loss of customers makes attribution of blame relevant, the matter of who should receive the blame is negotiable, owing to how both Melanie and members of Ronald's team have dealt with the customer recently. In the interaction, the participants also make references to Harry, who is one of Ronald's employees, and to Peter, a contact in one of the customer companies (ALIAS) who Ronald corresponds with.

We will focus on two aspects of this excerpt: first, how the question of Ronald and his employees' blameworthiness is negotiated in the interaction, and secondly, how interpersonal influence in the form of connecting leadership is accomplished in the here and now to project blame onto Melanie. Both aspects are intimately related to how the participants' roles are constructed in the setting, and for Ronald, this includes invoking external role relationships which would likely otherwise remain dormant in this setting.

Since the excerpt is quite long, it is relevant to outline what happens in it in broad terms before attending to the details of the participants' talk. Initially, Ronald raises the issue of two lost customer companies, the first being a retail firm (RETAIL) that was given an offer on financial services that they rejected, choosing instead another bank. In providing the example, Ronald focuses on how Melanie has failed to handle complaints from RETAIL to the company's satisfaction. Next, Ronald reports how the CEO (chief executive officer) of another customer (Peter at ALIAS) has experienced the contact with Melanie, giving his disappointment with her handling of the case as a cause for the company soliciting offers from competing banks. In the end, the branch manager Arthur aligns strongly with Ronald, expressing his disappointment, and explicitly telling about how saddening he feels the story is. Seemingly, this is the first time he hears the story. Thus, it seems that Ronald has managed to avoid blame for himself or his employees, at least for the time being, with the blame instead being placed on Melanie.

Looking in more detail on how this allocation of blame is accomplished, we now go through the excerpt again, focusing on the various role categories that are made relevant for Ronald. One such overall category is that of the group manager. This category is made relevant by the ongoing report that Ronald starts delivering at the beginning of the excerpt (lines 49–58), and which he returns to later (lines 69–79 and 82–94), highlighting both Ronald's privileged knowledge about the reported affairs and his overall accountability for handling problems related to these types of customer relations—a role aspect which we will return to later.

In addition, Ronald is also involved in two role relationships with potential targets of blame for the loss of customers: the first is as a superior to Harry, whose role in the events becomes introduced and managed in a side sequence to the overall report (lines 59-68). In line 59, Charles asks who handled the RETAIL case, a question which can be heard as foreshadowing evaluation or attribution of blame. Ronald responds with the name of one of his subordinates, Jenny, and Mary supplements with another name, Harry. In line 62, Ronald latches on to Mary's turn, naming Melanie and repeating Harry. Then, in line 64-67, Ronald produces a short expansion as a defense of Harry, thus showing that he indeed heard Charles's previous turn as attending to the accountability of those involved. In particular, Ronald argues that Harry is not to blame (lines 64–65: "no shade on Harry"), providing the account that Harry has

Excerpt 3

Ron: now we have two more cases eh:
RETAIL (.) is leaving us
(0.4)
on that side
(0.4)
going to BigBank
(0.8)
twenty-six thousand a month in fees
(0.4)
eh:::
Cha: who was it that had them↑
Ron: Jenny:
Mar: °Harry°=
Ron: =and Melanie be[sides Ha]rry
Mar: [°(   )°]
Ron: but there (.) is no (.)
shade on Harry there because I mean it is
(0.4)
historically (.) he has presented complaints
Art: °ye:s°
Ron: eh: it has gone through Melanie so that it
and then it was (.) it is gone and then Melanie came
again I mean there has been these turns
around the follow-up
>then I don't know< what has gone wrong really
so that
but anyway
he's (.) not satisfied with the follow-up
(0.4)
eh:: Melanie had been out to ALIAS now
met this n[ew] CEO
??: [mm]
(0.5)
Ron: and eh talk- I called Peter last week and eh:
(0.8)

.hh >she had made a< forced impression
sent an offer that was a bit incoherent
eh (.) that wasn't eh (.)in
in line with what she had presented
when she was out there verbally and eh: now they
were about to ask for a control offer from a competitor
(0.6)
eh:: so I have asked
everyone in the group to write down
(.)
with (.) different eh
Art: and that was a free kick [this one]
Ron: [yes] sure it was eh
yes eh it was ready
if we had just had a decent offer
made a good impression [( )]
Art: [I called] Melanie myself=
Ron: =yes
Art: and said that here is a customer
(0.7)
that you'll take
Ron: yes=
Art: =we have it all
they will give it all to you
(0.5)
Ron: mm=
Art: =arrange the meeting with them and [everything]
Ron: [mm (.) mm mm]
mm
(0.6)
??: °yes°
Art: AAahh:
Ron: ah it is so sa:d [I mean it ( )]
Art: [AH it] really makes one sad

already "made a complaint" (line 67) which positions Harry as a dissatisfied party, rather than the cause of the problematic events.

The second potential target of blame is of course Melanie. However, being an internal collaborator at the employee level, rather than a direct report to Ronald, the distribution of accountability and thus blameworthiness among them is somewhat less clear. One way to avoid blame in such as situation is to avoid being seen as placing blame oneself; as Bergmann states: "...moralization over some issue easily leads to accusations and other forms of (counter-) moralization" (1998, p. 288). What is visible in the extract is that Ronald employs various devices which can be used to manage potential criticisms that the description one is providing of a person or event, for example, is biased (Mueller & Whittle, 2011). Specifically, the way Ronald designs his report to revolve around seemingly factual descriptions in an emotionally "neutral" tone positions himself as an observer and downplays his own part in the situation and the description of it (Edwards & Potter, 1992). For example, in line 56, Ronald mentions the loss of "twenty-six thousand a month" in lost fee, rather than providing a more emotionally toned stance toward the events (e.g., by saying "we're losing a lot of money"). Also, the issue here is to be heard as the bank losing money, rather than for instance, that Ronald is disappointed or upset. Relatedly, the negative evaluations of Melanie's work are paraphrased as coming from Melanie's contact at RETAIL ("he" in line 76), and merely reported by Ronald. Ronald continues in line 82 to 89, reporting on what the ALIAS CEO has said about Melanie's actions and providing more details, thereby delegating the dissatisfaction and evaluation to the customer. However, the ALIAS CEO's reported description still performs category work by attributing the problems to Melanie's role performance as the customer's main contact. Ronald could thus be seen as "doing being objective" as a stance that is displayed for the other participants (Sacks & Garfinkel, 1970).

Another potential strategy for avoiding blame is of course to downplay one's own ability to influence the problematic situation (Whittle & Mueller, 2016). In claiming that he is not certain about the details of the events which led to the CEO of ALIAS criticizing Melanie (line 73), Ronald offers a version of his role where what has happened with the customer was outside of his scope of control. However, later in his report, Ronald begins describing an initiative he has taken as an upshot of the events involving Melanie and the customer (lines 91–94: "so I have asked"). While the initiative is not described in detail here, it was later formulated by Ronald in terms of collecting experiences from Ronald's direct reports about their collaborations with Melanie. While it is just as possible that Ronald's role-related accountabilities could be constructed in another way, especially given the general flexibility of role constructions in the bank, this is not the role construction that is established here. For example, the possibility could have been raised that Ronald should have kept a closer check on Melanie's handling of the customer. But rather than these responsibilities being given (for instance, as part of the organizational structure), they are open for negotiation, and here, they are tuned to Ronald's interactional project in the here and now: to provide an account for the events which have transpired which manages the risk of blame for the loss of the customers. Thus, Ronald could be said to perform a kind of indirect category work (since he is speaking as a group manager) in relation to his own role performance by framing himself as having trusted in Melanie to handle the case, but now showing diligence by reporting the situation to the other managers and having taken action to address Melanie's performance.

Constructing role responsibilities in the way Ronald does in the excerpt also has the potential to exercise influence in the here and now. Thus, as an additional interactional project, we argue that Ronald's contribution sets up an interactional environment which makes it relevant for his own superior, Arthur, to display readiness for action. More specifically, Ronald's construction of his role obligations outside of the current interaction is used as a *device* for producing influence from a subordinate "follower" position (Uhl-Bien & Carsten, 2018) in the current interaction, thereby engaging in what we call connecting leadership. We'll have a closer look at how this is accomplished.

While Ronald's report has described Melanie as the sole actor in dealing with RETAIL and ALIAS, and thus the only one to blame, Arthur's participation in the spoken interaction is quite minimal up until line 95. At this point, Arthur interrupts Ronald while Ronald is reporting on the initiatives taken to address the problem with ALIAS and assesses the circumstances regarding landing a contract with ALIAS as a "free kick" (i.e., as very favorable). Thus, Arthur's assessment suggests that the turn of events be attributed to Melanie, rather than the difficulty of the task, for example. Arthur's assessment is made relevant by Ronald's account: we see that even though Ronald has gone on with his report and is now describing his new initiative (lines 91–94), Arthur's assessment is fitted to the part of Ronald's report about Melanie's work with ALIAS. Because Ronald has merely reported events "neutrally," others are able to provide a more emotionally expressive assessment or evaluation of the situation first (Schegloff, 2007). Interestingly, Ronald even takes a short break before he transitions into describing his initiative (Line 90), thereby providing an opportunity for others to take the conversational floor with such an assessment (Sacks et al., 1974), although no one does so at that point.

Ronald's report is formulated as news to the recipients, who are positioned as not-knowing about the events concerning Melanie and ALIAS. When news are taken as surprising, various discursive features can often be seen in the recipients' responses: a surprise token (often in the form of an exclamation), which may be preceded by various *inserts* (Wilkinson & Kitzinger, 2006). Focusing on Arthur's talk in the excerpt, we see a surprise token in line 115 ("AAahh:") preceded by his assessment of the situation as a free kick and a description of a phone call with Melanie before she met with ALIAS (lines 95, 100, 102-104, 106-108, 110). Arthur thereby reaffirms the category work performed by the ALIAS CEO's reported description. The assessment and the description of the phone call can be seen as a form of *ritualized disbelief*, a highly common insert variant (for example in the form of "really?", "you're kidding," etc.). Ronald marks agreement with Arthur's assessment of the situation (lines 96–99) through his own expanded assessment (Pomerantz, 1984) and subsequently provides a number of alignment tokens (Lines 105, 109, 111–112) while Arthur is describing his phone call with Melanie, confirming Arthur's stance toward the events as surprising. In DeRue and Ashford's terms (2010), the sequence from lines 95–112 can thus be seen as granting Arthur a leader identity and claiming a follower identity for himself. In spite of Ronald's "neutral" emotional stance, his report had the effect of projecting attribution of blame to Melanie.

It is noteworthy that Ronald's role management toward Arthur changes somewhat toward the end of the excerpt: it is only when Arthur makes his surprise token as an explicitly disapproving evaluation of the situation (line 115: "AAahh") that Ronald take a more explicit negative emotional stance toward the reported events too (line 116: "ah it is so sa:d"), and Arthur recycles Ronald's description of feeling sad in his next turn, produced in partial overlap with Ronald. Thus, Arthur introduces the relevance of taking a more critical emotional stance toward the events involving Melanie and the customers. Ronald might have avoided such a stance in order to avoid becoming a potential target of accusations and counter-moralization, as we noted above. However, Ronald eventually leaves his emotionally "neutral" stance in order to affiliate with Arthur's allocation of blame to Melanie. Arthur and Ronald thus form a small alliance (or *operational unit*, Larsson & Lundholm, 2013), sharing the sadness and disappointment over a lost customer, and siding with each other in blaming Melanie for the problems.

Although the extract does not show any actions on Arthur's part in relation to Melanie or her division of the bank, his emotional engagement in the issue suggests that his obligations and commitment to the bank are made relevant to the interaction and that he is potentially being mobilized to act, like Ronald was. This mobilization is at least in part produced by Ronald's construction of his role responsibilities outside of the here and now (with Melanie and the CEO of ALIAS, Peter) and by how Ronald's contribution sets up a particular interactional environment which makes it relevant for Arthur to take a clear stance toward the transpired events. This is accomplished through Ronald's skillful monitoring of his emotional display, with his neutral stance opening for stronger emotional displays from Arthur, to which Ronald can subsequently align. Thus, from a follower position, Ronald invites his supervising manager to be mobilized in the direction of placing the blame on Melanie and to take action on the issue.

In sum, the excerpt sheds light on the intricacies involved in being a "connecting leader": these involve both addressing the different moral accountabilities associated with one's role categories and role relationships, and doing so in a manner which is attuned to how the relevancies of these categories and relationships shift within the interaction as dormant roles become enacted roles, previously enacted roles slip into the background, and the participants display and thus commit themselves to certain stances. However, the excerpt also shows how managers, while managing their own accountabilities, can also make others' role-based obligations relevant to the interaction, thereby shaping the interactional context so as to project certain actions in the future and in effect exercising connecting leadership.

DISCUSSION

In this chapter, we set out to challenge certain common understandings in the literature regarding managers' multiple roles and role relationships, namely the notion of the organizational context as given and fixed, and how the work of the connecting leader is seen as reconciling or managing different, possibly conflicting, role obligations. Instead, we suggested seeing the organizational context as being continuously talked into being in the here and now, and offered the concept of connecting leadership as the process of persuasively constructing a particular version of the context to accomplish influence in the here and now. In our empirical analysis, we set out to explore firstly how particular versions of the organizational context might be constructed and invoked in situated interactions, and secondly, the potential influence effects of such constructions.

Drawing on a conversation analytical approach, our analysis shows that roles are not simply invoked, but that their features, such as rights, obligations and other's expectations toward the role incumbent, are actively constructed and enacted in the setting. Participants do not construct their roles in a general, abstract version, but rather in a highly specific version, where particular aspects are highlighted. This specificity is indicated by the variability that can be seen in the data in relation to how roles are enacted: for example, there are clear differences between how Anita constructed her manager role in Excerpt 1 and how Nick constructed his in Excerpt 2 (both from Case 1), even though both are, in formal terms, managers of the team and hold the same level of rights and responsibility. Differences in role construction can also be more subtle, such as how Ronald shifted his stance in Case 2 by first providing a "neutral" account about the transpired events and only offering his personal critical comments about Melanie's work after Arthur, his boss, had done so. As discourse scholars point out, descriptions inherently have a "could-have-been-otherwise" quality (Edwards, 1997; see also Wetherell & Potter, 1988), and this is of course also the case for role constructions and constructions of role incumbents' performance.

An upshot of this quality is that we as analysts can attend to the interactional work that speakers perform by constructing a role one way rather than another. In our analysis, we have illustrated Grint's (2005) and Clifton's (2014) point that constructing the organizational context (in the sense of allowing different descriptions to be presented and different versions to be enacted) can serve an important leadership function. Specifically, we have focused on how connecting one's salient role in the current interaction to role relationships in other contexts can allow one to influence the current interaction. The particular construction of these role relationships works to shape possible actions and negotiations of role obligations in the here and now, or in the words of Grint, "limits the alternatives available such that those involved begin to act differently" (2005, p. 1471). An example of this is where Anita in Case 2 reported a quite unspecific "opening" provided by the intervention project as a warrant for further discussing Rod's suggestion. Anita of course holds a managerial position relative to the employees. But interestingly, her ability to lead in the situation was based on her status as a member in a project group championed by a high-ranking manager—a context in which she held a subordinate role. Still, invoking this role in the interaction constituted a resource which allowed her to influence the trajectory of the interaction toward keeping the suggestion on the table. Similarly, in Case 2, we saw Ronald drawing on his role as a group manager (and thus accountable for contracts with certain customers) and his relationship with a manager at ALIAS ("Peter") to provide an account which managed the matter of his own responsibility and that of his direct reports in losing the business while projecting a negative assessment of Melanie's performance as being relevant. Thereby, occupying different roles within the organization, and being able to invoke these effectively in one's interactions, may provide organization members with a rhetorical advantage that can be employed to try and shape the trajectory of the interaction.

Our analysis thus broadens the discussion about connecting leaders by highlighting and clarifying the role of the organizational context as a resource and a constraint, not only for general role performance (Ashforth, 2001), but more specifically for the practical accomplishment of leadership (Crevani et al, 2010; Larsson, 2017). While Graen and Uhl-Bien (1995) utilize the concept of a leadership structure to claim that relationships throughout the organization impact particular manager-subordinate dyads, our analysis shows in some detail how such impact might occur: rather than influencing the situation "from without," our notion of connecting leadership points precisely to how a particular rendering of a relationship extending beyond the current setting might contribute to accomplishing leadership in the here and now. How relationships develop over time, which is a focal topic for much of LMX research, is obviously outside the immediate scope of our form of close interaction analysis. However, we observe how role relationships elsewhere help make influence attempts both legitimate and morally defensible in the here and now (Grint, 2005), and these attempts will likely impact the development of the leader-follower relationship over time.

Although space precludes a detailed discussion of the topic, the processes we describe here can be seen as a subtle exercise of discursive power, similar to the asymmetries that others have described on the basis of conversation analytic studies (Heritage, 1997; Hutchby, 1996; Stevanovic & Peräkylä, 2014). The rendering of a particular version of role relationships outside of the current interaction might be particularly persuasive when the party presenting the information holds privileged access to the settings about which they speak, or what has been called the *epistemic authority* (Heritage & Raymond, 2005; Stivers & Sidnell, 2012). For example, by holding privileged access to the health and safety project group, Anita in Case 1 was able to present the implications of "opening" provided by the project in an authoritative manner which could be hard for the other participants to challenge. This form of authority is of course also available to employees who take up special roles in the organization, such as how Dennis in Excerpt 1 drew on his prior membership of the joint consultation committee to challenge Rod's suggestion.

In relation to the topic of power, critics of the interactional perspective may object that seeing the organizational context as constructed implies voluntarism by overstating the organization members' degrees of freedom in talking the organizational context into being. However, our point is that when trying to construct the context for action, competing voices can often be found, and the question of which one will prevail and gain (at least temporary) legitimacy is not given in advance. This also means that speakers risk resistance from the other parties to the discussion, especially if their constructions are not taken as credible (Clifton, 2014; Grint, 2005). For example, the fact that Nick distanced himself from Anita's position in Case 1, Excerpt 2 is an example that managers are not always successful in getting others to subscribe to their construction of the context.

Further, while the slow and detailed analysis might give an impression that actors are highly aware of their own strategies and that microlevel movements in interactions are premeditated and planned, this is not what we suggest. On the contrary, how we craft our ongoing contributions in conversations is not something we normally think much about—it is part of the "seen but unnoticed" (Garfinkel, 1967, p. 37) features of everyday interaction, and consequently not necessarily something that the participants can report on afterwards (which is one reason why recordings of interaction is needed for this kind of analysis). Following the ethnomethodological perspective, we see these tactics and movements as skilled but highly automated accomplishments that are closely fitted to the specific interactional environment and setting. Our perspective focuses on the interaction and relationships, rather than the individual minds of the participants. However, we do assert that actors are agentic (rather than cultural or psychological dopes; Garfinkel, 1967), that is, actively engaging in the evolving interaction, reflexively trying to pursue their various interactional projects and to avoid what they perceive as less attractive interactional outcomes on a turn-by-turn basis.

Returning to the topic of the connecting leader, the analysis also suggests that we should look beyond the "leadership triad" spanning the focal manager and their own superior and subordinates (e.g., Jaser, 2017) as managers may invoke (and thus "connect to") many different roles and role relationships in their interactions with others. In the cases presented here, these "external" roles included Anita's role as a steering group member (Excerpt 1) and Ronald's role as a manager toward an employee from another group (Melanie, Excerpt 3). The interactional perspective we employ here is sensitive not only to the specific roles that are relevant in the given situation, but also *how* these roles become relevant.

DeRue and Ashford's conceptualization of leader and follower identities as dynamic and potentially context specific is generally relevant to furthering our understanding of the work of connecting leaders (Jaser, 2017), and their description of how organization members engage in cycles of leadership (and followership) claims and grants in interaction can seem closely related to the EM/CA perspective we have presented here. However, there are important and significant differences. For one, while DeRue and Ashford claim to move "the leadership field away from a static and hierarchical conception of leadership and toward a more dynamic, social, and relational conception" (2010, p. 629), we have argued that their perspective still treats the organizational context as static. Thereby, DeRue and Ashford's approach is only to a certain degree compatible with Smircich and Morgan's (1982) point that leadership can be seen as the management of meaning: what is considered "manageable" is limited to certain aspects of the current situation, while a number of circumstances (such as which collectives exist in the workplace, or how the institutional structures shape the current interaction) are simply taken as given. Essentially, in DeRue and Ashford's (2010) theorizing, the institutional structure is treated as an antecedent, impacting the process of identity work without being a part of or affected by it. However, as our analysis suggests, particular aspects and versions of the organizational context are continuously and actively invoked as part of the ongoing negotiation of leader and follower identities. And, rather than being a fixed and given state, the organizational context seems to be a highly flexible resource, that can be told and retold in many different versions, where obligations are reinterpreted and portrayed in different ways, attuned to the interests of the participants' interactional projects in the here and now.

In closing, we have argued that the interactional perspective offers a number of specific insights to the study of connecting leaders and of leadership in general. In addition, the perspective provides a well-developed framework for conducting empirically grounded analyses of leadership in practice, as a social and situated behavior. Such analyses can suggest new ways to frame existing theoretical concepts and challenge current assumptions, thereby pointing toward new avenues to explore in future studies. Similarly, we hope that others will feel inspired to engage with the concept of connecting leadership and the influence that can be had through shaping the construction of the organizational context and the roles of its members.

NOTES

1. While the term *leader* is often used to refer to a person in a formal leadership position, we will instead use the term *manager* throughout the chapter. Our choice is guided by how current leadership theories are increasingly stressing that engaging in leadership as a form of social influence does not presume a certain position in the organizational hierarchy, and that from an interactional perspective, the same person might take both what could be called leader and follower roles at different times during an exchange (DeRue & Ashford, 2010; Larsson & Nielsen, 2017).
2. As readers of this volume are surely aware, a number of different definitions of the term leadership exist, and this can be a source of confusion and conceptual unclarity. Thus, we note that when writing of the leader-

ship literature, we refer to the wider academic field studying leadership across different paradigms and conceptualizations. When referring to other leadership theories, we will use the term in the same sense applied in the cited texts. However, within the perspective we apply in this chapter, leadership is understood as a social influence process that is produced by the participants in their interactions. From this perspective, leadership is not only exercised by people in a superior formal position over their subordinates—instead, the question of who is leading and who is following develops dynamically, sometimes on an utterance-by-utterance basis (Clifton, 2009, 2012; Whittle et al., 2015).

3. Within the leadership field, this understanding of social reality as actively constructed have provided inspiration for a number of studies under the headings of sensemaking and sensegiving, for example (Gioia & Chittipeddi, 1991; Humphreys et al., 2012; Pye, 2005). The focus on how speakers understand and make sense of what happens bears many similarities to the sensemaking perspective formulated by Weick (1995). Weick does draw on ethonomethodology, but essentially formulates a more cognitive and individual perspective on sensemaking (Neyland & Whittle, 2018). We thus acknowledge the many similarities, however, in our argument we draw on the ethnomethodological perspective.
4. Our use of the term *interactional project* should be understood pragmatically, that is, as a project which is inferable based on the person's actions across some stretch of interaction. This inference can be based on how speakers or recipients orient to specific turns as being part of an overall project, or through how the turns are formatted in a way which conventionally implies an overall project (Levinson, 2012). The projects are interactional in the sense that they aim to influence the trajectory of the interaction in some way and in getting other participants to contribute to this end, such as by progressing the talk toward producing a request or an invitation; on the other hand, getting other participants to comply with some course of action beyond the interactional setting (such as accepting the invitation) is typically not considered part of the project.

REFERENCES

Antaki, C., & Widdicombe, S. (1998). *Identities in talk*. SAGE.

Bergmann, J. R. (1998). Introduction: Morality in discourse. *Research on Language & Social Interaction*, *31*(3–4), 279–294.

Bittner, E. (1974). The concept of organisation. In R. Turner (Ed.), *Ethnomethodology: Selected readings* (pp. 69–81). Penguin.

Boden, D. (1994). *The business of talk: Organizations in action*. Polity.

Clifton, J. (2009). Beyond taxonomies of influence: "Doing" influence and making decisions in management team meetings. *Journal of Business Communication*, *46*(1), 57–79.

Clifton, J. (2012). A discursive approach to leadership: Doing assessments and managing organizational meanings. *Journal of Business Communication, 49*(2), 148–168. https://doi.org/10.1177/0021943612437762

Clifton, J. (2014). Being in the know: Socio-epistemics and the communicative constitution of a management team. *Organization Management Journal, 11*(1), 4–14.

Crevani, L., Lindgren, M., & Packendorff, J. (2010). Leadership, not leaders: On the study of leadership as practices and interactions. *Scandinavian Journal of Management, 26*(1), 77–86. https://doi.org/10.1016/j.scaman.2009.12.003

Dansereau, F., Graen, G. B., & Haga, W. J. (1975). A vertical dyad linkage approach to leadership within formal organizations. *Organizational Behavior and Human Performance, 13*, 46–78.

DeRue, D. S., & Ashford, S. J. (2010). Who will lead and who will follow? A social process of leadership identity construction in organizations. *Academy of Management Review, 35*(4), 627–647.

Drath, W. H., McCauley, C. D., Palus, C. J., Van Velsor, E., O'Connor, P. M. G., & McGuire, J. B. (2008). Direction, alignment, commitment: Toward a more integrative ontology of leadership. *The Leadership Quarterly, 19*(6), 635–653. https://doi.org/10.1016/j.leaqua.2008.09.003

Drew, P., & Heritage, J. (1992). Analyzing talk at work: An introduction. In P. Drew & J. Heritage (Eds.), *Talk at work: Interaction in institutional settings* (pp. 3–65). Cambridge University Press.

Edwards, D. (1997). *Discourse and cognition*. SAGE.

Garfinkel, H. (1967). *Studies in ethnomethodology*. Polity.

Garfinkel, H. (2002). *Ethnomethodology's program: Working out Durkheim's aphorism* (A. W. Rawls, Ed.). Rowman & Littlefield.

Gioia, D. A., & Chittipeddi, K. (1991). Sensemaking and sensegiving in strategic change initiation. *Strategic Management Journal, 12*(6), 433–448. https://doi.org/10.1002/smj.4250120604

Goffman, E. (1961). *Encounters*. Bobbs-Merrill.

Graen, G. B. (1976). Role making processes within complex organizations. In M. D. Dunnette (Ed.), *Handbook of industrial and organizational psychology* (pp. 1201–1245). Rand McNally.

Graen, G. B., & Scandura, T. A. (1987). Toward a psychology of dyadic organizing. *Research in Organizational Behavior, 9*, 175–208.

Graen, G. B., & Uhl-Bien, M. (1995). Relationship-based approach to leadership: Development of leader-member exchange (LMX) theory of leadership over 25 years: Applying a multi-level multi-domain perspective. *The Leadership Quarterly, 6*(2), 219–247. https://doi.org/10.1016/1048-9843(95)90036-5

Grint, K. (2005). Problems, problems, problems: The social construction of 'leadership.' *Human Relations, 58*(11), 1467–1494. https://doi.org/10.1177/0018726705061314

Halkowski, T. (1990). "Role" as an interactional device. *Social Problems, 37*(4), 564–577.

Hepburn, A., & Potter, J. (2011). Threats: Power, family mealtimes, and social influence. *British Journal of Social Psychology, 50*(1), 99–120. https://doi.org/10.1348/014466610X500791

Heritage, J. (1984). *Garfinkel and ethnomethodology*. Polity.

Heritage, J. (1997). Conversation analysis and institutional talk. In D. Silverman (Ed.), *Qualitative research: Theory, method and practice* (pp. 161–182). SAGE.

Heritage, J., & Raymond, G. (2005). The terms of agreement: Indexing epistemic authority and subordination in talk-in-interaction. *Social Psychology Quarterly, 68*(1), 15–38.

Housley, W. (1999). Role as an interactional device and resource in multidisciplinary team meetings. *Sociological Research Online, 4*(3), https://doi.org/10.5153/sro.315

Housley, W. (2000). Category work and knowledgeability within multidisciplinary team meetings. *Text-Interdisciplinary Journal for the Study of Discourse, 20*(1), 83–108.

Humphreys, M., Ucbasaran, D., & Lockett, A. (2012). Sensemaking and sensegiving stories of jazz leadership. *Human Relations, 65*(1), 41–62. https://doi.org/10.1177/0018726711424320

Hutchby, I. (1996). Power in discourse: The case of arguments on a British talk radio show. *Discourse & Society*, 7(4), 481–497. https://doi.org/10.1177/0957926596007004003

Hutchby, I., & Wooffitt, R. (2008). *Conversation analysis* (2nd ed.). Polity.

Jaser, Z. (2017). Pulled in two directions: Being in concert a leader to some and a follower to others. *Academy of Management Proceedings, 2017*(1), 16660. https://doi.org/10.5465/ambpp.2017.107

Jayyusi, L. (1984). *Categorization and the moral order*. Routledge & Kegan Paul.

Jefferson, G. (2004). Glossary of transcript symbols with an introduction. *Pragmatics and Beyond New Series, 125*, 13–34. https://doi.org/10.1075/pbns.125.02jef

Kahn, R. L., Wolfe, D. M., Quinn, R. P., & Snoek, J. D. (1964). *Organizational stress: Studies in role conflict and ambiguity*. Wiley.

Katz, D., & Kahn, R. L. (1978). *The social psychology of organizations*. Wiley.

Kitzinger, C. (2012). Repair. In J. Sidnell & T. Stivers (Eds.), *The handbook of conversation analysis* (pp. 229–256). https://doi.org/10.1002/9781118325001.ch12

Larsson, M. (2017). Leadership in interaction. *The Routledge Companion to Leadership*. Routledge.

Larsson, M., & Lundholm, S. E. (2013). Talking work in a bank: A study of organizing properties of leadership in work interactions. *Human Relations, 66*(8), 1101–1129. https://doi.org/10.1177/0018726712465452

Larsson, M., & Nielsen, M. F. (2017). The risky path to a followership identity: From abstract concept to situated reality. *International Journal of Business Communication*. https://doi.org/10.1177/2329488417735648

Levinson, S. C. (2012). Action formation and ascription. In J. Sidnell & T. Stivers (Eds.), *The handbook of conversation analysis* (pp. 101–130). https://doi.org/10.1002/9781118325001.ch6

Liden, R. C., Sparrowe, R. T., & Wayne, S. J. (1997). Leader-member exchange theory: The past and potential for the future. *Research in Personnel and Human Resources Management, 15*, 47–119.

Likert, R. (1961). *New patterns of management*. McGraw-Hill.

Llewellyn, N., & Hindmarsh, J. (Eds.). (2010). Work and organisation in real time: An introduction. In *Organisation, interaction and practice: Studies in ethnomethodology and conversation analysis* (pp. 3–23). Cambridge University Press.

Mueller, F., & Whittle, A. (2011). Translating management ideas: A discursive devices analysis. *Organization Studies, 32*(2), 187–210.

Neyland, D., & Whittle, A. (2018) Garfinkel on strategy: Using ethnomethodology to make sense of "rubbish strategy." *Critical Perspectives on Accounting, 53*, 31–42. https://doi.org/10.1016/j.cpa.2017.03.008

Peräkylä, A. (2011). Validity in research on naturally occurring social interaction. In D. Silverman (Ed.), *Qualitative research* (3rd ed.). SAGE.

Pomerantz, A. (1984). Agreeing and disagreeing with assessments: Some features of preferred/dispreferred turn shapes. In J. M. Atkinson & J. Heritage (Eds.), *Structures of social action: Studies in conversations analysis* (pp. 57–101). Cambridge University Press.

Pye, A. (2005). Leadership and organizing: Sensemaking in action. *Leadership, 1*(1), 31–49. https://doi.org/10.1177/1742715005049349

Sacks, H., & Garfinkel, H. (1970). On formal structures of practical action. In J. C. McKinney & E. A. Tiryakian (Eds.), *Theoretical sociology* (pp. 338–366). Appleton-Century-Croft.

Sacks, H., Schegloff, E. A., & Jefferson, G. (1974). A simplest systematics for the organization of turn-taking for conversation. *Language, 50*(4), 696–735.

Samra-Fredericks, D. (2010). Ethnomethodology and the moral accountability of interaction: Navigating the conceptual terrain of 'face' and face-work. *Journal of Pragmatics, 42*(8), 2147–2157.

Schegloff, E. A., & Sacks, H. (1973). Opening up closings. *Semiotica, 8*, 289–327.

Shamir, B. (2007). From passive recipients to active co-producers: Followers' roles in the leadership process. In B. Shamir, R. Pillai, M. C. Bligh, & M. Uhl-Bien (Eds.), *Follower-centered perspectives on leadership: A tribute to the memory of James R. Meindl* (pp. 9–39). Information Age.

Sluss, D. M., & Ashforth, B. E. (2007). Relational identity and identification: Defining ourselves through work relationships. *Academy of Management Review, 32*(1), 9–32.

Smircich, L., & Morgan, G. (1982). Leadership: The management of meaning. *Journal of Applied Behavioural Science, 18*(3), 257–273.

Stevanovic, M., & Peräkylä, A. (2014). Three orders in the organization of human action: On the interface between knowledge, power, and emotion in interaction and social relations. *Language in Society, 43*(2), 185–207.

Stivers, T., Enfield, N. J., Brown, P., Englert, C., Hayashi, M., Heinemann, T., Hoymann, G., Rossano, F., de Ruiter, J. P., Yoon, K.-E., & Levinson, S. C. (2009). Universals and cultural variation in turn-taking in conversation. *Proceedings of the National Academy of Sciences, 106*(26), 10587–10592. https://doi.org/10.1073/pnas.0903616106

Stivers, T., & Sidnell, J. (Eds.). (2012). *The handbook of conversation analysis*. Wiley.

Stryker, S., & Statham, A. (1985). Symbolic interaction and role theory. In G. Lindzey & E. Aronson (Eds.), *Handbook of social psychology* (3rd ed., Vol. 1, pp. 311–378). Random House.

ten Have, P. (2007). *Doing conversation analysis*. SAGE.

Uhl-Bien, M., & Carsten, M. (2018). Reversing the lens in leadership: Positioning followership in the leadership construct. In I. Katz, G. Eilam-Shamir, R. Kark, & Y. Berson (Eds.), *Leadership now: Reflections on the legacy of Boas Shamir* (pp. 195–222). Emerald.

Uhl-Bien, M., Riggio, R. E., Lowe, K. B., & Carsten, M. K. (2014). Followership theory: A review and research agenda. *The Leadership Quarterly*, *25*(1), 83–104. https://doi.org/10.1016/j.leaqua.2013.11.007

Weick, K. E. (1995). *Sensemaking in organizations* (Vol. 3). SAGE.

Wetherell, M., & Potter, J. (1988). Discourse analysis and theidentification of interpretative repertoires. In C. Antaki (Ed.), *Analysing everyday explanation. A casebook of methods* (pp. 168–183). SAGE.

Whittle, A., Housley, W., Gilchrist, A., Mueller, F., & Lenney, P. (2014). Power, poitics and organizational communication: An ethnomethodological perspective. In F. Cooren, E. Vaara, A. Langley, & H. Tsoukas (Eds.), *Language and communication at work: Discourse, narrativity, and organizing* (pp. 71–94). Oxford University Press.

Whittle, A., Housley, W., Gilchrist, A., Mueller, F., & Lenney, P. (2015). Category predication work, discursive leadership and strategic sensemaking. *Human Relations*, *68*(3), 377–407. https://doi.org/10.1177/0018726714528253

Whittle, A., & Mueller, F. (2016). Accounting for the banking crisis: repertoires of agency and structure. *Critical Discourse Studies*, *13*(1), 20–40. https://doi.org/10.1080/17405904.2015.1074598

Wieder, L. (1988). From resource to topic: Some aims of conversation analysis. *Annals of the International Communication Association*, *11*(1), 444–454. https://doi.org/10.1080/23808985.1988.11678701

Wilkinson, S., & Kitzinger, C. (2006). Surprise as an interactional achievement: Reaction tokens in conversation. *Social Psychology Quarterly*, *69*(2), 150–182. https://doi.org/10.1177/019027250606900203

Yukl, G., Seifert, C. F., & Chavez, C. (2008). Validation of the extended Influence Behavior Questionnaire. *The Leadership Quarterly*, *19*(5), 609–621. https://doi.org/10.1016/j.leaqua.2008.07.006

APPENDIX: TRANSCRIPTION LEGEND

(.)	audible break (“.” indicates short break, numbers indicate seconds)
( )	unintelligible speech
(( ))	transcription comments
[ ]	overlapping speech
=	no pause between speaker turns
:	elongated speech
> <	utterance spoken at a higher pace than surrounding talk
° °	phrase spoken at low volume
CAPITALS	sounds are louder than those surrounding it
-	speech is cut off

↑	soft rise in intonation
?	sharp rise in intonation
.hh	audible inbreath

CHAPTER 7

THE CONNECTING LEADER AND MANAGERIAL STANCES AT WORK

A Practice Perspective

Roddy Walker
Copenhagen Business School, Department of Organisation

ABSTRACT

Informed by a generative approach to social practice theories, this chapter suggests the idea of "managerial stances" as a productive concept for investigating and understanding the work of connecting leaders as it unfolds. An ethnographic study following middle managers at work provides the point of departure for an exploration of the shifting identities manifesting in their managerial practices, enabling them to navigate the varying interests of staff, immediate superiors, and wider organizational agendas. Rather than perceiving leadership and followership as traits assigned to particular organizational positions, the approach undertaken in this chapter operationalizes leading and following as the adoption of *managerial stances* emerging within and across the different situated practices in which managers participate. In doing so, the figure of the connecting leader is perceived in practice, hosting a horizon of leader and follower identities

The Connecting Leader: Serving Concurrently as a Leader and a Follower
pp. 191–217

brought into relief on the background of participation in organizational practices.

INTRODUCTION

The position of the middle manager, betwixt and between the hierarchy presented in typical organizational and bureaucratic "charts," emphasizes the importance and complexity of their work, particularly within leadership processes and the implementation of change initiatives. They are "controlled and controllers, and resisted and resisters" (Harding et al., 2014) working with subordinates and superiors having, so to speak, a foot in both camps. Their work involves navigating potentially contradictory interests from above and below. As such, how they maneuver in this organizational space is important; the orientation of their work can be directed toward different ends. This has implications for how they approach organizational change initiatives: opposing them, supporting them or mediating between these two positions (Floyd & Wooldridge, 1997; Rouleau, 2005; Rouleau & Balogun, 2011), and therefore potentially influencing the eventual outcomes of these. Focusing on middle managers in this way provides a potent point of departure for studying the work of the connecting leader empirically.

To do so, this chapter takes inspiration from an integration of Schatzki's social practice theory (Schatzki, 2002) and critical psychology (Dreier, 2009) to conceptualize the situated managerial work of connecting leaders. A bifocal analytical perspective is developed, capable of appreciating how the practices of this managerial work are coordinated within a wider and complex organizational plenum, while simultaneously preserving an important space for the manager as a distinct practitioner within this complex. Drawing on inspiration from Dreier's idea of *personal stances* (2008, p. 3), the concept of "managerial stances" is developed and presented as a fitting theoretical tool for working with the complexity of the (re)orientations of situated managerial work emerging within broader organizational dynamics.

The chapter provides an empirical and analytical approach to studying the connecting leader at work, where the concept of managerial stances offers a way of understanding the situated identities of the connecting leader, as both leader and follower; the manner in which connecting leaders oscillate between actively leading and following becomes discernible. The chapter begins by considering connective leadership and the connecting leader, before moving on to a fundamental exploration of literature pertaining to aspects of followership within management studies, using this as a background upon which the theoretical exercise can proceed. The elements comprising the theoretical integration are then introduced and operationalized, working toward a qualification of the concept of "managerial stances" within situated managerial work. This theoretical exercise is then furnished with an empirical illustration, utilizing transcriptions of audio recordings collected during intervals of shadowing a middle manager at work. This provides the opportunity to demonstrate an operationalization of the concept in analysis, while simultaneously providing insight into the empirical footings from which it is developed.

UNDERSTANDING THE MIDDLE MANAGER AS A CONNECTING FIGURE

The notion of "connective leadership" (Lipman-Blumen, 2000) is a propitious way of understanding the position and potential influence of middle managers, placing emphasis on their work in securing wider organizational coherence, by developing interpersonal connections with subordinates, superiors and peers, serving as "the threaded needle stitching together multiple shorter term alliances" (p. 23). Here, middle managers can work as "intrapreneurs" (Pinchot, 1985) in undertaking this task, seeking to innovate and navigate between the differing interests of groupings within the larger organizational plenum. This emphasizes the importance that the work of the middle manager can have and the importance of this in terms of leadership processes, where middle managers must be simultaneously capable of both leading and following (Jaser, 2017) in order to operate effectively within these conditions. While the notion of connective leadership is appealing, a more detailed consideration of the actions of the middle manager as a connecting leader can provide insight into the possible influence and implications of this at the organizational level: what does it look like in practice and how can it be recognized? Greater emphasis on empirical studies examining connective leadership and the connecting leader at work can illuminate how connecting leaders approach their work, and the possible implications of this for leadership processes.

Understanding leadership as a relational process (Hogg, 2005) comprising the social relations and interactions (Fairhurst & Uhl-Bien, 2012) between participants, draws attention to its inherent fluidity and dynamism. This focuses analytical attention toward activities and relations emerging within unfolding situated interactions, rather than emphasizing individual roles, traits, competences and skills more typical in traditional leader-centric approaches (Lord & Hall, 2005). A processual understanding of leadership demands, therefore, an appropriate consideration of followership (Carsten et al., 2010; Uhl-Bien et al., 2014) as a contingent element of any leadership process. For leading to take place, following must also arise. The fluidity and emergent nature of such a processual understanding calls for a constructivist approach to studying how individuals adapt followership behavior, regardless of their official role—rather than focusing on performance of role expectations within a formal hierarchical organizational structure (Uhl-Bien et al., 2014). Here, the manner in which leader and follower identities are claimed and granted (DeRue & Ashford, 2010) through interaction becomes the unit of analysis, where leadership involves an attempt to actively influence others, while followership is understood to be a similarly active acceptance of being directly influenced by others (Uhl-Bien & Pillai, 2007). Such an understanding of transient identities presents a challenge in leadership and management studies, particularly in terms of how it can inform approaches to studying the connecting leader empirically.

Studying identity work (Sveningsson & Alvesson, 2003) and the exploration of provisional selves (Ibarra, 1999) offer salient conceptual resources for exploring the manifestation of different identities, how these may be achieved, and to what end. However, as emphasized by Coupland and Brown, (2012) such approaches concentrate primarily on "'epistemological spaces' that discourses offer individuals and collectives in their efforts to construct their selves" (p. 2), drawing primarily on data from interviews. This focus is illustrated in a review of extant literature pertaining to identity and identity work in the journal organization studies (Brown, 2018), where the production of "identity narratives" (p. 10) through interviews provide specific accounts of "an edited past, a preferred present and a desired future" (Wright et al., 2012, p. 1471) for analysis. Approaching identity in this manner becomes an introspective project, at the expense of a more dialectic approach to studying how identities may be tied to organizational processes and particular outcomes in situated work (Coupland & Brown, 2012).

The empirical and analytical approach developed in this chapter aligns more with the understanding of identity work presented in (DeRue & Ashford, 2010) focusing on the manner in which leadership and followership identities are constructed through "reciprocal and mutually reinforcing claims and grants" (p. 637) in social interactions. However, an alternative understanding of identity and context is presented, more attuned to studying the manifestation of different identities in the work of connecting leaders, providing insight into how these arise and how they can influence situated managerial and organizational practices. The remainder of this chapter will develop an analytical approach geared toward studying situated identities of connecting leaders and the manner in which their managerial work is oriented and reoriented in practice.

Operationalizing practice theory allows for an understanding of the connecting leader as situated firmly within organizational processes, considering how these activities are coordinated and establishing a perspective from which the manifestation of different leader and follower identities can be studied. The development of the concept of *managerial stances* offers a theorization of the situated identities of connecting leaders and their managerial work, concurrently leading and following, influencing and being influenced within a wider organizational plenum. This represents a novel approach to understanding the work of connecting leaders, beginning empirical study in the midst of their work. A practical understanding of identity is developed, capable of responding to appeals to locate "the study of identity within a study of organizing" (Coupland & Brown, 2012, p. 3).

ESTABLISHING A PRACTICE THEORY PERSPECTIVE: A GENERATIVE APPROACH TO PRACTICES AND PRACTITIONERS

The adoption of a practice theory approach represents a choice to approach social phenomena in a certain way (Nicolini, 2012, p. 13). Focus is trained upon the primacy of practice in the production of meaning, and in the understanding of social activity and interaction (Buch et al., 2015). Interest in the study of leadership and management as "practice" has increased in recent times (Blackler & Regan, 2009; Carroll et al., 2008; Corradi et al., 2010; Nicolini, 2012; Raelin, 2016), reflecting a desire to focus on, and understand, these processes as they emerge through situated activities in the workplace. This growing interest can be perceived as a direct response to the wider aim of "bringing work back in" (Barley & Kunda, 2001) to academic analyses by studying work in situ. By choosing this approach, the character and nature of managerial and leadership practices are brought to the fore—how are these practices coordinated: what do leaders and managers actually *do* within these situated practices, how can these doings be understood, and what difference can they potentially make? Such an approach is immediately appealing and relevant for studies aiming to gain insight into the work of the connecting leader.

The specter of practice theory has, however, often haunted these attempts, rather than supported them. While most practice theorists are concerned with connecting the activities of people to the organization of social practices, representing the social context in which they proceed (Schatzki, 2017c) it is not a unified theory, comprising instead a multitude of different approaches and, often conflicting, understandings. The varying positions and perspectives of which it is comprised reflects a "practice turn" (Schatzki et al., 2001) within the wider realm of social sciences. The character of this hotly disputed theoretical field (Gherardi, 2015) can give rise to confusion. When this confusion is coupled with the tendency for practice theories to encourage abstraction, and the folly of marginalizing the people involved in these practices (Schatzki, 2017b)—the practitioners—these theories have been accused as metaphysical, thereby inflicting "collateral damage" (Schmidt, 2018) on the study of practice. Empirical analysis is obscured rather than sharpened.

However, a generative approach to the operationalization and adaptation of different practice theories can also provide a productive tension in analysis (Nicolini, 2009, 2017), provided that the implications of these theories and their relationship to one another are considered carefully. Such a generative approach offers the opportunity to study situated activities, without divorcing them from a wider context, approaching practices as "constituting a point of connection between abstract structures and their mechanisms, and concrete events—between society and people living their lives" (Chouliaraki & Fairclough, 2007, p. 21). This can provide an analytical perspective embracing social practices, how these are organized and interconnected, as well as the significance of the people populating them—a perspective capable of taming the complexity of the study of situated activities without vanquishing it completely. This presents the opportunity to develop an analytical approach capable of studying the connecting leader at work, considering how their activities are coordinated within a wider organizational plenum, focusing upon how they navigate this coordination and the manner in which their horizon of possible identities manifest in particular ways.

APPLYING SCHATZKI: THE SOCIAL WORLD AS A PLENUM OF INTERCONNECTED PRACTICES

Compared to posthumanist positions in practice theory focusing on symmetry between humans and nonhumans (see Feldman & Orlikowski, 2011), Schatzki's social practice theory (2002; 2012) affords primacy to humans, allowing analytical focus to include the practitioners. This "agential humanism" (Schatzki, 2002, p. xv) acknowledges the importance of nonhuman entities but trains focus on the activities of humans in using these, and how they bring them into play within practices, thereby potentially reinvigorating an understanding of human agency. This is no attempt to deny that nonhuman entities can have agency (can do things), but that the meaning of these doings will depend on human understandings of them. "Objects, if you will, make a contribution, but the nature of that contribution depends on us" (Schatzki, 2002, p. 117).

This foregrounds the "doings and sayings" of participants in analysis, allowing for consideration of how these activities are coordinated within practices. While Schatzki is reluctant to be drawn on methodological and empirical issues of studying social practices, his theory offers conceptual handles with which to grasp the inherent complexity of them, focusing on how they are organized, how they interconnect and represent the "site of the social" within which people and things achieve identity and meaning (Schatzki, 2002, p. 38). This affords researchers a license to adapt and apply his theoretical models, but also assigns them with responsibility for ensuring consistency and coherence in the application.

Practices, according to Schatzki, are organized nexuses of actions, ordered in four ways: through (1) practical understandings, (2) rules, (3) a teleoaffective structure and (4) general understandings (Schatzki, 2002, p. 77). In other words, practices unfold and emerge through a shared practical understanding among participants of how the practice should be undertaken, an awareness of any explicit rules that must be followed, a teleoaffective structure normatively guiding its appropriate means and ends, and a set of general understandings providing the practice with its fundamental meaning.

Schatzki maintains that practices should not be perceived independently of the material conditions within which they take place, or the tools of which they make use. He introduces the term "arrangements" to address the material entities to which people react and/or manipulate (Schatzki, 2012, p.16) in the undertaking of any given practice. Arrangements therefore focus on how entities—such as people, artifacts and things, hang together. The meaning[1] of these entities is derived from their role and position within the practice-arrangement bundle (ibid; 38). Social life then, is fundamentally comprised of a nexus of interconnected practice arrangement bundles interconnecting into one all-encompassing plenum of practices. It becomes conceivable to trace how the activities taking place in an observable practice are simultaneously emergent and coordinated: reliant upon the practitioners undertaking them in situ, while responsive to influences and organization from outwith. Understanding social life in this way provides a dynamic theoretical framework for understanding the varying contexts, groupings, activities and interests within which the connecting leader must navigate. By perceiving the organization as an interconnected bundle of practice-arrangements, the scope for empirical investigation of the connecting leader is sharpened: what are the characteristics of the practices within which they participate, how are these coordinated, how does the connecting leader act, and what are the implications of these actions?

This brings the study of practices to the fore, while acknowledging the significance of the people populating them. While an understanding of the person as an intrinsic element of social practices, an organic entity with consciousness and memory; with cognitive capacities within the "continuity of a life" (Schatzki, 2017b, p. 41) is emphasized, persons remain rather shadowy and more must be done to enlighten an appropriate understanding of the person in practice theories (Schatzki, 2017b). How can people's agency—their doings and sayings—within these practices be understood, and how can this agency impact upon the manner in which these practices play out? More emphasis on persons and the manner in which they negotiate and move between these interconnected practice bundles can provide greater analytical scope. The following section will engage Schatzki's practice theory with ideas from critical psychology to enable such considerations to be elaborated and developed, allowing the actions of the connecting leader as a practitioner within and across interconnected organizational practices to be considered.

PRACTITIONERS: PERSONAL TRAJECTORIES THROUGH STRUCTURES OF SOCIAL PRACTICES

How, then, can the person, the practitioner, be understood within particular practices and the overarching plenum of practice-arrangement bundles? How can the connecting leader—in the particular case of this exercise, the middle manager—be perceived and understood amidst the flurry of organizational practices within which they operate? The understanding of the person offered by critical psychology,[2] and particularly Ole Dreier (1999, 2003; 2008, 2009a) and Klaus Holzkamp (2013) is useful here. This builds on the premise that, in order to gain a more detailed insight into the person, one must avoid attempting to look directly at the person, and instead perceive the person as a participant in a world composed of structures of social practices (Dreier, 2009a, p.41). While there are ontological tensions, the presentation of the person offered by Dreier is potentially compatible with a Schatzkian perspective (Schatzki, 2017a). The combination of these approaches offers the opportunity for a bifocal perspective in analysis– capable of capturing the practical circumstances offering coordination of the actions of participants, while simultaneously focusing on these participants as active practitioners, as historical and agential persons capable of effecting change. Such a focus is particularly appropriate in the study of connecting leaders and the manner in which their actions can effect proceedings in the workplace.

Dreier contends that the social world exists because of participants reproducing and changing it: human activity is the dynamic middle which connects subject and social worlds, where both are reproduced and changed in practice (Dreier, 2009b, p. 22). People have the possibility to shape their participation within and across the multitude of practices within which they participate.

> In short, due to various structural arrangements, personal lives must unfold in movement through diverse contexts in the existing structure of social practice. Persons must shape their lives and pursue their concerns, including those for learning, by linking and separating their diverse participation in diverse contexts, and they must vary their modes of participating by taking the various arrangements of local contexts into account. (Dreier, 2008, p. 8)

The capacity to shape "modes of participating," in personal trajectories through structures of social practices delineates an agential space for the person in practice, where they have the possibility to follow different courses of action (Schatzki, 2017a) qua their doings and sayings. The manner in which they strive to shape this participation can have implications for the identities that it becomes legitimate for them to pursue, as well as how the ongoing practice develops and unfolds. The understanding of identity offered here is useful and, to a certain extent, picks up where the Schatzkian framework stops, providing a more detailed understanding of the person compatible with an analytical point of departure in the primacy of practice. While Schatzki describes practices as "spaces of intelligibility," (Schatzki, 2005, p. 469) within which people and things can achieve identity and meaning, the nature and condition of personal identities is not discussed. Practices offer resources for experiencing identity, and are spaces in which identity can manifest—but what about the condition of personal identities capable of traveling across practices, and having a tangible influence on how they play out? How can the connecting leader, traversing a multitude of organizational practices and negotiating the varying interests of the participants within them be appreciated? Here, Dreier offers a concept of identity focused on opening up the understandings of person, and personal actions in social practices. Central to this is his idea of "personal stances."

Dreier suggests the concept of *personal stances* (Dreier, 2008, p. 3) as the manner in which participants understand, shape and orient their activities in practices. These stances enable an integration of conceivable identities, allowing for the possibility of consistent and coherent personal actions and decisions within and across practices, by regulating and mediating personal pursuits (Dreier, 2009b, p. 44). These stances, however, are not to be understood as divorced from practice, or the social, in that they also relate to the concerns of other participants. Dreier explains that this idea of personal stances leans on a definition of identity provided by Charles Taylor:

> "As defined here, stances come close to Taylor's definition of identity, since he stresses the significance of what we stand for." To know who I am is a species of knowing where I stand. My identity is defined by the commitments and identifications which provide the frame or horizon within which I can try to determine from case to case what is good, or valuable, or what ought to be done, or what I endorse, or oppose. In other words, it is a horizon within which I am capable of taking a stand (Taylor, 1985b, p. 27). (Dreier, 2009b, p. 43)

This provides an understanding of personal identity as a horizon of possible understandings of the self, which informs the person's doings and sayings: a repertoire of potential stances emergent within situated practices shaping ongoing participation in the given practice and thereby potentially shaping the practice itself. This is a horizon of possibilities from which an understanding of self can be drawn, and from which actions proceed. Dreier adds the notion of personal stances as the possible positions that can be adopted within this identity horizon, contingent primarily upon the nature of the social practices within which they are situated: "To adopt stances also means to take sides in the conflicts and contradictions of social practices" (Dreier, 1999, p. 14). The relevance of such a situated understanding of managerial identity is particularly salient when considering the practice of connecting leadership and the connecting leader, working toward securing organizational coherence, concomitantly leading and following.

This stance-taking can be regarded as a strategic and conscious choice, but it can also be an instantaneous and unconscious reaction to the complexity of ongoing situated activities, where the organization of the practices within which the person is participating at the given time offer cues which can be taken up in different ways by participants. This embraces the Schatzkian understanding of agency as "doings," which can be more or less deliberate, more or less intentional. The issue of intentionality is not the key interest, instead the doings and sayings, and what they accomplish in situated practices are foregrounded. Understanding the adoption of stances as expressions of identity and the taking of sides within structures of social practices allows investigation of the directions in which managerial work and the work of the connecting leader becomes oriented in practice.

Managerial Stances at Work

The potential to operationalize the idea of *stances* as emerging between the individual cognition of the person and the social, while difficult, is appealing. This provides the opportunity for an appreciation of the duplicity of persons and social practices in the analysis of situated activities, privileging neither individual cognition, nor the coordination of practices. Instead, the manner in which stances emerge in situated practices becomes the object of study, offering an empirical and analytical approach capable of opening up the situated work of middle managers, how they lead and follow, navigating between the interests of subordinates, peers and superiors—between local interests and those of the wider organization. The idea of managerial stances allows investigation of the orientation of participant's activities, while appreciating the character of the situated practices within which they find themselves and how these nest within a wider organizational plenum. In understanding the connecting leader, and the fluctuating orientation of their work, this ongoing and emergent orientation, the taking of sides, presents a useful conceptualization. An operationalization of this approach will now be undertaken, where a close analysis of situated managerial work is unfolded. In order to frame this analysis meaningfully, the ethnography from which the empirical material is drawn is briefly introduced.

THE SETTING AND THE DATA

A detailed ethnographic study (Walker, 2018) investigating the organizational influences of a leadership development program (LDP) provided for managers in the Danish public sector provides the empirical footing for the present chapter. This study spanned 2 years: observations were conducted in the final module of the LDP, exam papers produced by participants within the LDP were collected and analyzed, and interviews were conducted with them, their staff and superiors. Furthermore, a key element of the ethnographic approach involved shadowing (Czarniawska, 2007) selected participants in the workplace at several intervals during and after participation in the LDP. In considering eventual organizational influences of the LDP, findings from the study point toward an increased propensity among participants to engage actively and pragmatically with organizational initiatives and changes introduced by superiors. The LDP was found to be propitious in encouraging *followership* among middle managers to wider organizational goals, but—and perhaps more surprisingly—also to the interests and opinions of peers and subordinates. The claim, therefore, is not that the LDP simply tamed these middle managers, domesticating them as compliant organizational lackeys. Rather, they became more capable and inclined to accepting the changing organizational conditions and environments within which they worked, seeking to understand the underlying rationale and potential utility of such changes, while also becoming more conscious of the importance of the opinions and interests of their own teams and staff. The managers were therefore found to become adept at functioning as "double agents," gaining, as it were a third position from which to perceive their work: neither as organizational robots nor disciples of their profession. Instead, they gained a middle ground, a capacity to perceive situations from these different perspectives, informed by their different rationales, broadening their repertoire of actions and responses that could potentially be deemed appropriate. Applying the continuum of managerial work in relation to organizational reform suggested by Kellog (2014), the managers were found to both actively "broker" and "buffer" between local concerns of subordinates and the wider organizational strategizing introduced by superiors: connecting and/or disconnecting the interests of different stakeholders in specific situations. This proved to be a crucial element of their situated managerial work.

The methodological approach to the collection and analysis of the empirical material used was inspired by Dorothy Smith's Institutional Ethnography (Smith, 2005); a method of inquiry beginning in the actualities of people's lived lives. This posits that in order to gain qualified insight into the complexity of ongoing social life, it is first necessary to identify a particular experiential *standpoint* from which observations can proceed, allowing the *problematics* identified from this standpoint to guide ethnographic inquiry thereafter. This approach encourages the researcher to strive to discover situated orderings, rather than imposing them (Smith, p. 162). In the empirical excerpt chosen here, the standpoint identified is that of Eve,[3] a middle manager of a day-care institution in the municipality of Copenhagen. In order to provide an illustration of the empirical conditions within which the concept of managerial stances was adapted, as well as an example of the application of the suggested theoretical approach in analysis, an investigation of managerial work in situ will now be undertaken.

AN EMPIRICAL AND ANALYTICAL ILLUSTRATION: EVE AS THE CONNECTING LEADER WITHIN AND ACROSS INTERCONNECTED ORGANIZATIONAL PRACTICES

Eve was initially employed as a pedagogue in the day-care institution, comprising approximately 39 members of staff and 150 children between the ages of 0–6, before being promoted to the position of "institutional manager," a position she held for more than 10 years. Due to managerial restructuring within the municipality, Eve's job title had recently changed to that of "educational manager," her institution being grouped together with four similar institutions in a so-called "cluster." An element of this restructuring involved the introduction of a new managerial position—the "cluster manager" assuming overall of control of budgetary and staffing areas of the member institutions of each cluster. Therefore, this change in structure involved a marked encroachment on Eve's autonomy, where she now reported directly to her cluster manager—her immediate superior.

Analysis of exam papers produced by Eve throughout the LDP provided insight into her ongoing reflections about this change in circumstances. These papers detailed her gradual, but increasing acceptance of the involvement of the cluster manager in the institution and growing awareness of the implications of her position within the wider organizational structure of the municipality, rather than solely as manager of the local institution. In the period since the introduction of the cluster reform, the cluster manager had introduced structural and organizational changes to the member institutions. The most prominent of these changes arose in the summer of 2014, with the decision to depart from the traditional arrangement of dividing the children in the preschool department of the institution into three groups of approximately 20 members, where each group was assigned their own room and a group of three pedagogues, responsible for the workings of this room. Instead the building would now be divided into three "zones" with nine pedagogues rearranged into a larger, more flexible, team charged with coordinating all of the 60-plus children in a more fluid manner. This was the central problematic identified by Eve in her approach to everyday work, and over the course of her participation in the LDP.

The stated intention of this restructuring had been to reduce the child-to-adult ratio, allowing the pedagogues to work with the children in smaller groups. This flexibility would also enable and allow the children to find their peers among the wider group, and reduce the unavoidably large developmental gap between 3–6 year olds, inherent within the more traditional "room" structure. Observations revealed that Eve, and her employees perceived the restructuring fundamentally as "yet another cost-cutting exercise" and general opposition to the changes was palpable. The shifting forms of coordination resulting from this restructuring had created discernible difficulties and confusion for all of the actors involved—the managers, the staff, the children and their parents. It was difficult for them to identify a pattern to decode how daily operations were to proceed, and where each child should be, with whom and at what time.

Following Subordinates: Buffering Through a Managerial Stance

The following section focuses empirically on the work of Eve as a connecting leader in the ongoing conflict and unrest in the institution, arising from the team restructuring. During the month of April 2016, the institution had slavishly followed a stringent schedule imposed by the cluster manager, in which the new team structure was to be the rationale driving daily operations. The interactions presented below arise within an emergency meeting called by Eve in response to what she sensed was an increasingly strained atmosphere and working environment, resulting from the staff's difficulties in accepting and adapting to this strict new iteration of the team structure. It is worth noting that, at this point in time, the institution had been working with this "new" team structure for over 2 years, emphasizing the inertia that continued to plague attempts to actualize the changes.

The introduction of the team structure had wide reaching implications for the daily work of the pedagogues. The flexible structure and division of the children and staff into zones meant that the pedagogues expressed frustration at losing "feeling" with the children—they no longer had a specific group of children that they followed all day, every day. They were assigned to consistent "contact groups," but these children were now often spread across the different zones and activities in the institution, with staff complaining that it was difficult to keep up with what they were doing and how they were getting along. Eve called the emergency meeting in response to a perceived escalation in staff complaints and confusion around their daily routines and schedules. She explained that she regarded the emergency meeting as an attempt and opportunity to get to the bottom of things, stating that she had learned that it was a good idea to take these pressing issues as they developed, rather than waiting for the next designated meeting.

Analysis of situated interactions within the meeting will provide insight into how Eve strives to lead her staff in a particular direction to ensure progress in daily operations, but more importantly, how she actively encourages and engages their attempts to influence her approach and understandings, in order to achieve this. The meeting began with the team members voicing their frustrations with the new team structure, comparing it unfavorably to the steadiness of the old room structure. Closer analysis of the interactions taking place within the meeting illustrates how the idea of *managerial stances* is capable of opening up the situated managerial work taking place; specifically the manner in which Eve's followership shifts in orientation. This illustrates how studying the emergence of different managerial stances within the horizon of a broader managerial identity unfolding in situated practice allows focus to fall on the very *doings* of the connecting leader.

We join the interaction during the emergency meeting as Eve attempts to summarize comments from the team members, as to how they would suggest they are to proceed in working with the "new" team structure.

The participants in the meeting are Eve (E) and the team of nine pedagogues, of whom Claire (C), Lizzy (L), and Beth (B) make audible contributions. At times, it is impossible to verify the identity of the speaker in the audio recording; these are therefore marked as Unknown (U). There are also times when many of the participants voice their agreement; this is marked as Many (M).

31. E: If we play with the idea that we have our rooms and we have our groups divided by age—how then,
32. can we do other things across the different rooms?
33. B: The same way that we did last December with those functions. Where there was one person on a trip
34. and there were other activities in the house which were mixed, both with the adults and the children—I
35. actually think that that worked really well.
36. M: [Loudly voice their approval]
37. E: But, but I need to have it like
38. U: We can just call them 'functions'
39. M: [Inaudible comments]
40. E: [Raises her voice] Well that would mean that you meet in your room with your three adults, and do
41. some kind of activity in the morning across the different rooms, where someone takes a mixed group on
42. a trip, someone makes biscuits with a mixed group and the others do something else across the groups.
43. Then you come back and eat your lunch in your room and kind of figure out how the day should proceed
44. from there. On Tuesday, we had the groups divided by age almost all day, right? ... Aaahh, no we didn't
45. but you could maybe play with the idea that you are in your age group, and that it was first in the
46. afternoon that you went into your room, or that you were just in your age-groups, right? And on
47. Thursday, you would just do it as a room because there would be staff reflections and meetings
48. M: Mmmm
49. E: On Friday, you would just like on Monday, meet in your room and the do some activities across the
50. groups.
51. U: YES!
52. **B:** That would make much more sense!
53. E: I hear you!
54. U: That would be worth a million!
55. B: That would make so much more sense
56. **E**: But I hear you all [Exuberantly]

By looking more closely at the ongoing practice, and considering the doings and sayings of the practitioners, Eve's work as the connecting leader can come to the fore. On Line 31, Eve summarizes the comments made so far, and indicates a willingness to engage with them, without committing to them, stating, "if we play with the idea that we have our rooms." Eve acknowledges the team members' overwhelming and unanimous desire to maintain the traditional room structure. She then invites the group to come up with concrete suggestions as to how they envisage accommodating elements of the team restructuring. This point of departure is consistent with the "Heliotropic principle" and appreciative inquiry approaches advocated in the LDP, and drawn on by Eve in her exam papers, where the manager should focus on "dreams rather than frustrations" and possible solutions rather than problems. Here the energy of the group is to be focused on how to make things better, rather than remaining stuck in the criticism of problematic circumstances. Eve invites further explication from her staff, as to how they envisage an optimal solution.

Beth suggests, on Line 33, that a structure capable of accommodating elements of the desired flexibility while remaining faithful to the traditional room structure would be the optimal solution. Her reference to "last December" makes it clear that this is an approach that they have previously adopted. Previous observations conducted confirm this and provide insight into the fact that this involved a deliberate and clandestine deviation from the instructions of the cluster manger. Eve had essentially sanctioned a return to the old room structure, working with the new team system only in limited intervals, disguising this in any administrative trails visible to the cluster manager. Beth's suggestion has overwhelming approval in the team, expressed clearly in Line 36. The team presents a collective vision for their ideal course of action.

In Line 40, Eve audibly raises her voice and takes the position of speaker, processing the staff's comments by reciting how such a daily routine would play out. Emphasis is repeatedly placed on when the children would be within the more familiar room structure, with a steady team of three pedagogues—for example Lines 42+3 "then you come back and eat your lunch in your room." The significance of the room structure becomes increasingly important within the daily structure under negotiation—a shift met with great approval by the group, reflected in Lines 51, 52, 43 and 55. Eve's statements at Line 51, "I hear you," and Line 56 "but I hear you all!" are significant in the meeting. This is expressed in a manner of delight, Eve appears excited by the fact that she is engaging with the staff in this manner, and that she is displaying her capacity to listen to the staff and acknowledge their opinions. This fits with the managerial approach of appreciative inquiry championed in the LDP, where the recognition of employees and their opinions should be central in managerial work, providing an explanation for the jubilant manner in which Eve celebrates the fact that she "hears" her employees. The manner in which Eve formulates a renegotiation of the team structure more akin to the old room system is used to strengthen her claim that she "hears" the staff—by actively drawing on their contributions in order to formulate a local iteration of the team restructuring, erring from the plan put in place by her superior, the cluster manager. Eve is actively inviting the staff to articulate their vision, and drawing on the information provided to form the planned course of action.

ADOPTING STANCES IN SITUATED MANAGERIAL PRACTICE

Eve, in her role as middle manager is making the opinions of her staff heard, and granting legitimacy to their suggestions. A negotiation is under way in relation to the coordination of the team structure imposed by the cluster manager, suggesting that it may be possible to circumvent this, and come closer to the practical wishes of the staff. The managerial stance taken by Eve is oriented toward that which makes sense in the given circumstances, creating a distancing or decoupling between the team structure schedule implemented by the cluster manager, and the actualities of the daily routine in the institution. Here, Eve can be seen to actively take sides in the structures of social practices within which she participates, prioritizing professional principles and opinions rather than organizational directives. She follows the influence of her staff, listening attentively before reformulating and articulating their suggestions, the adoption of a managerial stance which facilitates *buffering*, minimizing the interference of the external restructuring on the actualities of their daily institutional work. From the horizon of possible and conceivable identities available to her, she adopts a particular stance, legitimizing a particular course of action and shaping the manner in which the practice unfolds. Here, Eve engages actively with attempts by her staff to influence her and the unfolding proceedings, what can be perceived as an instance of active followership.

Schatzki's vocabulary opens up for study of the emergent practice of managing taking place and how the activities within it are coordinated, without being determined. There are shared *understandings* between the participants that this managerial practice must accommodate the restructuring implemented by the cluster manager, and an awareness of the authority of the rules that govern their activities. However, the *teleoaffective structure*—the norms guiding the appropriate means and ends of the practice within which they are participating are seen to be open for negotiation. Rather than the managerial practice simply enforcing predetermined rules, the purpose becomes different. Instead, the most important end becomes achieving a working solution for the participants present. It is possible to see middle managing and the work of the connecting leader unfolding as a situated practice, where Eve establishes and maintains a leadership identity by actively following her subordinates.

FOLLOWING SUPERIORS: BROKERING THROUGH A MANAGERIAL STANCE

In the next section of the analysis, attention is dawn to the manner in which the managerial stance adopted by Eve shifts within the ongoing practice. In previously adopting a stance conducive to *buffering*, Eve had listened attentively to the suggestions made by the staff, deliberately displaying and indeed emphasizing her willingness to follow their influence, ultimately sanctioning an alternative working structure, and deviating from the stringent model imposed by the cluster manager. The new team structure is made malleable, to incorporate elements of the previous room structure. While the pedagogues are clearly pleased with this decision, as the meeting progresses, they are unsure whether it is acceptable for them to depart from the collective guidelines introduced by the cluster manager in this way. Eve strives to reassure them, explaining and justifying her approach.

The idea of managerial stances enlightens the shifting orientation of Eve's work as a connecting leader. We rejoin the interactions arising within the meeting as Eve responds to a direct inquiry from one of the pedagogues, as to whether their planned course of action is, in fact "legal." Again, **(E)** denotes turns taken by Eve, while **(U)** denotes turns taken by other participants, where it is not possible to discern which person is speaking (Unknown).

67. **(E)** Well you could say that I am going in and saying 'well, what is the
68. thinking behind this?' **[the new team structure]** About 'how do we get control of the children, how
69. can we, what's it called?...develop them and challenge them in the best way
70. possible across the different things.' And you can say that part of the
71. thinking behind working across teams is that you can't just stare blankly at
72. your own room, and agree upon the fact that 'it's just because that's the
73. way Mohammed is.' But that you are challenged to say 'it may well be that
74. we experience Muhammed does certain things in this context, so therefore
75. we should challenge him in other ways because we have a lot of colleagues
76. we can work together with around him, so it should be possible for other
77. perspectives to be taken. Because, you could say that part of the things
78. which have been difficult about rooms in the old days, was that you were
79. chained together to these children, and there were some children that

simply fell through the gaps, that weren't seen. Here the experiment was
kind of to say that you had to break that up, and that you couldn't only
focus on your own children, like 'your own' children.
U: Yes
(E): But you have to, like, know that many perspectives are taken, so if you
were a piss-poor pedagogue, then there would be a colleague who notices
that you were doing shitty work.
(U): Mmmm, yeah
(E): ...**[pause of 3 seconds]** So that's basically what it's all about.

In this section, Eve begins by addressing a member of staff's concerns about whether the suggestion that they depart from the organizationally prescribed approach specified by the cluster manager is acceptable or not. Informed by Schatzkian understandings, this is a direct reference to, and articulation of, the recognized *rules* by which the ongoing practice is potentially coordinated. The organizational authority of the instructions put in place by the cluster manager, and the scope of the managerial practices in light of these are brought into play. In response to this, Eve offers an articulation of the teleoaffective structure guiding the ongoing managerial practice, fastening the appropriate means and ends informing it. The authority of the organizational rules is recognized, but the stance adopted by Eve makes them—to a certain extent—open to interpretation.

Indeed, she strives to make this approach explicit, taking responsibility for the deviation from the official design of the organizational restructuring. At Line 67, she emphasizes that "I am going in and saying, 'what is the thinking behind this?'" Eve continues, in Lines 70 to 82 to articulate her interpretation of the intentions of the new team structure, literally providing a translation of the organizational directives for the pedagogues. She engages actively with the municipal agenda and the underlying principles and motivation guiding it, but does not insist on slavishly implementing the initiative regardless of the practical implications. Eve explains how, and that, their revised approach will still follow the fundamental goals of the restructuring, but in a way that is appropriate for their local setting and working conditions.

At this point, Eve can be seen to actively *broker* (Kellogg, 2014) between the organizational agenda and the local actualities, providing an explanation for the changes, and why they were deemed to be necessary. This brings forward the possible drawbacks of the old room structure, and the potential benefits of the new team structure. Eve seeks to provide a bigger organizational picture and emphasizes what it is that the initiative is trying to achieve, once again taking sides in the structures of social practices within which she participates: in this instance prioritizing organizational directives before professional principles and opinions. Here, she adopts and displays a critical distance to elements of her previous profession, suggesting that resistance to change can also legitimately be seen as problematic. The room structure favored by the pedagogues is described as being too static, where the revised team structure offers dynamism; the children are to be followed by a wider community of pedagogues, giving them optimal opportunities to grow and develop, while also ensuring an ongoing collective supervision of the pedagogical practices taking place in the institution. At the same time, Eve's use of language in Lines 85 and 86 is particularly striking, and may be perceived as a deliberate attempt to underline her position "in the trenches," as it were, removing herself from possible recriminations of adopting municipal newspeak, or being perceived as the cluster manager's puppet.

Eve can be seen to actively adopt a managerial stance within the practice, shaping the manner in which it proceeds. In detailing the underlying principles of the team restructuring, Eve indicates an acceptance of these, and a willingness to engage with them: to follow the influence of her superior—the cluster manager. Eve adopts a stance conducive to *brokering*, following the influence of her superiors in order to define and explain the overall intentions behind the team restructuring. This stance enables her to adopt a different perspective and approach, brokering between the conflicting interests of her superiors and her staff, in order to achieve a practical solution. This works toward ensuring that daily operations can continue in a manner that is locally acceptable, and at the same time broadly in accordance with the wider organizational edict put in place by the cluster manager.

Eve articulates the very nature and purpose of her work, thus claiming a particular space by adopting an explicit position, acknowledging and responding to the external coordination of their activities. She is seen to ultimately influence and lead her subordinates by delineating the space available to her and articulating the reasons for her decision and the activities taking place. Eve maintains a leadership identity, by explicitly following: following the explicit influence of *both* her immediate superiors and subordinates. Engaging actively with these influences and navigating them, enables her to lead her staff in a new direction. This clarifies the way in which operations are to proceed, making a new direction locally acceptable and actionable, without denying the intentions and value of the restructuring efforts themselves. By illuminating the different dimensions or "sides" in these structures of practices and recognizing the legitimacy of both her immediate superiors and subordinates, she communicates and mediates between them, opening up an avenue in which their work can proceed in a practically appropriate manner.

IMPLICATIONS

Theorizing managing as a situated and emergent practice sharpens focus on the actions of a middle manager as a connecting leader at work, and the manner in which her shifting orientations, conceptualized as the adoption of different managerial stances, can give rise to new potentialities influencing the manner in which the ongoing leadership process and change initiative plays out. The empirical analysis illustrates that, by being equipped and prepared to engage actively with attempts to influence her—to follow—she can establish and maintain legitimate grounds for her to lead, recognizable to the other practitioners. By engaging with others in this way, and drawing on a repertoire of potential managerial stances, she is able to perform as a connecting leader, by being an active and engaged follower.

By beginning in practice, the middle manager is perceived as a practitioner shaping, and shaped, by the practices in which they participate. From this perspective, identity is to be considered in a particular way, where the meeting between practices and practitioners offers a horizon of possible understandings of the self, providing an evolving repertoire of potential managerial stances. This offers a practical approach capable of responding to calls (Coupland & Brown, 2012) to position the exploration of identities within the study of organizing. The situated and ongoing identity work of the connecting leader can be perceived in the midst of their work, at the intersection of interconnected organizational practices. In this case the "buffering" and "brokering" (Kellogg, 2014) being undertaken between these practices and the practitioners populating them is perceived as the expression of managerial stances; the manager taking sides in the social practices within which they participate. The study of identity and identity work is situated within organizational processes, rather than through the production of identity narratives isolated from practice. The ethnographic approach informing this chapter, and particularly the insight gained through shadowing managers at work, secured a thorough and rigorous body of empirical material capable of responding to specific appeals for detailed qualitative study of situated identity work (DeRue & Ashford, 2010, p. 641), providing a grounded approach to studying connecting leaders in action.

In the analysis, Eve strives to influence her staff and lead them in a particular direction to ensure that local operations can progress. She is perceived to do this by adopting shifting stances, where, in particular, the orientation of her followership changes. In the first part of the excerpt, she willfully follows her staff, explicitly articulating that she is listening to them and valuing their input. This informs the solution developed in the meeting; a "buffering," through which Eve actively follows her subordinates, facilitating a disconnection between the stringent details of the organizational restructuring program and the local interests and opinions presented by her staff. In the second part, focusing on an empirical excerpt taken at a slightly later point in the same sequence of interaction, the orientation of her followership shifts. Here Eve, adopts a managerial stance which enables "brokering," actively engaging with the reforms and wishes of her superiors and translating these into the local setting, striving to make them meaningful for her staff. The orientation of Eve's followership is altered. The idea of stances provides insight into how the orientation of Eve's managerial work shifts, while maintaining a leadership identity capable of encouraging involvement from her staff. She opens up for their influence, while simultaneously aligning with the organizational reform and influencing staff to do the same. The two stances identified and contrasted in the present analysis are not intended to represent definitive or binary positions available for middle managers in situated practice. Rather the idea of managerial stances can encourage open investigation of situated managerial work, a sensitizing concept capable of appreciating the multiplicity of positions that may be identifiable in empirical analysis.

The analysis contributes to understandings of "nonstatic" leader and follower identities emerging through a social construction process (DeRue & Ashford, 2010, p. 628) in two ways. Firstly, the idea of managerial stances allows analytical focus to remain on Eve, the middle manager, working as a connecting leader by investigating how different identities as leader and follower manifest in situated practice. Consideration of her organizational role and privileged status in the proceedings can be preserved, while the manner in which she establishes and maintains a leadership identity in practice through dynamic followership is highlighted. Secondly, the operationalization of practice theory establishes a sensitive approach to the understanding of the manner in which identities are "embedded in specific contexts" (DeRue & Ashford, p. 629). An understanding of practices as "the site of the social" (Schatzki, 2002) provides analytical handles for understanding how activities are coordinated in practices, but also how activities have the potential to change these practices. Rather than solely accepting that social interaction is embedded in specific contexts, it is also possible to study how social interactions can shape and influence these specific contexts.

Approaching the study of managerial work in this way allows for appreciation of how it is coordinated within a wider organizational plenum, while bringing the doings and saying of the connecting leader to the fore, by considering them within the unfolding practice. The work of the connecting leader becomes observable in situ. Attention is drawn to the work of the connecting leader in engaging actively, but critically with attempts by others to influence and lead them—neither ignoring, nor blindly accepting such attempts: a "constructive dissent" rather than "destructive consent" (Grint, 2005). This is seen to be an engaging, but critical, followership of superiors and subordinates alike, underlining the insights that can be gained from such a practical understanding of situated managerial identities. The understanding of middle managers as connecting leaders is sharpened, underlining the importance of the capacity to follow, as well as lead, in their work (Carsten, 2017; Jaser, 2017). This compliments existing literature focusing on the intricate relationship between leading and following (Carsten, 2017; Carsten et al., 2010; DeRue & Ashford, 2010; Jaser, 2017; Uhl-Bien & Pillai, 2007; Uhl-Bien et al., 2014) in leadership and management studies, offering the concept of managerial stance as an analytical tool to trace shifting orientations in managerial work. In the present analysis, Eve is seen to actively adopt leader and follower identities, responding to the situation—shaping and being shaped by the managerial practices within which she is participating. This allows an appreciation of the work of middle managers in connecting interests of a multitude of organizational stakeholders, by concomitantly leading and following in their situated managerial practices.

Overall, the approach developed in this chapter takes the application of practice theory in a different direction to that of the "bandwagon" of practice-based studies in leadership and management studies described by Corradi et al(2010). An empirically grounded application of practice theory is developed, addressing the kinds of abstractions (Schmidt, 2018) which have often plagued such attempts. The integration of Schatzki's social practice theory and critical psychology, allows the organizational conditions guiding managerial work to be appreciated, while maintaining a space in which the manager as a practitioner is capable of shaping their actions and modes of participation within these organized practices. The introduction of the concept of managerial stances, draws analytical attention specifically to the space between the coordinated activities of managerial practices and the actions of practitioners.

In doing so, the process through which a middle manager can act as a connecting leader, the "threaded needle" (Lipman-Blumen, 2000, p. 23) bringing differing interests of organizational subordinates and superiors together, can be studied in situ. Eve's work as a connecting leader emphasizes her capacity to navigate differences in the expectations and priorities of other participants, drawing attention to the importance of her selective and controlled *dis*connections. This demonstrates the potential of the empirical and analytical approach developed to facilitate rigorous investigation and analysis of the doings and sayings within the workplace, where detailed examination of situated identities at work can potentially provide the opportunity for new directions in the study and understanding of connecting leaders.

NOTES

1. Critical psychology is inspired by critical theory, emphasizing power relations and the implications of this in the understanding of subjectivity (Dreier,1979; Holzkamp et al, 2013). A core element in the general critical psychological conception of human functioning concerns the subject's development of a personal action potency vis a vis his or her immediate situation in the social structure (Dreier, 2003).
2. Eve is one of the three middle managers—or standpoints—followed over the course of the original ethnography.

REFERENCES

Blackler, F., & Regan, S. (2009). Intentionality, agency, change: Practice theory and management. *Management Learning, 40*(2), 161–176. https://doi.org/10.1177/1350507608101227

Brown, A. D. (2018). Identities in organization studies. *Organization Studies, 40*(1), 7–22. https://doi.org/10.1177/0170840618765014

Buch, A., Andersen, V., & Klemsdal, L. (2015). Turn to practice within working life studies. *Nordic Journal of Working Life Studies, 5*(3a), 1. https://doi.org/10.19154/njwls.v5i3a.4830

Carroll, B., Levy, L., & Richmond, D. (2008). Leadership as practice: Challenging the competency paradigm. *Leadership, 4*(4), 363–379.

Carsten, M. K. (2017). Followership development: A behavioral approach. In M. G. Clark & C. W. Gruber (Eds.), *Leader development deconstructed* (pp. 143–161). https://doi.org/10.1007/978-3-319-64740-1_7

Carsten, M. K., Uhl-Bien, M., West, B. J., Patera, J. L., & McGregor, R. (2010). Exploring social constructions of followership: A qualitative study. *The Leadership Quarterly, 21*(3), 543–562. https://doi.org/10.1016/j.leaqua.2010.03.015

Chouliaraki, L., & Fairclough, N. (2007). *Discourse in late modernity: Rethinking critical discourse analysis*. Edinburgh University Press.

Corradi, G., Gherardi, S., & Verzelloni, L. (2010). Through the practice lens: Where is the bandwagon of practice-based studies heading? *Management Learning, 41*(3), 265–283. https://doi.org/10.1177/1350507609356938

Coupland, C., & Brown, A. D. (2012). Identities in action: Processes and outcomes. *Scandinavian Journal of Management Scandinavian Journal of Management, 28*(1), 1–4.

Czarniawska, B. (2007). *Shadowing, and other techniques for doing fieldwork in modern societies*. Copenhagen Business School Press.

DeRue, D. S., & Ashford, S. (2010). Who will lead and who will follow? A social process of leadership identity construction in organizations. *The Academy of Management Review*, *35*(4), 627–647.

Dreier, O. (1979). *Den kritiske Psykologi: Artikler* [Critical psychology: Articles]. Rhodos.

Dreier, O. (1999). Personal trajectories of participation across contexts of social practice. *Outlines?: Critical Practice Studies*, *1*(1), 5–32.

Dreier, O. (2003). Learning in personal trajectories of participation. In N. Stephenson (Ed.), *Theoretical psychology: critical contributions* (pp. 20–29). Captus University Publications.

Dreier, O. (2008). Learning in structures of social practice. In S. Brinkmann & C. Elmholdt (Eds.), *A qualitative stance essays in honor of Steinar Kvale* (pp. 85–96). Aarhus Universitetsforlag.

Dreier, O. (2009a). Persons in structures of social practice. *Theory & Psychology*, *19*(2), 193–212.

Dreier, O. (2009b). *Psychotherapy in everyday life*. Cambridge University Press.

Fairhurst, G. T., & Uhl-Bien, M. (2012). Organizational discourse analysis (ODA): Examining leadership as a relational process. *The Leadership Quarterly*, *23*(6), 1043–1062. https://doi.org/10.1016/j.leaqua.2012.10.005

Floyd, S. W., & Wooldridge, B. (1997). Middle management's strategic influence and organizational performance. *Journal of Management Studies*, *34*(3), 465–485. https://doi.org/10.1111/1467-6486.00059

Gherardi, S. (2016). To start practice theorizing anew: The contribution of the concepts of *agencement* and formativeness. *Organization*, *23*(5), 680–698. https://doi.org/10.1177/1350508415605174

Grint, K. (2005). *Leadership*. Palgrave Macmillan.

Harding, N., Lee, H., & Ford, J. (2014). Who is 'the middle manager'? *Human Relations*, *67*(10), 1213–1237. https://doi.org/10.1177/0018726713516654

Hogg, M. A. (2005). Social identity and leadership. In R. M. Kramer & D. M. Messick (Eds.), *The psychology of leadership: new perspectives and research*. Erlbaum.

Holzkamp, K., Schraube, E., Osterkamp, U., Abbott, A., & Sloan, T. (2013). *Psychology from the standpoint of the subject: Selected writings of Klaus Holzkamp*. Palgrave Macmillan.

Ibarra, H. (1999). Provisional selves: Experimenting with image and identity in professional adaptation. *Administrative Science Quarterly*, *44*(4), 764–791. https://doi.org/10.2307/2667055

Jaser, Z. (2017). Pulled in two directions: Being in concert a leader to some and a follower to others. *Academy of Management Proceedings*, *2017*(1). Retrieved from https://www.worldcat.org/title/pulled-in-two-directions-being-in-concert-a-leader-to-some-and-a-follower-to-others/oclc/7174686814&referer=brief_results

Kellogg, K. C. (2014). Brokerage professions and implementing reform in an age of experts. *American Sociological Review*, *79*(5), 912–941. https://doi.org/10.1177/0003122414544734

Lipman-Blumen, J. (2000). *Connective leadership: Managing in a changing world*. Oxford University Press.

Lord, R. G., & Hall, R. J. (2005). Identity, deep structure and the development of leadership skill. *The Leadership Quarterly The Leadership Quarterly, 16*(4), 591–615.

Nicolini, D. (2009). Zooming in and out: Studying Practices by switching theoretical lenses and trailing connections. *Organization Studies, 30*(12), 1391–1418. https://doi.org/10.1177/0170840609349875

Nicolini, D. (2012). *Practice theory, work, and organization an introduction*. Oxford University Press

Nicolini, D. (2017). Is small the only beautiful? Making sense of 'large phenomena' from a practice -based perspective. In A. Hui, T. Schatzki, & E. Shove (Eds.), *The nexus of practices: connections, constellations and practitioners* (1st ed.). Routledge, Taylor & Francis Group.

Pinchot, I. G. (1985). *Intrapreneuring. Why you don't have to leave the corporation to become an entrepreneur*. Harper & Row.

Raelin, J. A. (2016). *Leadership-as-practice: Theory and application*. Routledge.

Rouleau, L. (2005). Micro-practices of strategic sensemaking and sensegiving: How middle managers interpret and sell change every day. *Journal of Management Studies, 42*(7), 1413–1441. https://doi.org/10.1111/j.1467-6486.2005.00549.x

Rouleau, L., & Balogun, J. (2011). Middle managers, strategic sensemaking, and discursive competence: Middle managers and strategic sensemaking. *Journal of Management Studies, 48*(5), 953–983. https://doi.org/10.1111/j.1467-6486.2010.00941.x

Schatzki, T. (2002). *The site of the social a philosophical account of the constitution of social life and change*. Pennsylvania State University Press

Schatzki, T. (2005). Peripheral vision: The sites of organizations. *Organization Studies, 26*(3), 465–484. https://doi.org/10.1177/0170840605050876

Schatzki, T. (2012). *A primer on practices: Theory and research*. In J. Higgs, R. Barnett, S. Billett, M. Hutchings, T. Franziska (Eds.), *Practice-based education: Perspectives and strategies*. Sense.

Schatzki, T. (2017a). Practices and learning. In P. Grootenboer, C. Edwards-Groves, & S. Choy (Eds.), *Practice theory perspectives on pedagogy and education* (pp. 23–44). Springer Singapore.

Schatzki, T. (2017b). Practices and people. *Teoria e Prática Em Administração*, 7(1), 26–53. https://doi.org/10.21714/2238-104X2017v7i1-32735

Schatzki, T. (2017c). Sayings, texts and discursive formations. In A. Hui, E. Shove, & T. Schatzki (Eds.), *The nexus of practices: connections, constellations and practitioners* (1st ed.; pp. 126–140). Routledge.

Schatzki, T., Knorr-Cetina, K., & Savigny, E. von (Eds.). (2001). *The practice turn in contemporary theory*. Routledge.

Schmidt, K. (2018). Practice theory: A critique. In V. Wulf (Ed.), *Socio-informatics: A practice-based perspective on the design and use of IT artifacts* (1st ed.). Oxford University Press.

Smith, D. E. (2005). *Institutional ethnography: A sociology for people*. AltaMira Press.

Sveningsson, S., & Alvesson, M. (2003). Managing managerial identities: Organizational fragmentation, discourse and identity struggle. *Human Relations, 56*(10), 1163–1193. https://doi.org/10.1177/00187267035610001

Uhl-Bien, M., & Pillai, R. (2007). The romance of leadership and the social construction of followership. In J. R. Meindl & B. Shamir (Eds.), *Follower-centered perspectives on leadership: A tribute to the memory of James R. Meindl* (pp. 187–210). Information Age.

Uhl-Bien, M., Riggio, R. E., Lowe, K. B., & Carsten, M. K. (2014). Followership theory: A review and research agenda. *The Leadership Quarterly, 25*(1), 83–104.

Walker, R. (2018). *Leadership development as organisational rehabilitation: Shaping middle managers as double agents* (Doctoral dissertation). Copenhagen Business School, Frederiksberg, Denmark.

Wright, C., Nyberg, D., & Grant, D. (2012). "Hippies on the third floor": Climate change, narrative identity and the micro-politics of corporate environmentalism. *Organization Studies, 33*(11), 1451–1475. https://doi.org/10.1177/0170840612463316

PART 4

LEADER AND FOLLOWER AS ONE

CHAPTER 8

LEADERSHIP AND FOLLOWERSHIP AS ONE

Connecting Leaders in the Military

Melanie A. Robinson
HEC Montréal

Nicole Bérubé
Royal Military College of Canada

Ann Langley
HEC Montréal

ABSTRACT

Many people occupy roles of leader and follower in their jobs and are expected to juggle these effectively. This dynamic is particularly salient in the military, where people often switch between leader and follower roles depending on the situation. In this study, we sought to better understand how members of the military interpret and engage in these 2 roles. We interviewed 10 individuals who were either employed at or attending the

The Connecting Leader: Serving Concurrently as a Leader and a Follower
pp. 221–243

Royal Military College of Canada and who held positions encompassing both leadership and followership. Two key themes emerged. First, unexpectedly, we found that members not only recognized the importance of the 2 roles, but also described them in ways that seemed to fuse them together: in other words, leadership and followership were seen as 1. We also found that far from attempting to maintain distance and authority with respect to subordinates and trainees as might have been expected, respondents emphasized mentoring and modeling mechanisms implying closeness and proximity, thus bridging the distance between leaders and followers. Our findings reveal the distinctive form that "connecting leadership" may take in the military. We conclude with a discussion of the transferability of these findings to other settings.

INTRODUCTION

Yes sir, ma'am! A common perception of the military context is the image of the strong, directive leader and obedient followers—a context where leaders are trained to give orders that followers are expected to execute. At first glance, leadership and followership in the military therefore seem to be very different phenomena. And yet, in this hierarchically organized context, leaders in one situation are likely to have to shift gears and become followers in the next. As Latour and Rast (2004) note, members of the military engage in both roles during their careers. Indeed, the more general literature suggests that people must alternately demonstrate leadership and followership in their jobs (e.g., Carsten, 2017; Jaser, 2017; Kelley, 1992) and are expected to juggle the two roles effectively. Jaser (2017) refers to such individuals as *connecting leaders*, who engage in both leadership and followership roles, linking people from various levels together. But how do such leaders manage the switch between roles effectively? More specifically, in this chapter, we ask: how do leaders in hierarchical settings such as the military interpret and engage in leadership and followership roles, given the need for both in the course of their work?

To address this question, we conducted an exploratory qualitative study in which we interviewed 10 leaders at the Royal Military College of Canada (RMC), to understand how they interpret and engage in leadership and followership roles. Given the central focus on leadership training at RMC, we also sought to explore how these leaders help others develop the skills required for these two roles, which are essential for their military careers. We found, surprisingly, that these military leaders tended to view leader and follower roles as fused together: in other words, almost as one. We also found that far from attempting to maintain distance and authority with respect to junior members as might have been expected, the leaders in our study emphasized approaches to mentoring and modeling, implying closeness and proximity, bridging the distance between leaders and followers. Thus, our study reveals the distinctive form that connecting leadership (Jaser, 2017) may take in the military context.

In the following sections, we first review the literature on leadership and followership, in particular in relation to hierarchical or military settings, before presenting the methodology and findings of the study.

LITERATURE REVIEW

Connecting Leadership: Combining Leadership and Followership Roles

Leadership and followership have been conceptualized as distinct, such that leaders make decisions and followers execute objectives set by leaders. However, several authors argue leadership and followership can be intertwined (e.g., Bjugstad et al., 2006; Carsten, 2017) and collaborative (e.g., Chaleff, 2003; Rost, 2008). Notably, some scholars have discussed how "followers actively have an influence over leaders" (Oc & Bashshur, 2013, p. 919), thus blurring the boundaries between the two roles (e.g., Kelley, 2008).

Given the prevalence with which leadership and followership intersect in the workplace, understanding how individuals experience their leadership and followership roles, as well as foster the skills required to manage them successfully, is highly important. However, while these two roles are often intertwined with individuals acting as "connecting leaders" in the workplace (Jaser, 2017), considerably more focus had tended to be placed on leadership development in organizations (Carsten, 2017).

One theoretical framework that may assist in better understanding the interplay between leadership and followership when these roles are played by the same individuals is De Rue and Ashford's (2010) theory of the social construction of leader and follower identities. De Rue and Ashford argued that mutual influence within leader-follower relationships shapes one's identities with respect to each of these roles. These are developed through interactions by which members *claim* and *grant* leader and follower identities for themselves and others. These claiming and granting interactions (which can differ with respect to the extent that they are both "verbal/nonverbal and direct/indirect" (p. 632), as well as the recognition or reinforcement of one's identities related to each role, occur at multiple levels. This implies that the ability to play both leadership and followership roles successfully depends on mutual understanding among interacting individuals of when each of these roles is in play, and of which kinds of conditions and behaviors are associated with the claiming and granting of leadership and followership. Specifically, De Rue and Ashford (2010) note that shared schemas conceptualizing leadership as more hierarchical may facilitate the *internalization* of relevant identities (pp. 633–634)—an example that is particularly relevant to the context of the present study, which we now explore more deeply in relation to the notion of connecting leaders.

The Emphasis on Leadership and Followership in the Military

The evidence suggests that the military context is clearly traversed by "connecting leadership" (Jaser, 2017) roles, even though this is rarely recognized in training programs. For example, while Neal and colleagues (2015) identified several military organizations from different countries that "have identified and embraced the concept of followership" (p. 8), other authors have noted that followership is the focus of fewer professional development programs in military settings (Latour & Rast, 2004). Illustrating the latter point, we performed an exploratory search on the National Defense and the Canadian Armed Forces website (Government of Canada, *Canadian Army*, 2019) using the keywords "leadership" and "followership." Interestingly, the search using the term "leadership" revealed a total of 5,418 results, whereas only 3 results emerged when the search was performed with the term "followership." The disparity in the number of results generated with respect to each term is striking.

This emphasis on leadership seems at first sight congruent with the organizational structure of the military, which remains characterized by tall hierarchies with one long chain of command, an emphasis on formal authority, and rules of engagement (Wong et al., 2003). However, some strands of the literature have also begun to suggest that the unique nature of the military might, in effect, subsume followership as an integral part of leadership, thus bringing the two roles closer together rather than separating them. For example, in a study of peer nominations for roles of leadership and followership among naval cadets, Hollander and Webb (1955) found evidence that those nominated by their peers as good leaders also tended to be considered as good followers, suggesting some similarities in perceptions associated with the two roles. In a recent longitudinal study, Peters and Haslam (2018) compared self-nomination for leadership and followership among a sample of marine recruits with attributions of leadership and followership, as rated by both their commanders and by their peers. They found that while commanders' attributions were largely congruent with self-reports, peers tended to perceive those who had identified themselves primarily as followers, as leaders.

These findings suggest that there may be greater overlap between the characteristics of effective followers and leaders than usually thought. This observation seems partly congruent with Kalimuddin's (2017, p. 2) description of the "effective follower" in the military as a person who can "rise to the challenge of exercising disciplined initiative," rather than as "a sheep."

Thus, despite the hierarchical context and emphasis on leadership over followership discourse in training programs, the literature reviewed above suggests that the conceptualization of these roles as clearly distinct may not be an accurate reflection of how they play out in practice, and, in particular, in the military context (e.g., Hollander & Webb, 1955; Peters & Haslam, 2018). In the present study, we aim to further explore this puzzle by investigating how a sample of military leaders both experience and interpret the leadership and followership roles in which they engage in their work.

METHODS

Research Context and Design

The military, with its hierarchical structure, use of an "internal promotion system" (Wong et al., 2003, p. 673), and emphasis on training and development, combined with the opportunity for members engage in both leadership and followership within their careers (Latour & Rast, 2004), provides an ideal setting through which to explore how members juggle leadership and followership roles (i.e., act as connecting leaders; Jaser, 2017) and develop the skills to achieve this in others.

To investigate our research question, we interviewed leaders at the Royal Military College of Canada, a full-degree granting university within the Department of National Defense that has been educating and training residential students (officer cadets) for careers as commissioned officers in the Canadian Armed Forces since 1876. The undergraduate degree at RMC is composed of four pillars: the academic degree, second language proficiency, physical fitness, and military training. The latter includes opportunities for officer cadets to learn and experience leadership and followership, under the direction of the Training Wing, which is comprised of officers and senior noncommissioned officers serving in the Canadian Armed Forces. The structure of the cadet chain of command (Cadet Wing) reflects that of the Training Wing. In this manner, officer cadets learn and experience leadership and followership through the guidance and the example of both members of the Training Wing and their peers as they advance through the program.

Sample

Data were collected via semistructured interviews with 10 participants (eight men, two women) who were either employed at or attending RMC, and who held positions that encompassed both leadership and followership roles. Seven interviewees held formal staff/training roles at various hierarchical levels at the institution. These participants were part of the military training unit within the college and were not faculty members, who are part of a parallel, but separate unit. They included four officers and three noncommissioned officers, with a broad range of backgrounds, averaging 25 years of military experience (SD = 6.43). All three branches—Army, Navy, and Air Force—were represented. The three other interviewees were senior officer cadets attending RMC who held an assigned leadership role within the cadet chain of command at the time of the interview. To preserve the anonymity of respondents, each interviewee was given a code (Participant A-J, see Table 8.1) to which we refer throughout this chapter.

Participation was completely voluntary. All interviews were conducted in person by one of the authors, a faculty member at RMC. However, except for one participant who helped facilitate access to the sample, the interviewer only formally met the interviewees at the time of the interview. Respondents were contacted by email when they agreed to participate and were subsequently sent the interview protocol to review prior to the meeting. At this meeting, the protocol was again reviewed and signed

Table 8.1. Sample Characteristics

Participant Code	*Role*	*Language of Interview*	*Years of Military Service*
Participant A	Training Wing	English	22
Participant B	Training Wing	English	12
Participant C	Training Wing	English	26
Participant D	Training Wing	English	27
Participant E	Training Wing	French	31
Participant F	Training Wing	English	27
Participant G	Training Wing	English	30
Participant H	Officer Cadet	English	3.5
Participant I	Officer Cadet	French	5.5
Participant J	Officer Cadet	French	4.5

Note: Quotes drawn from the three participants for whom interviews were conducted in French were translated for this chapter by a member of the research team.

consent was obtained from all respondents prior to the commencement of the interview. As we were interested in learning about participants' perceptions related to their leadership and followership roles, we did not define either construct during the interviews. The interviews lasted from 75 to 90 minutes and were conducted in either English or French, according to the preference of the interviewee. Each was also recorded and later transcribed.

Ethics approval was obtained from the institutions of each of the researchers prior to data collection. Approval to conduct the study was also obtained from top management at RMC. During this process, we provided the senior staff member at the institution with an overview of the study and a copy of the interview questions (see Appendix A). This senior staff member further supported the study by helping us to solicit potential respondents across hierarchical levels within the facility and, additionally, by participating as an interviewee. As such, we used a purposeful sampling strategy to recruit participants for the project (Patton, 2003).

Data Analysis

The 10 interviews were transcribed, resulting in a total of approximately 170 pages of textual data. To conduct our analysis, we proceeded in a series of steps, described below.

We began by reading through eight of the interviews and preparing detailed contact summaries (3–5 pages in length) of the information presented in each (Miles et al., 2014). At the same time, an initial database was created using Excel, in which we assigned preliminary codes related to all elements discussed by participants in relation to our research question. This first step allowed us to hone our understanding of the data and examine initial commonalities across the interviews. The most striking observations across the interviews were (a) the degree to which most respondents referred to leadership and followership as similar (as reflected in specific in vivo codes within our spreadsheet as "similarities in leadership and followership roles" and "followers can demonstrate leadership"), (b) described oscillating between leadership and followership (as captured by the code "moving between roles"), (c) noted the importance of supporting one's leader (as represented by such codes as "supporting the leader" and "providing advice"), and (d) the importance leaders seemed to accord to closeness or proximity with followers when discussing both training and leadership more generally (as reflected in such initial codes such as "leading by example," "modeling," "engaging with students," "mentoring," and "providing advice").

Inspired by these initial insights in light of the existing theory on connecting leadership and leadership identity construction (Jaser, 2017; De Rue & Ashford, 2010), one of the authors next conducted a more detailed coding process for all 10 interviews, honing in on these ideas and the commonalities that we saw across the interviews. At this stage, we developed 188 in vivo codes that were very close to the data,[1] grouping them with respect to leadership, followership, and training roles/contextual elements, and focusing on specific activities mentioned (e.g., setting an example, mentoring, building trust, etc.) and skills (e.g., respect, communication, accountability, discipline, etc.) identified by respondents. An analysis of the list of codes allowed us to identify 18 first order codes that captured the essence of respondents' interpretations of leadership and followership. Drawing on the methodology suggested by Gioia et al. (2013), we then examined the codes to determine which could be grouped together to a higher conceptual levels of abstraction, thus creating the data structure presented in Figure 8.1, composed of five second-order themes and two aggregate dimensions: "leadership and followership as one" and "bridging the distance." The numbers presented in brackets next to the first-order codes in this diagram represent the number of interviews in which this code appeared. The aggregate dimensions and second order themes that compose them are discussed in detail in the findings section that follows.

FINDINGS

Overall, as mentioned, our findings suggest that participants perceived leadership and followership roles as highly synergistic, a theme that we discuss under the label *leadership and followership as one*. They also revealed an emphasis on behaviors (such as modeling, interaction, and engagement) that reflect a focus on *bridging the distance* between roles, notably (but not only) in the context of training. We discuss each of these overarching themes in the sections that follow.

Leadership and Followership as One

At its crux, the overarching theme *leadership and followership as one* represents the degree to which participants in the study described their leader and follower identities as deeply intertwined. In essence, the recognized importance of both roles allows them to meld them together seamlessly, such that the respondents expect, practice, and value leadership and followership in their jobs. Indeed, as we shall see, they do not

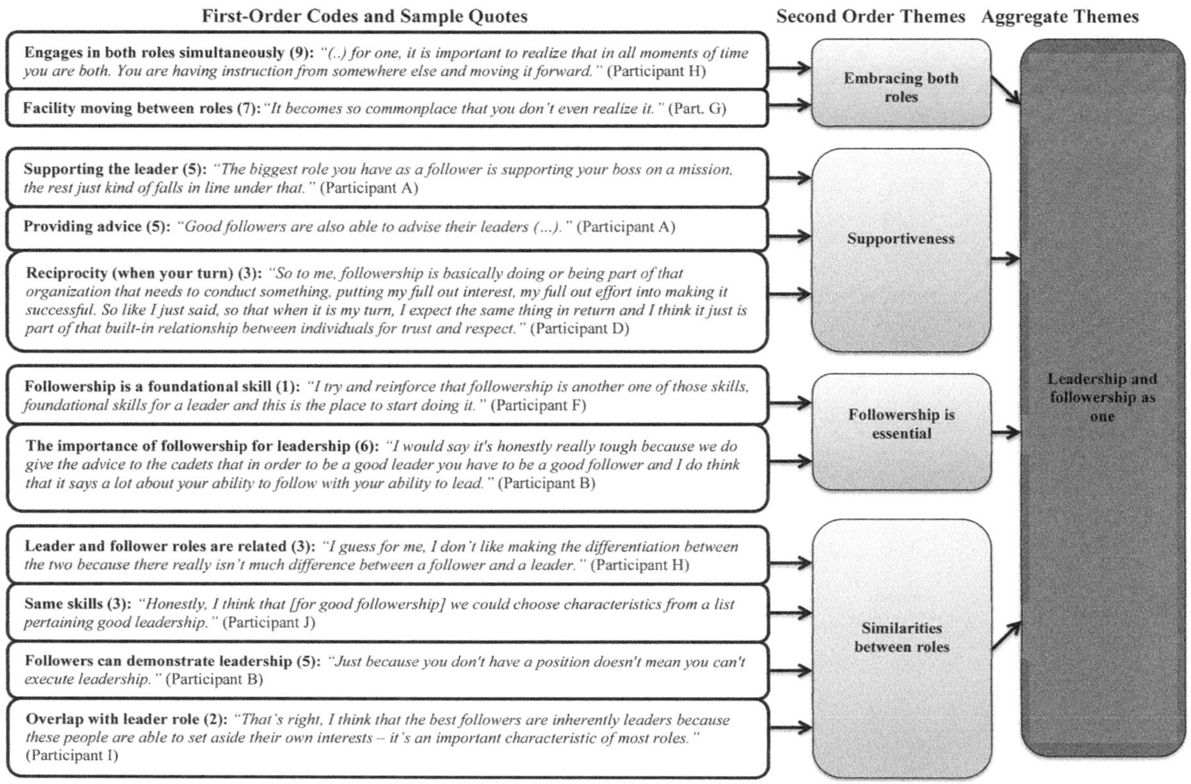

Figure 8.1. Data structure.

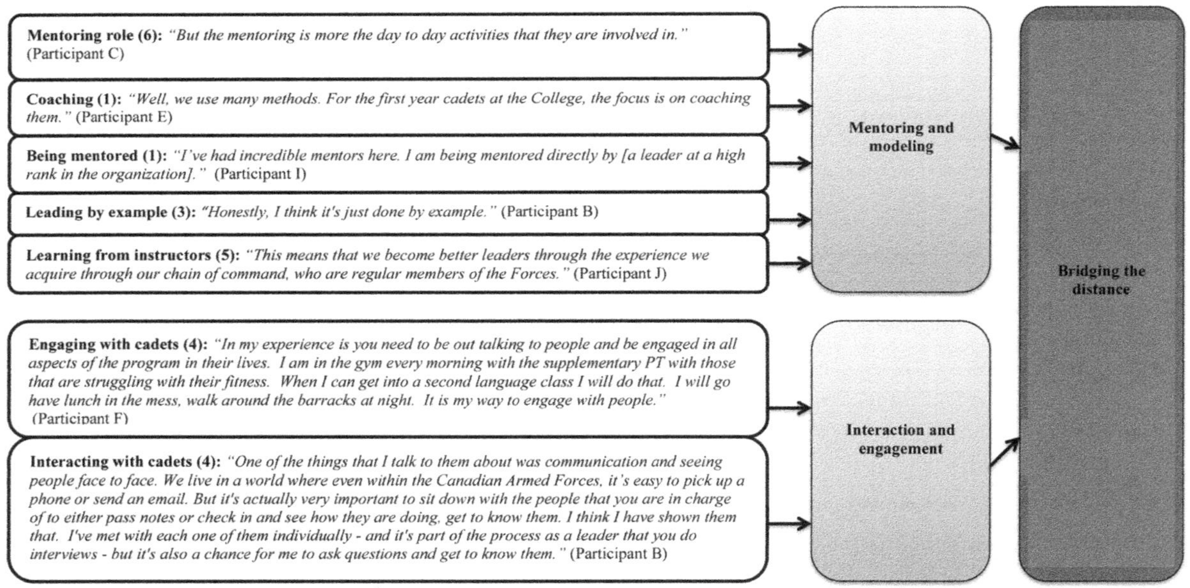

Figure 8.1. (Continued)

appear to be particularly conscious of "switching" or "juggling" roles, but rather see them as a smoothly integrated into what they do and who they are.

Contributing to the emergence of this theme, participants across several interviews described engaging in or embracing both roles, the importance placed on supporting one's leader when in the followership role (sometimes qualified by noting that this supportiveness will then hopefully be reciprocated when one steps into a leader role), the essential nature of followership, and similarities or overlap in the characteristics of the two roles. Together, these elements suggest synergistic roles that meld together within their everyday experience to reflect a perception of *leadership and followership as one* (see Figure 8.1).

Embracing Both Roles Simultaneously. The importance placed by participants upon both leadership and followership roles was clearly articulated across the interviews. Indeed, all 10 interviewees either described how they enacted or embraced both roles and/or the ease with which they moved between them. For example, one participant noted:

> I will reiterate, I think that leadership and followership almost always happen simultaneously. You are never not a follower when you are a leader. (Participant A, Training Wing)

In responding to a question about whether leadership and followership roles are integrated, another respondent rejected the "juggling roles" metaphor ("there is nothing to drop"), describing instead a natural fusion into "who you are as a professional," as well as a proactive followership role orientation (Carsten et al., 2010):

> I feel it is. I also think it makes your life that much simpler. If it is juggling, and I think juggling is probably a really good visual—you are trying to keep various things in the air and not drop them. Whereas if you view it as very much integrated or majority of those qualities of those traits are the same, there is nothing to drop. It is who you are, your profession. This is how I am as a professional. You just tell me what role, responsibilities you need me to do and I will decide when I am a follower and when I am a leader based on my assessment of the situation. (Participant F, Training Wing)

The hierarchical context of the military, which may lead members to develop expectations related to ranks and behaviors, likely facilitates the ease with which respondents switch between leadership and followership roles. This is illustrated by the quote below, in which one interviewee describes not only the importance of the two roles, but also how the chain of command seems to facilitate the movement between them:

> So from my subordinates' perspective, it's clear I'm a leader, but from my superiors' perspective, I'm a follower. So if a division commander tells me to do something by a certain time, I do it. (Participant J, Officer Cadet)

Supportiveness. Although participants described a wide variety of ideal characteristics of leaders and followers, one element that stood out across several interviews was the importance of supporting the decisions of leaders once made. This is illustrated in the following quote:

> Followership, I think, is being respectful to those who are in a superior position. It's about providing them with the right support. (Participant B, Training Wing)

Some participants also discussed supporting one's leader, even if the respondent disagreed. For example, consider the following excerpt from an interview with a member of the Training Wing, in which the participant describes the importance of supporting the superior's directions, though they may not always be in line with the interviewee's recommendations.

> Once I come away from a discussion with them [leadership], their ideas become my ideas and no one will make me change my mind about whether they are the right approach. The attitude I was told to have—not to question the leadership—I support what they tell me to do and then try to do the best I can to fulfill their intentions. (Participant E, Training Wing)

The discussion of supportiveness was also sometimes qualified by referring to the presumed ethical nature of leaders' decisions or justified by arguments of reciprocity: one should become the follower that one would like to have when one becomes the leader, as reflected in the following two statements:

> Quite simply followership to me is being that person who is always supportive of a leader, regardless of whether they are strong or not. As I just explained I see it as a personal investment. It is almost a way of respecting that person's way as a leader. What they are doing, their service to their country. I feel, as a follower, the least I can do is support that person in every way shape or form. The underlying assumption there is they are following our ethos, they are giving lawful orders, and if that assumption is made, is a foundation of who you are supporting as a follower, that is a duty to give them everything you can to support them and their leadership. To make them better, to push them to be better. (Participant F, Training Wing)

> Imagine that we put someone in a fairly high leadership position at the college. If his peers observed him as a follower and saw him break rules, or not show the level of ethical behavior that we expect ... those peers will be likely

> to reproduce his behavior when they are his subordinates. You know, followers mimic the prior behaviors of their leaders. They tell themselves: "Well, when he was a follower, he allowed himself to act in this way, so I can do it now that he is a leader. I will follow his example." (Participant E, Training Wing)

Note how the need for reciprocity expressed in the above quotes again emphasizes the intertwined nature of leadership and followership. When your formal position may have to change from one role to the other from moment to moment, effective followership behaviors become the *sine qua non* condition for effective leadership, as revealed further in the next theme.

Followership Is Essential. Many respondents also noted the importance of followership as an essential element for leadership. The following excerpts illustrate this point:

> There's no doubt, there's no argument that you have to be a good follower to be a good leader. Period. And you're doing both at the same time, almost always. (Participant A, Training Wing)

> No one ever talks about followership. I think again they [leadership and followership] go hand in hand. Especially in the military you are a follower but at some point in your chain you are also a leader. Again, you can't be a good follower without being a good leader. It is only when you understand both properly and the dynamic between them properly that you can move forward. (Participant H, Officer Cadet)

Similarity Between Roles. Finally, participants discussed surprising similarities between their understandings of leadership and followership and the skills required for both. Some interviewees also highlighted that followers can demonstrate leadership, which further speaks to similarities in how the two roles are conceived and enacted.

> It goes right back to what I had mentioned way back, like five hours ago when we first started this conversation of how leadership and followership are equal and they interchange with one another. (Participant D, Training Wing)

> Each follower will be a leader in their area; will be a leader in a particular task; will demonstrate leadership to peers, by ... simply by showing everyone a good example of followership. A good follower demonstrates leadership.... A good leader and a good follower will demonstrate leadership. (Participant E, Training Wing)

> We don't need titles to be leaders. And we don't need titles to be followers, either. (Participant I, Officer Cadet)

Collectively, these themes illustrate the synergies our respondents clearly saw between leadership and followership roles, and their fusing together within their experience and identities.

Bridging the Distance

The popular image of the relationship between leaders and followers in the military is one of distance and authority. The second overarching theme that emerged from our data revealed a pattern of relationships that was quite different, reflecting proximity rather than distance. This is no doubt related in part to the training context in which the study was conducted. However, overall, it was striking to see participants highlighting the importance of mentoring and modeling, as well as a focus on interacting and engaging with followers (often, but not always the cadets) directly. These actions, centering on proximity and closeness, reflect mechanisms that aim to *bridge the distance* between leaders and followers as well as between trainers and trainees (see Figure 8.1).

Mentoring and Modeling. Several interviewees discussed the importance of mentoring (either engaging in mentorship or being mentored), as well as leading by example and learning through observation as mechanisms for leadership and training.

Indeed, several of the members of the Training Wing who participated in the study referenced mentoring and leading by example. Notably, all of the interviewees who described mentoring or leading by example in this context also discussed the importance of either leading by example or setting the example with respect to leadership more generally. Setting or leading by example therefore appear to be viewed as essential leadership actions by these participants, which also translates into how they enact their training roles with respect to leadership development as well. Consider the following illustrative citations:

> One of the things ... and I do all the time when we are walking around if we see garbage we stop, pick it up and put it in the garbage can. Simple things like that, leading by example—and it is starting to rub off. Sometimes I say, "I don't have time, but would you mind emptying that garbage can, it is overflowing and I have a meeting right now?" "Ok, I don't mind. I have a spare right now." Then I thank them for it. Once they realize it is their home, and their unit, they have pride in it. They want the campus to look good and if they see people throwing garbage on the ground they will say, "Hey, do you mind picking that up? This is my home." I grew up in that pride in your unit, and I want that on board here but it takes time. I could yell at them all the time, but if I bend over and pick it up right in front of them 1,000 officer cadets walk past it every day en route to the dining hall—

> but—if [names a member of the Training Wing] and I walk past and pick it up that is setting a good example. (Participant G, Training Wing)

Thus, mentoring is described as a practice that can help bring people together (i.e., bridge the distance). Surprising, some interviewees discussed how mentoring can be enacted in multiple directions. Consider the following two excerpts, in which the interviewees explain how followers mentor or influence them:

> Let's go on record; people try to make mentoring this big formal deal—here is a manual on mentorship. Mentorship happens or it doesn't, and I know sometimes that relationships are formalized after some time, though you know that you may have someone you follow through your career who may be your mentor. At the onset, either mentorship happens or it doesn't, I think, through normal interactions. So, I think, for example, that our [names a position at the college] is a very good mentor to me but he's not my official mentor in the CAF [Canadian Armed Forces]. I lean on him a lot. I get a lot of mentorship from him. I (also) lean on my [names a specific position at the college, who reports to the participant] a lot because in this environment, when I got here, I was lucky to be paired with her, because she understands the training environment more than I did at the time. Good followers are able to figure out how to mentor their leaders. But sometimes, leaders are not receptive to that, and that's poor leadership." (Participant A, Training Wing)

> I learn every day from the officer cadets and they teach me to be a better follower as well. If we circle back to the ego bit, I think one of the main obstacles we have is trust and the officer cadets trying to trust what we are saying is actually for their benefit. To make them better and enable their success. You can't buy experience—you have to go through it, make mistakes, live through it. It isn't a contest of egos; we are all a team, so leverage our strengths. We are trying to make each other better. (Participant F, Training Wing)

Furthermore, several respondents—including all three of the officer cadets—discussed learning by observing members of the Training Wing, as highlighted in the quote below.

> The only way you learn it at RMC is through decent examples and them testing those examples for yourself. For myself, I look at how [names a member of the Training Wing] has done things and then try and apply it to what I am doing and see if it works or fails. (Participant H, Officer Cadet)

Interaction and Engagement. Some participants described the importance of engaging and interacting with followers directly, often but not only in the context of training relationships. As demonstrated in the excerpts below, such interactions—thus getting to know others—appear to be viewed as important considerations.

> But for me, I try to get to know my subordinates personally—it's something that I try to do as much as I can, in my position as .... (Participant I, Officer Cadet)

> I like to get to know people and like to just out of the blue, just start a conversation with one of the young officer cadets here and just to find out what makes them tick. Um, I don't have that fear of doing that. I don't care what they say and how it comes across.... It demonstrates to them that I'm actually interested in them, which is true. I want to know what makes them tick because it makes them better. So I think that's a skill set that needs to be. I don't think you can teach it. I think it's just something that's kind of brought upon yourself. (Participant D, Training Wing)

> It is the patience and taking the time to interact with them. I know the more I can interact with them and give exposure to what being a [name of position] is all about is good. If they don't get it right away, or understand it, it might be [stay] in the back of their minds. (Participant C, Training Wing)

Finally, another interviewee explicitly related interaction to mentorship, as reflected in the quote below. This emphasizes the importance of actively interacting with followers, as it facilitates being seen as approachable.

> Instead of staying in the office all day, plugging away at the desk, you have to be approachable and be out. No matter what rank you are people have to be able to come up to you. There is a chain of command ..., I think, it has transitioned into a mentorship, coaching role.[2] (Participant G, Training Wing)

In summary, respondents emphasized in different ways proximity and closeness rather than distance and authority in their relationships with followers (cadets and others), through modeling and mentoring, interaction and engagement behaviors, even in this military context, where the presence of hierarchy was clearly ingrained and unquestionable.

DISCUSSION

In this chapter, we asked, "How do leaders in hierarchical settings such as the military interpret and engage in leadership and followership roles, given the need for both in the course of their work?" Although we were open to any themes that would arise from this research, we anticipated at the outset that proficiency with leadership and followership would facilitate the development of relevant skills in others. What we did not anticipate, however, was the degree with which participants would describe the roles as being so closely construed that they almost seemed to merge into one, as well as the emphasis placed on leadership and training mechanisms that implied closeness and proximity with followers (and particularly with cadets), rather than distance and authority. This may initially seem somewhat paradoxical, in the context of an organization known for its emphasis on hierarchy and obedience, represented in the uniforms that members wear (which include symbols that communicate the members' rank to others; e.g., Wong et al., 2003) and the way in which the organization is structured. Yet our main findings, which centered around perceptions of *leadership and followership as one* and the importance of *bridging the distance*, highlight the significance of these attitudes and behaviors for the members of our sample, and confirm prior suggestions that leadership and followership in the military may be more closely intertwined than usually thought (e.g., Hollander & Webb, 1955; Peters & Haslam, 2018).

First, the focus on *leadership and followership as one* reflects the degree to which interviewees embraced both roles, described an agility with respect to moving between them, acknowledged the importance of followership, described similarities between leadership and followership, and discussed the importance of supporting one's leader when in the followership role. Indeed, all participants in the study either described engaging in both roles or discussed the ease with which they switched between them.

In line with De Rue and Ashford's (2010) argument that schemas centered on the hierarchical manner in which leadership should be organized can impact how leader and follower identities develop, the hierarchical nature of the military (e.g., Wong et al., 2003) likely facilitates the manner in which the two roles are embraced within the study. Whereas some authors have noted that followership can sometimes be perceived negatively (e.g., Kelley, 1992), none of the participants in the present study communicated any negative personal perceptions related to the role (though one interviewee did recall an incident where a person had been offended when referred to as a follower). In discussing people who inhabit both roles, whom she describes as "connecting leaders", Jaser (2017) notes that juggling leadership and followership roles simultaneously can be difficult, and may lead to tension—proposing "awareness and acceptance" (p. 4) of both roles as a potential avenue through which this tension may be mitigated. Interestingly, our findings do not reveal any of the tension or difficulties mentioned by Jaser (2017). However, this may well be due to the fact that the structure of the military chain of command incites members to develop expectations related to the roles that they will undertake in their careers (schemas of leadership structure, as described by De Rue & Ashford, 2010), which enable members to be conscious of and embrace both roles and move smoothly between them. Indeed, as suggested by Jaser (2017), this context allows them to view alternating roles as natural, complementary, and seamless—such that interviewees did not appear to describe any strain associated with this process.

Second, the emphasis placed on elements related to *bridging the distance* captures the consistency with which interviewees described the proximity and closeness between leaders and followers, via such actions as mentoring, modeling, and engagement with members, as key mechanisms that they used when training and developing officer cadets. By engaging in these behaviors, members of the Training Wing are essentially modeling a key skill that cadets will be required to demonstrate in their careers, given their future connecting leader roles—how to bridge the distance between members in different roles within the groups that will be part of in their jobs.

In addition to mentoring, several participants also described actions that center on modeling, or leading by example, when training others. Through modeling, leaders demonstrate desired behaviors and reinforce the expectations for followers, allowing the leadership and followership roles to become more fluid. Notably, elements of the particular context in which the data for this study were collected—such as the hierarchical structure of the military and the quick rotation of individuals in leadership positions at the college (described in more detail below)—provide an environment in which members are exposed to a number of leadership styles and observe a variety of leader-follower interactions. Effective role models are thus crucial in this environment. Indeed, the impact of modeling in military settings has been noted in the literature—for example, modeling desired behaviors by leaders and setting clear expectations has been linked to effective followership in battlefield military settings (Warner & Appenzeller, 2011).

This finding therefore maps well onto the extant literature on leader development in military settings, which has identified mentoring (e.g., Lester et al., 2011) and interactions (e.g., Larsson et al., 2006) as potentially influential elements when developing leaders. Notably, the importance of interactions has been highlighted in literature that is not specific to military contexts as well. Swindall (2011), for example, underscores the value of the leader's personal presence and involvement with subordinates to increase their engagement at work. Our study reinforces this perspective, as respondents indicated that they found their leadership to be more effective when based on personal engagement and interaction with followers.

These points may also be linked to De Rue and Ashford's (2010) proposition that our perceptions related to the potential rewards and hazards related to our actions can influence how we develop leadership and followership identities. Indeed, by observing others and integrating expectations via our social interactions, we are able to discern which actions will be valued by key others in our environment, thus influencing how members will choose to claim and grant identities related to both roles.

Facilitative Context

In line with De Rue and Ashford's (2010) assertion that organizational structures can influence how individuals claim and grant leader and follower identities, several respondents pointed to contextual elements related to the institution at which the data were collected that serve to facilitate the development of leadership and followership skills. Examples include *the deliberately choreographed switching of roles among trainees*, through such mechanisms as the rotational leadership opportunities built into the program at the college and different leadership opportunities provided to officer cadets. Some participants also mentioned the *challenge of leading one's peers*. Others noted a more explicit *emphasis on leadership, rather than followership*, at RMC, despite the omnipresence of follower roles in practice.

In addition to the contextual elements described by respondents, *the short rotational leadership appointments at RMC* are an important consideration. All officer cadets occupy leadership positions during their 4 years at the college, with third- and fourth-year cadets switching leadership roles at varying levels each semester. Moreover, the staff positions in the military chain of command generally change every 2 years—where these rotations involve staff arriving from other military units and leaving the campus. As such, different individuals occupy staff positions at each rotation.

As individuals in leadership positions at the college change, subordinates (staff and officer cadets) must adapt to different leadership styles. While our findings underscore the importance of leading by example in the training environment, it is possible that the emphasis placed on mentoring and modeling, for example, may change with different administrations.

Strengths, Limitations, and Future Research Directions

Although our sample size was small, participants in our study had experience in a variety of roles. Seven interviewees held positions within the Training Wing (which included respondents with backgrounds from all three branches of the Canadian Armed Forces) and three interviewees were presently attending RMC, holding leadership roles at the time of the interviews. This allowed us to obtain the perspectives of participants in a variety of roles at the college, enabling us to identify interesting themes that emerged across respondents.

However, it is important to acknowledge that the data were collected from participants at a single facility, which limits the generalizability of the findings. Additionally, respondents were invited to participate based on their leadership roles and in conjunction with a list of potential interviewees suggested by a senior staff member, rather than randomly selected among staff members and officer cadets. Future research may endeavor to examine the experience of both being in, as well as training others for, leadership and followership roles across a variety of military learning facilities or similar environments. Moreover, future research could provide better insights on the development and interplay of these roles by adopting a more longitudinal perspective, following participants over a period of their careers and examining their experiences within leadership and followership roles during this time. Finally, future studies may examine similarities and differences in how participants interpret, engage in, and train others for leadership and followership across both military and nonmilitary samples.

CONCLUSION

Contributing to the literature exploring how individuals experience and interpret joint leadership and followership roles (e.g., Jaser, 2017) and develop skills related to each role within a military context (e.g., Larsson et al., 2006; Lester et al., 2011), we examined how leaders at the Royal Military College of Canada construed their roles and trained others. Overall, we found that interviewees embraced and valued both roles and described agility with respect to moving between them. While respondents described many different ways in which they, and others, helped officer cadets to develop skills related to each role, several interviewees highlighted engagement and interaction with officer cadets as an important mechanism for leader development. Future research may conduct similar studies in other organizational contexts to compare and contrast themes across different environments.

NOTES

1. Note that the codes from this stage are not necessarily the same as the preliminary codes, given that the coding process was more detailed and focused.

2. Note that the final sentence within this quote was coded as "mentoring role" (see previous second-order theme).

REFERENCES

Bjugstad, K., Thach, E. C., Thompson, K. J., & Morris, A. (2006). A fresh look at followership: A model for matching followership and leadership styles. *Journal of Behavioral and Applied Management, 7*(3), 304–311, 313–319

Chaleff, I. (2003). *The courageous follower: Standing up to and for our leaders* (2nd ed.). Berrett-Koehler.

Carsten, M. K. (2017). Followership development: A behavioral approach. In M. G. Clark & C. W. Gruber (Eds.), *Leader development deconstructed: Annals of theoretical psychology* (Vol. 15, pp. 143–161) Springer.

Carsten, M. K., Uhl-Bien, M., West, B. J., Patera, J. L., & McGregor, R. (2010). Exploring social constructions of followership: A qualitative study. *Leadership Quarterly, 21*, 543–562.

De Rue, D. S., & Ashford, S. J. (2010). Who will lead and who will follow? A social process of leadership identity construction in organizations. *Academy of Management Review, 35*(4), 627–647.

Gioia, D. A., Corely, K. G., & Hamilton, A. L. (2013). Seeking qualitative rigor in inductive research: Notes on the Gioia methodology. *Organizational Research Methods, 16*(1), 15–31.

Government of Canada (2019). *Canadian Army*. www.army-armee.forces.gc.ca/en/index.page.

Hollander, E. P., & Webb, W. B. (1955). Leadership, followership, and friendship: an analysis of peer nominations. *The Journal of Abnormal and Social Psychology, 50*(2), 163–167.

Jaser, Z. (2017). Pulled in two directions: Being in concert a leader to some and a follower to others. A paradox model of dynamic equilibrium in the leadership triad. *Academy of Management Proceedings*, 2017(1), 1–6.

Kelley, R. (1992). *The power of followership*. Doubleday.

Kelley, R. (2008). Rethinking followership. In R. E. Riggio, I. Chaleff, & J. Lipman-Blumen (Eds.), *The art of followership: How great followers create great leaders and organizations* (pp. 5–14). Jossey-Bass

Kalimuddin, M. (2017, September 29). The practical application of leadership theory in mission command. *Military Review*. https://www.armyupress.army.mil/Journals/Military-Review/Online-Exclusive/2017-Online-Exclusive-Articles/Follower-ship-Theory/

Latour, S. M., & Rast, V. J. (2004). Dynamic followership: The prerequisite for effective leadership. *Air & Space Power Journal, 18*(4), 102–110.

Larsson, G., Bartone, P. T., Bos-Bakx, M., Danielsson, E., Johnansson, E., & Moelker, R. (2006). Leader development in a national context: A grounded theory approach to discovering how military leaders grow. *Military Psychology, 18*(Suppl.), S70–S81.

Lester, P. B., Hannah, S. T., Harms, P. D., Vogelgesang, G. R., & Avolio, B. J. (2011). Mentoring impact on efficacy development: A field experiment. *Academy of Management Learning & Education, 10*(3), 409–429.

Miles, M. B., Huberman, A. M., & Saldaña, J. (2014). *Qualitative data analysis: A methods sourcebook*. SAGE.

Neal, D. J., Boutselis, P. S., & Bennett, J. (2015). The United Kingdom Ministry of Defence—The case for followership as a key element of leadership development. *Strategic Management Quarterly, 3*(4), 1–22.

Oc, B., & Bashshur, M. R. (2013). Followership, leadership and social influence. *The Leadership Quarterly, 24*, 919–934.

Patton, M. Q. (2002). *Qualitative research and evaluation Methods*. SAGE.

Peters, K., & Haslam, S. A. (2018). I follow, therefore I lead: A longitudinal study of leader and follower identity and leadership in the marines. *British Journal of Psychology, 109*(4), 708–723.

Rost, J. (2008). Followership: An outmoded concept. In R. E. Riggio, I. Chaleff, & J. Lipman-Blumen (Eds.), *The art of followership: How great followers create great leaders and organizations* (pp. 53–64). Jossey-Bass.

Swindall, C. (2011). *Engaged leadership: Building a culture to overcome employee disengagement* (2nd ed.). Wiley.

Warner, C. H., & Appenzeller, G. (2011). Engaged leadership: Linking the professional ethic and battlefield behaviors. *Military Review*, September–October, 61–69.

Wong, L., Bliese, P., & McGurk, D. (2003). Military leadership: A context specific review. *The Leadership Quarterly, 14*, 657–692.

APPENDIX A:
INTERVIEW QUESTIONS (SEMISTRUCTURED INTERVIEWS)

1. Could you please describe your key responsibilities in your current position?
2. What does leadership mean to you? What does followership mean to you?
3. Can you give some examples of how you play the role of a leader in your job?
4. Can you give some examples of how you play the role of a follower in your job?
5. How do you juggle both?
6. What skills are required to successfully play the role of leader, and how are they developed?
7. In your training role, how do you help others to develop their leadership skills? Can you give us some examples of how you do this? Can you give us some precise elements in the curriculum that focus on developing leadership skills?

8. What skills are required to successfully play the role of follower, and how are they developed?
9. In your training role, how do you help others to develop their followership skills? Can you give us some examples of how you do this? Can you give us some precise elements in the curriculum that focus on developing followership?
10. How would you describe the relative emphasis on leadership and followership in the training that you give to students?
11. How are leadership and followership perceived in the military?
12. How are the two roles balanced in the program for students?

Note: These questions were developed as a guide for the semi-structured interviews. Questions were rephrased or presented in a different order, depending on the interview discussions.

CHAPTER 9

EVERYDAY LEADERSHIP AND ENGAGED FOLLOWERSHIP

Two Sides of the Same Construct

Ronald E. Riggio
Claremont McKenna College

Zhengguang Liu
Beijing Normal University and Claremont McKenna College

Rebecca J. Reichard
Claremont Graduate University

Dayna O. H. Walker
San Francisco State University

ABSTRACT

In this chapter, we introduce the idea of an everyday leader or an individual who, regardless of formal title or authority, influences others to achieve shared objectives for the good of the collective. We view everyday leadership and engaged followership as two sides of the same construct. More specifically, we conceptualize everyday leadership as multidimensional and pro-

The Connecting Leader: Serving Concurrently as a Leader and a Follower
pp. 245–267

pose two strategies for assessing it. First, using traditional self-report survey measures, we define everyday leadership with five dimensions—leadership work duties, taking charge, voice, individual innovation, and civic engagement. Second, using an assessment center method, we define everyday leadership through four behavioral dimensions—pathways, people, and place, problem solving, and positive persuasion—all within the context of a community-based simulation. Providing clear conceptualization and multiple measurements on the new construct of everyday leadership will offer future researchers a solid foundation for examining it.

Traditional notions of leaders and followers view them as very different, and, in many ways, opposites. When people think of the term *leader*, they might often picture a top executive wearing a suit and tie commanding a large organization, or might conjure an image of an elected head of a nation, addressing a crowd at a political rally and making important policy decisions. In the same vein, when considering the term *follower*, it can conjure an image of a low-level employee, without a mind of his/her own, sheepishly adhering to a leader's commands. However, contemporary scholars have pointed out that these images are generally one sided. In this sort of traditional, stereotypic thinking, we ascribe too much of the leadership that takes place in organizations and collectives to the leader (Meindl, 1995), and we tend to neglect the important role that followers play in coconstructing leadership (Carsten et al., 2010; Uhl-Bien et al., 2014). These terms refer to a process of influence that flows between members of a group. A formal position of authority is not required to enact positive influence, and a formal position of subordination is not required to be influenced to follow another. In fact, the formal organization itself does not even require such divisions of power and influence. Leadership and followership can occur both within the workplace context as well as outside of it—in every corner in our everyday life, including the family and the community.

In this chapter, we introduce the construct of *everyday leadership,* a new concept that fits well into the theme of this book, which focuses on serving concurrently as a leader and a follower. While a connecting leader acts as one person who occupies the role as a leader to some, and a follower to others (Jaser, 2017), an everyday leader is an individual who, regardless of formal title or authority, influences others to achieve shared objectives for the good of the collective. The everyday leader engages in proactive and prosocial citizenship at work and in nonwork settings such as the family and the community. In terms of roles, the everyday leader may be a formal leader, an informal leader, an individual contributor, or even a proactive follower. Followers, who are engaged, proactive, and who are instrumental in the attainment of goals, are, by our conceptualization, acting as everyday leaders. In this way, we equate everyday leadership and engaged followership, viewing them as two sides of the same construct. In this chapter, we portray everyday leadership as one form of connecting leadership to capture how everyone, in their daily lives, is both a leader and a follower in unexpected ways.

Why Is Everyday Leadership Important?

Interest in leadership has never been greater. Kellerman (2012) captures this in her discussion of the *leadership industry*, where she cites the tremendous and ongoing growth of programs to identify and develop leaders, not just in work organizations, but in a host of other areas, from schools to sports, to communities and politics. Consider education. As early as elementary school, there is an emphasis on fostering leader development in children (Reitan & Stenberg, 2019). Certainly, identification of student leaders, and leader development programs are quite common in secondary or high schools. But it does not stop there. The mission statements of many colleges and universities in the United States (and in many other countries) refer to the development of leadership in their students. And, while business schools have purported to develop leadership in MBA programs for a long time, the past 2 decades have seen an increase in graduate programs in the study and development of leadership, with many of these programs offering online degrees in organizational leadership, educational leadership, and leadership and change management. Note that many of these programs are not necessarily preparing students for specific leadership positions. Instead, they are intended to increase leadership capacity that will presumably serve them in future leadership positions, but also in their community endeavors.

The past few decades have also seen a flattening of our hierarchical systems in work organizations, including a decrease in the power distance between leaders and followers (Scott et al., 2018). Rank-and-file employees in many organizations are recognized when they demonstrate initiative or innovation with a variety of leadership awards. For example, in one organization an excellence in leadership award is given to employees who: "inspire others to work collaboratively and creatively; demonstrate initiative, promote a work environment that is respectful, collegial and supportive and fosters pride" in the organization.

In politics, spurred on by the populist movement in the United States, we have seen an increase in the number of first-time candidates for a variety of local, state, and even federal elected offices. There is a perception that current politicians are not demonstrating effective leadership, and those politicians need to be replaced. Grassroots community organizations and nonprofit organizations are on the rise. People are stepping up and taking the lead to solve a variety of social ills (Barisione, 2016; Schmitz, 2011), and in many instances, these individuals do not have formal leadership roles or titles. Take, for example, the student survivors of the mass shooting at Marjory Douglas Stoneman High School in Parkland, Florida. Several of these students engaged in leadership behaviors as mere citizens by speaking out about the need for gun control, appearing at demonstrations and media events, and lobbying legislators to enact stricter gun control measures.

All of these efforts, whether they be educational programs designed to foster leader development in students, employees who are recognized for demonstrating leadership in the workplace, or community members who are leading political and social change, involve what we refer to as *everyday leadership*. Yet, each of these groups—students, rank-and-file employees, and community members—would best be characterized as followers, not as formal leaders. To our main point, we can also view these individuals, who are demonstrating everyday leadership, as engaged (and exemplary) followers. As stated, everyday leadership and engaged followership are two sides of the same construct.

Conceptualizing Everyday Leadership

When individuals take on leadership roles, their implicit models of a leader and leadership play an important role in guiding their behavior (Lord & Maher, 1991). Likewise, when people choose to follow a leader, their implicit views about the follower role shape their behavior (Shondrick & Lord, 2010). Indeed, the true acquisition of both leader and follower roles is a complex process. DeRue and Ashford (2010) argue that the construction of leader and follower roles takes place through reciprocal claiming and granting—an individual lays claim to the role of leader, and others agree and grant the leader role. Likewise, individuals choose to follow a leader and claim the follower role, which the leader, in turn, grants. In other words, the identities of leaders and followers can be mutually and dynamically reinforced by each other (Shondrick & Lord, 2010).

What are the behaviors that define the leader and follower roles? Decades of research on leadership have suggested a wide range of behaviors and has led to the creation of taxonomies of effective leader behaviors (Yukl, 2012). These include task-oriented behaviors (e.g., planning, monitoring, problem solving), relationship-oriented behaviors (e.g., supporting, empowering, developing), and change-oriented behaviors (e.g., advocating for change and encouraging innovation). This search for critical leader behaviors goes back to the behavioral theories of leadership studied by researchers at Ohio State University and the University of Michigan in the post-World War II era (e.g., Halpin & Winer, 1957; Kahn & Katz, 1960), to more recent attempts to compile and categorize leader behaviors (Behrendt et al., 2017).

Conversely, scholars have given much less attention to identifying follower behaviors. From a traditional point of view, the role of followers is considered to be about obedience and compliance with directives from the leader. However, research has suggested that followership does not solely include this passive stereotype. It also includes proactive and participative notions of followership (Carsten et al., 2010). Effective followers should challenge the leader when they believe the leader's action or direction is wrong (Chaleff, 1995, 2009; Uhl-Bien et al., 2014). Exemplary followers, however, should also assume responsibility for the common purpose, self-manage, be self-motivated, take the initiative, and be innovative (Chaleff, 2009; Kelley, 1988, 2008). In short, there is an overlap between the behaviors of effective leaders and exemplary followers. Both should be committed to the shared purpose, initiate positive actions, and innovate when necessary.

Effective leaders and exemplary followers not only share some behaviors that provide value for the collective, but they may also move between the leader and the follower role. Leaders in organizations, for example, may play the leadership role when overseeing subordinates but may switch to the follower role when interacting with their superiors. Even when interacting with subordinates, leaders may defer to followers when they have special expertise, or some novel ideas or contributions—allowing the followers to temporarily take the lead role with the leader following along. Indeed, the very best leaders also tend to be good followers (Agho, 2009; Hollander, 1995). Some theories of leadership, such as Servant Leadership (e.g., van Dierendonck, 2011), even argue that effective servant leaders facilitate the achievement of goals for the collective in a sort of blurring of leader and follower roles. For those in the follower role, being an exemplary follower—including being self-motivated, innovative, collaborative, credible, and dedicated to the team's mission—is the path to attaining a formal leadership position (Blackshear, 2003). Indeed, an exemplary follower is well prepared to step up and take on a leadership role when so called.

This construct of everyday leadership is consistent with the whole-person approach, which emphasizes the holistic nature of human beings and suggests that an individual is an integrative organism (Taysum, 2003). Every one of us plays various roles in daily life. For instance, one individual may have the role of a leader in a company, a parent at home, a grassroots organizer in the community, and a key player in a recreational sports team. When it comes to leadership, it may be more dependent on the behavior that one performs, rather than the nature of the formal role that one is holding.

Much of leadership research focuses primarily on the leader and overemphasizes leading in the context of the workplace (Hammond et al., 2017). With the everyday leadership construct, we view leadership more broadly, suggesting that the same sorts of leadership behaviors that identified leaders display are performed by individuals who are not in leadership positions but are in the follower or member role in a collective. This approach recognizes that leadership is cocreated (Carsten & Uhl-Bien, 2012), with followers or regular members sometimes initiating efforts that result in leadership. Finally, everyday leadership-engaged followership is not limited to the confines of formal work organizations but extends to other domains such as the broader community itself.

Everyday Leadership and Related Constructs

In defining everyday leadership, it is important to consider existing overlapping constructs. One construct that overlaps with everyday leadership is *active citizenship*. Whereas being a citizen of a nation or a community means that an individual is a legitimate member of that nation or community, *active citizenship* goes beyond mere membership and suggests that the individual takes the initiative to be actively engaged in the community (Sherrod & Lauckhardt, 2009). Active and engaged citizenship is defined "as someone who has a sense of civic duty, feeling of social connection to their community, confidence in their abilities to effect change, as well as someone who engages in civic behaviors" (Zaff et al., 2010, p. 737). What this suggests is that active citizens go beyond their role of being members of a community and engage in behaviors that connect with other members, and that they are motivated to work toward bettering the community, and are effecting change—all behaviors that are consistent with the proactive, other oriented, and change-related behaviors that are typically performed by effective leaders.

Another well-researched construct that has connections to everyday leadership in the workplace is *organizational citizenship behaviors* (OCBs). OCBs are behaviors in the workplace that go beyond what the job role requires and have a positive impact on the organization and its goals (LePine et al., 2002; Organ, 1988). Categories of OCBs include altruistic behaviors, such as volunteering to help a coworker, conscientious behaviors, such as using one's time wisely and efficiently, maintaining a sense of fairness and *sportsmanship*, and being deeply committed to the organization, in what is termed *civic virtue* (Organ, 1988). Both leaders and followers in the organization can perform OCBs, which represent both excellent leadership and exemplary followership. For the most part, researchers have emphasized OCBs as an outcome in research on organizational behavior. Indeed, there is a body of literature that suggests that outstanding leaders, as represented by leaders who are transformational or engage in positive leader-member exchange relationships lead groups that engage in higher levels of OCBs (e.g., Ilies et al., 2007; Podsakoff et al., 1990). Yet, employees, regardless of their positions in the organization, who regularly engage in OCBs are likely the same individuals who could be considered everyday leaders.

Even though there is evident overlap between everyday leadership and the two constructs above, everyday leadership is different from them in the following ways. First, the scope of everyday leadership is larger than that of active citizenship or individuals simply engaging in OCBs. Everyday leadership can exist in almost every corner of our daily lives, whereas active citizenship only exists in the community, and OCBs only exist in organizational settings. Second, everyday leadership, as one type of connecting leadership, has its corresponding concept of followership, and the perpetrators of everyday leadership behaviors, by nature, include both identified leaders and followers. Finally, from the perspective of outcomes, we view everyday leadership more from the effectiveness perspective, whereas we view active citizenship or OCBs more from the virtue-based perspective. In other words, everyday leaders get good things done; active citizens do good things.

THE ASSESSMENT OF EVERYDAY LEADERSHIP

In leadership research, we typically begin with the identification of some group of *leaders* who will be studied. Possession of a leadership position or title is the standard—what scholars refer to as *leader role occupancy* (e.g., Li et al., 2011). If we are studying business leaders, we identify persons in the organization(s) with the title of *manager*, at whatever level, and if we want to assess the quality of their leadership, we survey their direct reports (or their superiors). We could also measure leader effectiveness more objectively, such as obtaining assessments of the productivity of the group, department, or organization. In this case, however, we would not be measuring leader performance per se but would be using the collective efforts and output of the followers as a means to measure the leader's effectiveness and impact. In short, the way that we typically study business leadership has limitations.

Likewise, if we are interested in political leaders, we focus on elected or appointed officials, and to measure their leadership effectiveness, we might poll their constituents. If we want more objective assessments of leader effectiveness, we could look at legislative success, but this often goes beyond the leader's individual efforts and involves the cooperation and coordination with other members (and constituents). If we are working in a more controlled, experimental setting, we might bring a group together (e.g., MBA students, undergraduates) have them elect (or we might appoint) a leader, and study that leader's behavior. In short, for the vast majority of leadership research, we are studying people who are in an identified leadership role. In addition, when we measure a leader's effectiveness, we are actually looking at the combined efforts of the leader and followers or others.

But what if we want to study leadership in people who do not necessarily have an identifiable leadership position? Assessing leadership in those without a formal role would also be the case if we were intent on studying student leader development or the acquisition of leadership capacity in employees or members of the community. Assessing leadership in those without a formal role was one challenge that we faced that stimulated our interest in everyday leadership. We argue that you don't have to study formal leaders to research leadership.

Everyday Leadership Self-Report Survey

We initially proposed that the everyday leadership construct consisted of five components: *leader work duties,* or the performance of behaviors at work that would typically be performed by a designated leader, such as training or mentoring someone, *civic engagement, taking charge*, such as being in charge of a project, *individual innovation,* which included coming up with new ideas, or setting a new course, and *voice*, which involved having a voice in decision making or agenda setting. These five dimensions, together, seemed to capture the construct of everyday leadership/engaged followership.

We began by focusing on leader work behaviors that could be, and frequently are, enacted by proactive followers. This focus led to the development of a scale of leader work duties. Items on this scale included having taken charge of a special project, representing a team's position to management, planning or coordinating a special event, presenting the results of a special project, and coaching/mentoring other employees—all tasks that would be routinely performed by leaders. This scale was used as an assessment of leadership in previously published studies examining early life precursors of adult leadership (Guerin et al., 2011; Reichard et al., 2011). Engaging in leader work duties in the workplace, regardless of whether or not an individual is in a formal leadership role, we suggest, is one element of everyday leadership.

The second component of everyday leadership is demonstrating leadership in the community through civic engagement. Given the community is the place where human capital and social capital are embedded (Apaliyah et al., 2012), people usually exhibit their social influence and responsibility by engaging in community activities. In fact, many people develop their leadership or followership through experiences in the community, either informally (Hammond et al., 2017), or formally (Azzam & Riggio, 2003). This scale includes detailed information about civic engagement, including the frequency of community service/volunteering, taking part in political activities, working on neighborhood problems, and participating in fund-raising for charity.

The other three components that went into our assessment of everyday leadership asked about the frequency of "everyday leadership activities" that they engage in at work, or outside of work (typically in the community or volunteer organizations). We clustered these self-rating scales into specific areas: taking charge behavior (e.g., instituted new methods or procedures, implemented solutions); individual innovation (e.g., communicated views even if they differed from others' views, encouraged others to get involved); voice (e.g., championed ideas to others, secured funds to implement new ideas, developed adequate plans and schedules to implement new ideas). Taking charge emphasizes voluntary efforts that improve work processes or procedures (Morrison & Phelps, 1999). An everyday leader might take charge of his or her work group by streamlining a cumbersome work flow or using meeting facilitating techniques to drive consensus on a controversial proposal. Individual innovation involves coming up with and implementing new ideas, including building a coalition of supporters to embrace the new ways of working (Scott & Bruce, 1994). For instance, everyday leaders might employ creative solutions to technical problems facing the organization. Gaining momentum around the idea and gathering the resources to implement it would take considerable skill. Lastly, voice entails speaking up and making constructive suggestions, even when it may be controversial to do so (Van Dyne & LePine, 1998). For instance, voice could include recommending additional safety precautions to be put in place to prevent injury or abuse. Although speaking up may incur personal risk or may differ from the opinions of others, everyday leaders communicate their perspectives on issues that matter and offer helpful solutions to the problems they see.

We chose taking charge, individual innovation, and voice as core components of everyday leadership because, together, they comprise proactive work behaviors (Parker & Collins, 2010). Proactivity involves anticipating future needs of a group as well as acting on those needs.

Rather than wait for others to address challenges or responding only once crises come to a head, proactive individuals initiate change themselves early and often. Proactive behaviors are anticipatory rather than reactionary; they address future problems or opportunities. Importantly, proactive behaviors can be performed without managerial title or authority and therefore are well suited to everyday leadership.

Each of the proactive behaviors we measure as part of everyday leadership can be performed both within and outside of a person's actual job description. That is, everyday leaders might take on additional responsibilities outside of their day-to-day volunteer or work duties, but they may also fulfill these added responsibilities within an expanded, evolving definition of their role. Consistent with research on proactive work behavior (Parker & Collins, 2010), we suspect that everyday leaders take an expansive approach to their roles and do not feel restricted by the activities listed on their actual job descriptions. Everyday leaders in volunteer roles may be especially inclined towards defining their role broadly because volunteer roles may or may not have written job descriptions. Regardless of whether the work is paid employment, volunteer efforts, or civic engagement, everyday leaders likely continuously update their role to include additional activities they pick up as needed.

Taken together, these proactive work behaviors—taking charge, individual innovation, and voice—are the sorts of behaviors that we believe are central to members of a collective stepping up and demonstrating leadership, regardless of whether they hold any formal leadership position. It also suggests that everyday leadership is related to, but distinct from, other leadership constructs such as transformational leadership. Beyond that, we have been trying to longitudinally examine the developmental precursors of everyday leadership with the aim of developing everyday leadership.

Everyday Leadership Assessment Center

We have also designed, developed, pilot tested, and revised a developmental assessment center (AC) to assess everyday leadership. Three primary simulations with accompanying written instructions and materials have been developed, namely an in-basket activity, a leaderless group discussion, and a one-on-one conflict resolution role-play session (see Table 9.1 for an overview). The AC scenario (described below) is an everyday situation that any adult could find himself/herself in.

Unlike managerial assessments, we explicitly designed this AC to measure everyday leadership. Therefore, we situated the AC simulations within the context of a home owner's association (HOA) in which the person we are assessing is meant to lead constituent homeowners with limited formal authority. HOAs are common in planned community housing developments and condominium buildings. Dues-paying HOA members are the individuals who purchase homes in the community. Thus, each homeowner has a financial stake in the HOA and the surrounding community.

Each AC simulation presents the leader with unique challenges relevant to leading in everyday contexts. The person we are assessing is assigned the role of an HOA vice president. HOA vice presidents are tasked with leading the community, yet do not possess hierarchical authority over homeowners as would a manager. Instead, HOA vice presidents are tasked with carrying out the community's vision regarding visual standards for yard and building maintenance, safety, and community engagement. Each simulation represents a unique yet common context for leading, either via written emails, via group meetings, or via a one-on-one conversation, and thus provides a broad array of opportunities for the person being assessed to demonstrate everyday leadership behaviors. Taken together, the AC simulates an everyday leadership context relevant and accessible to anyone who might influence others in pursuit of shared goals.

The three AC simulations were designed to assess specific dimensions of everyday leadership behavior (Lievens, 1998). In each simulation,

Table 9.1. Overview of AC Structure

Timing	*Activity*	*Description*
00:00–01:00	In-basket simulation	A written simulation in which participants work individually on a computer to respond to memos from supervisors, constituents, and coworkers.
01:15–02:15	Leaderless group discussion	A leaderless group discussion consists of 4–5 participants presenting and then deliberating the contents of proposals to submit for funding.
02:30–03:30	Role-play meeting with a follower	A one-on-one meeting in which each participant engages in a conversation with a problem subordinate (one of our actors playing the role of the participant's follower).
1–3 weeks later	Email feedback report	A five-page detailed feedback report emailed to participants. The report is designed to increase participants' self-awareness of their leadership strengths and areas in need of improvement and may form as basis for future leadership development efforts. Ideally, report is coupled with a coaching debriefing meeting.

leader behaviors are coded using behaviorally anchored rating scales (BARS; see Appendix A for an example BARS). In total, the AC contains 17 BARS, culminating in four overarching dimensions of leadership behavior—*pathways, people and place, problem solving,* and *positive persuasion* (see Table 9.2 for a breakdown of the BARS constructs by simulation). *Pathways* reflects execution and is defined as accomplishing goals, getting things done, and driving solutions forward. We define *people and place* as establishing and maintaining interpersonal relationships. We define *problem solving* as analytical, creative, and strategic thinking. *Positive persuasion* involves clear, convincing, and influential oral and written communication. Together, *pathways, people and place, problem solving,* and *positive persuasion* are some of the traditional leadership dimensions assessed in executive leadership ACs. They also map onto the two broad categories of leadership behavior noted earlier in the classic Ohio State and University of Michigan studies, task (i.e., pathways) and relationship maintenance (i.e., people and place) functions. In our AC, these four dimensions of leadership behavior are made relevant for everyday leaders who may or may not have held leadership positions nor had formal leadership experience in organizations.

In-Basket Task. In the in-basket simulation, we task the everyday leader with responding to emails from homeowners with differing yet equally strong viewpoints on contentious issues within given time constraints. For instance, one resident complains about the size and placement of a flag in a neighbor's yard. No clear answer exists; the leader must balance individual property rights with community norms. Therefore, the leader has

Table 9.2. Breakdown of BARS Constructs by Simulation

Everyday Leadership Dimension	*In-Basket Exercise*	*Leaderless Group Discussion*	*Role-Play (1 on 1)*
Pathways	• Email management • Planning and organizing	• Initiation of group structure	• One-on-one meeting facilitation
Problem-solving	• Analytical processing	• Group decision-making	• Collaborative problem solving
People and place	• Relationship correspondence	• Group communication • Team focus	• Individual consideration • Relational transparency
Positive persuasion	• Written communication	• Group influence	• Dyadic influence • Dyadic communication

an opportunity to display everyday leadership behaviors in their written responses. As indicated in Table 9.2, the in-basket exercise covers all four leadership dimensions of *pathways, people and place, problem solving,* and *positive persuasion* (Fredericksen, 1962; Wollowick & McNamara, 1969). Because we time the exercise, the leader must plan, organize, and prioritize email responses by importance, thereby displaying *pathways* behaviors. We assess *problem-solving* behaviors via the extent to which the leader uses resources at his/her disposal (e.g., HOA community guidelines) to analyze the specific problem at hand. Leaders exhibiting *people and place* behaviors maintain healthy and productive relationships while making sure to complete tasks via email. Lastly, the email format of the in-basket task allows the leader to display *positive persuasion* skills via written communication; raters look for coherent yet concise arguments as well as polite salutations and closings when assessing this skill.

Leaderless Group Discussion. In the leaderless group discussion, the everyday leader represents his or her own neighborhood "zone" in a group budget discussion. We task the group with coming to consensus on how to allocate limited HOA funds to various proposals, ranging from safety to aesthetics to a neighborhood block party. The leaderless group discussion was designed to assess interpersonal skills such as listening, cooperation, influencing, and problem-solving skills (Bass, 1954; Wollowick & McNamara, 1969). In our AC and as shown in Table 9.2, this simulation provides the everyday leader an opportunity to display *pathways, people and place, problem solving,* and *positive persuasion* behaviors. Raters assess pathways skills by the extent to which the leader initiates the discussion around a specific topic. In our experience, there have been times when an AC participant never said a word in the meeting or only responded to others' comments, thereby neglecting their own neighborhood zones' priorities. Raters would mark this passivity as low on the BAR called initiation of structure. In another stand-out case at the other end of the spectrum, an AC participant not only brought forth her neighborhood zone's concerns but also skillfully invited discussion of other representatives' concerns, ultimately identifying a creative win-win solution. Such behavior would rank high on initiation of structure as well as interpersonal communication and team focus. Similarly, leaders who talk too much, interrupt others, or speak so softly that the microphone barely picks up their voice would receive low ratings on oral communication and team focus.

One-on-One Conflict Resolution Role-Play. In the role-play simulation, the HOA leader meets with a homeowner who has become delinquent on paying HOA dues. Although the HOA guidelines contain procedures for these types of situations (e.g., late fees), the leader ultimately has the discretion to resolve the situation in the manner they see fit. In this role-play, the leader must first understand the homeowner's situation before helping to resolve it. The role play session was designed to assess a participant's ability to resolve conflict, including framing the issue at hand, communicating pertinent information clearly and diplomatically, and identifying and/or creating pathways toward resolution of the conflict (Borman et al., 1983; Dill, 1972; Streufert et al., 1988). In our AC, the one-on-one conflict resolution role play assesses *pathways, people and place, problem solving,* and *positive persuasion*.

As shown in Table 9.2, the majority of BARS assessed in this simulation fall under people and place. A critical juncture in this role-play often occurs if/when the everyday leader asks the actor (playing the delinquent homeowner) why he/she is late on the HOA dues. If they inquire, the leader learns additional information about the homeowner's situation that could lead to resolution. The extent to which the leader takes ownership over any misunderstandings, speaks honestly and candidly about his/her discretion, and encourages the homeowner to speak openly about their situation informs their rating on relational transparency (see Appendix A for an example of Relational Transparency BARS). Likewise, we assess individual consideration by the extent to which the leader uses his/her discretion to find a customized solution versus applying HOA rules in a blanket fashion. Sometimes, participants in our AC attempt to persuade the delinquent homeowner through "hard tactics" such as coercion, threats, and standoffish body language. Such behavior yields low ratings and rarely leads to successful resolution because the leader fails to elicit key information from the homeowner. In contrast, other participants open the conversation with a question and then later can use that additional information to find common ground and a path forward.

Although all of the simulations are challenging, our experience suggests that everyday leaders who experience our AC find the one-on-one role play the most difficult and enlightening. In leadership workshops we have facilitated using the AC, participants often eagerly compare notes with each other on how they handled "the Alex conversation" (Alex is the fictitious name of the delinquent homeowner). Some would be surprised to discover that their peers uncovered additional, pertinent information about Alex's situation. Aha moments tend to arise when participants realize they too could have accessed this information, if only they had asked Alex his perspective. This informal sensemaking prepares participants for the formal feedback they receive based on two or more trained assessors' ratings.

Assessment Center Validity. Based on a pilot study with 175 nonprofit leaders across 13 separate AC occasions averaging 12.5 leaders per AC session (min = 7, max = 21) and 1,575 hours of assessor coding (i.e., 9 hours per leader across two assessors), we refined the AC procedures and BARS. Specifically, in the implementation of the AC, we followed best practices by standardizing simulation and assessment procedures, using professional role players who actively seek to elicit behaviors from participants that are related to the dimensions of behavior under investigation, and informing participants which dimensions of performance we will assess (Lievens, 1998). Further, in the revisions of the BARS coding scheme, we followed the recommendations of Lievens (1998) by coding a small number of dimensions of performance, selecting dimensions that are unrelated to each other, and defining each dimension concerning the position of responsibility in question. We designed the BARS to provide assessors with observational aids such as checklists, operationalize each dimension's checklist with at least six behaviors but not more than 12, and group checklist behaviors in naturally occurring clusters.

Assessor Training. Research indicates that the validity of ACs increases when assessors are psychologists (rather than line managers, for example; Gaugler et al., 1987; Spychalski et al., 1997). In addition, the reliability of ACs increases with the training of assessors in behavioral observation, evaluation, and feedback techniques (Richards & Jaffee, 1972). Training of assessors is particularly important in cases where complex judgments are required as training mitigates against cognitive biases which tend to arise during complex judgments (Gaugler & Rudolph, 1992; Gaugler & Thornton, 1989; Lance et al., 2004). Training in behavioral coding is an effective way of mitigating such biases (Lance et al., 2004).

As such, we trained psychology graduate student assessors following the *Guidelines and Ethical Considerations for Assessment Center Operations* (International Taskforce on AC Guidelines, 2009). We provided particular instruction on the hypothetical organization and roles involved in the simulation, assessment techniques, dimensions of the behavior of interest and typical behaviors in the simulations in question, recording and classifying behavior, rating and data integration, feedback procedures, and frame of reference training (Lievens, 1998).

At least two assessors rated each simulation, allowing us to examine interrater reliability. Raters discussed any discrepancies larger than 1 point on a 5-point rating scale and, if necessary, called in an expert to arbitrate and retrain. Based on the BARS, leaders participating in the AC received a feedback report along with targeted developmental suggestions for improvement. In this way, we are both assessing everyday leadership and providing feedback for the future development of participants' everyday leadership/engaged followership capacity.

The two research methodologies—our multifactor self-report measure of everyday leadership and the everyday leadership assessment center have allowed us to examine leadership in persons without any identifiable leadership position. These two measuring methods can be utilized independently according to the specific goals and the cost budget in the research or practice on everyday leadership. After all, the self-report measure saves more money and energy investment at the sacrifice of its validity. Certainly, they may also be used together to act as the cross-evidence of validation for each other. Research using both of these methods is ongoing.

Implications of Everyday Leadership for Research and Practice

The everyday leadership construct has important implications for our thinking about leadership, leadership research, and leadership development. A constant criticism of leadership scholarship is that it focuses too much on the leader and gives little attention to the role that followers and situational elements play in the leadership equation (Riggio, 2019). This was a major thrust of Meindl's (1995; Meindl et al., 1985) *Romance of Leadership* idea—the fact that we overattribute the cause of outcomes to the part that the leader played, and that we have romanticized ideas about leaders. This perspective led to calls to pay more attention to followers in leadership –"reversing the lens" to better understand followers' roles in coproducing leadership (La Pierre & Bremner, 2010; Uhl-Bien & Carsten, 2018).

Everyday leadership suggests that leader behaviors are not only emitted by persons in recognized leader roles but that followers also engage in leader behaviors. In some instances, leadership takes place without any formal leaders being present. Such situations are what spurred research on *substitutes for leadership* (Hackman, 1990; Kerr & Jermier, 1978) and *shared leadership* (Pearce & Conger, 2003). In these cases, it is assumed that the members of the collective are pulling together to enact leadership, absent the presence of any designated leaders.

The everyday leadership construct is also consistent with the idea of *leadership potential*. Organizational research has focused on identifying employees in organizations who are labeled as having high potential to assume leadership positions (Conger & Fulmer, 2003). Indeed, many large companies have structured programs designed to identify such *high potentials* and provide leader development experiences for them so that they can later assume leadership positions within their organizations (Armagoh, 2009; Fulmer et al., 2009).

It is within educational systems that we see a growing amount of attention to developing leadership potential in students. Although students may fill designated leadership roles in their schools (e.g., class officer, student council member, student ambassador) leadership development is often a part of the curricular or cocurricular program, so that all students, regardless of whether they have an actual leader role, are targeted for the development of leadership potential. This emphasis on student leader development has been a part of higher education for decades (e.g.,

Ayman et al., 2003), but in recent times leadership development has been a focus of all levels of education, from high school, to middle school, and even elementary schools are instituting leadership development activities and programs (Liu et al., in press).

In addition, the construct of everyday leadership has important implications for the various communities in which we live. Whether it is the local homeowners association, some city or county political initiative, volunteer work with a civic organization, or community engagement on a larger basis, these all involve everyday leadership but are also representative of highly engaged followers/members of these various communities.

SUMMARY AND CONCLUSION

This chapter contributes to the field of leadership and followership in the following ways. First, we advance emerging perspectives on leadership development outside of the work context (Hammond et al., 2017). Although leadership is fundamentally a social influence process independent from positional authority, traditional leadership research has tended to use managerial work samples and, in so doing, has conflated influence and positional authority. However, as we argue in this chapter, leadership is a more fundamental influence process that is aided by but does not require formal managerial authority. In investigating leadership beyond managerial work positions, we take a more expansive view of leadership and followership processes that may have implications for informal communities (e.g., homeowner's and neighborhood associations, volunteer activities, and political organizing) and nonhierarchical workplaces. Second, we integrate research on leadership and followership by furthering the notion that leaders and followers mutually reinforce one another. That is, instead of a unidirectional process (e.g., leaders influencing followers or followers influencing leaders), viewing leadership and followership as two sides of the same construct proposes a multidirectional process whereby a collection of followers not only influence a leader but also influence each other and the context in which the group operates.

Finally, in today's uncertain climate and the widening gap between rich and poor and the powerful and powerless, the development of everyday leadership is an important responsibility. What is needed in today's society is not strong, charismatic leadership in top positions in organizations. What is needed today is everyday leadership; people, who, regardless of position, proactively enact positive influence and speak up both at work and in their community to improve society.

REFERENCES

Agho, A. O. (2009). Perspectives of senior-level executives on effective followership and leadership. *Journal of Leadership and Organizational Studies, 16*(2), 159–166.

Apaliyah, G. T., Martin, K. E., Gasteyer, S. P., Keating, K., & Pigg, K. (2012). Community leadership development education: Promoting civic engagement through human and social capital. *Community Development, 43*(1), 31–48.

Armagoh, F. (2009). Leadership development and leadership effectiveness. *Management Decision, 47*(6), 989–999.

Ayman, R., Adams, S., Fisher, B., & Hartman, E. (2003). Leadership development in higher education institutions: A present and future perspective. In S. E. Murphy & R. E. Riggio (Eds.), *The future of leadership development* (pp. 201–222). Erlbaum.

Azzam, T., & Riggio, R. E. (2003). Community based civic leadership programs: A descriptive investigation. *Journal of Leadership and Organizational Studies, 10*, 55–67.

Barisione, M. (2016). Leadership, political. In G. Mazzoleni (Ed.), *International encyclopedia of political communication* (pp. 636–648). Wiley-Blackwell.

Bass, B. M. (1954). The leaderless group discussion. *Psychological Bulletin, 51*, 465–492.

Behrenedt, P., Matz, S., & Goritz, A. S. (2017). An integrative model of leadership behavior. *The Leadership Quarterly, 28*(1), 229–244.

Blackshear, P. B. (2003). The followership continuum: A model for fine tuning the workforce. *The Public Manager, 32*(2), 25–29.

Borman, W. C., Eaton, N. K., Bryan, D. J., & Rosse, R. (1983). Validity of army recruiter behavioral assessment: Does the assessor make a difference? *Journal of Applied Psychology*, 68, 415–419.

Carsten, M. K., & Uhl-Bien, M. (2012). Follower beliefs in the co-production of leadership: Examining upward communication and the moderating role of context. *Zeitschrift fur Psychologie, 220*(4), 210–220.

Carsten, M. K., Uhl-Bien, M., West, B.J., Patera, J. L., & McGregor, R. (2010). Exploring social constructions of followership: A qualitative study. *The Leadership Quarterly, 21*(3), 543–562.

Chaleff, I. (1995). *The courageous follower*. Berrett-Koehler.

Chaleff, I. (2009). *The courageous follower* (3rd ed.). Berrett-Koehler.

Conger, J. A., & Fulmer, R. M. (2003, December). Developing your leadership pipeline. *Harvard Business Review, 81*(12), 76–84.

DeRue, S. D., & Ashford, S. J. (2010). Who will lead and who will follow? A social process of leadership identity construction in organizations. *Academy of Management Review, 35*(4), 627–647.

Dill, W. R. (1972). What management games do best. In E. L. Deci, B. V. H. Gilmber, & H. W. Karn (Eds.), *Readings in industrial and organizational psychology* (pp. 442–451). McGraw-Hill.

Fredericksen, N. (1962). Factors in in-basket performance. *Psychological Monographs, 76*(541).

Fulmer, R. M., Stumpf, S. A., & Bleak, J. (2009). The strategic development of high potential leaders. *Strategy & Leadership, 37*(3), 17–22.

Gaugler, B. B., Rosenthal, D. B., Thornton, G. C., III, & Bentson, C. (1987). Meta-analysis of assessment center validity. *Journal of Applied Psychology, 72*, 493–511.

Gaugler, B. B., & Rudolph, A. S., (1992). The influence of assesse performance variation on assessors' judgments. *Personnel Psychology, 45*, 77–98.

Gaugler, B. B., & Thornton, G. C., III. (1989). Number of assessment center dimensions as a determinant of assessor accuracy. *Journal of Applied Psychology, 74*, 611–618.

Guerin, D. W., Oliver, P. H., Gottfried, A. W., Gottfried, A. E., Reichard, R. J., & Riggio, R. E. (2011). Childhood and adolescent antecedents of social skills and leadership potential in adulthood: Temperamental approach/withdrawal and extraversion. *The Leadership Quarterly, 22*(3), 482–494.

Hackman, J. R. (1990). *Groups that work (and those that don't)*. Jossey-Bass.

Halpin, A. W., & Winer, B. J. (1957). A factorial study of the leader behavior descriptions. In R. M. Stogdill & A. E. Coons (Eds.), *Leader behavior: Its description and measurement*. Ohio State University Bureau of Business Research.

Hammond, M., Clapp-Smith, R., & Palanski, M. (2017). Beyond (just) the workplace: A theory of leader development across multiple domains. *Academy of Management Review, 42*, 481–498.

Hollander, E. P. (1995). Ethical challenges in the leader-follower relationship. *Business Ethics Quarterly, 5*(1), 55–65.

Ilies, R., Nahrgang, J. D., & Morgeson, F. P. (2007). Leader-member exchange and citizenship behaviors: A meta-analysis. *Journal of Applied Psychology, 92*(1), 269.

International Task Force on Assessment Center Guidelines. (2009). Guidelines and ethical considerations for assessment center operations. *International Journal of Selection and Assessment, 17*(3), 243–253.

Kahn, R. L., & Katz, D. (1960). Leadership practices in relation to productivity and morale. In D. Cartwright & A. Zander (Eds.), *Group dynamics: Research and theory* (2nd ed., pp. 554–571). Row, Peterson

Kellerman, B. (2012). *The end of leadership*. Harper-Collins.

Kelley, R. E. (1988). In praise of followers. *Harvard Business Review, 66*(6), 142–148.

Kelley, R. (2008). Rethinking followership. In R. E. Riggio, I. Chaleff, & J. Lipman-Blumen (Eds.), *The art of followership* (pp. 5–15). Jossey-Bass.

Kerr, S., & Jermier, J. (1978). Substitutes for leadership: Their meaning and measurement. *Organizational Behavior and Human Performance, 22*, 375–403.

Lance, C. E., Foster, M. R., Gentry, W. A., & Thoresen, J. D. (2004). Assessor cognitive processes in an operational assessment center. *Journal of Applied Psychology*, 89, 22–35.

La Pierre, L. M., & Bremner, N. (2010). *Reversing the lens: How can followers influence their leader's behavior*. Working Paper WP.10.14. Telfer School of Management.

LePine, J. A., Erez, A., & Johnson, D. E. (2002). The nature and dimensionality of organizational citizenship behavior: A critical review and meta-analysis. *Journal of Applied Psychology, 87*(1), 52.

Li, W., Arvey, R. D., & Song, Z. (2011). The influence of general mental ability, self-esteem and family socioeconomic status on leadership role occupancy and leader advancement: The moderating role of gender. *The Leadership Quarterly, 22*(3), 520–534.

Lievens, F. (1998). Factors which improve the construct validity of assessment centers: A review. *International Journal of Selection and Assessment, 6,* 141–152.

Liu, Z., Riggio, R. E., Day, D. V., Zheng, C., Dai, S., & Bian, Y. (2019). Leader development begins at home: Over-parenting harms adolescent leader emergence. *Journal of Applied Psychology, 104*(10), 1226–1242.

Lord, R. G., & Maher, K. J. (1991). Cognitive theory in industrial and organizational psychology. In M. D. Dunnette & L. M. Hough (Eds.), *Handbook of industrial and organizational psychology* (Vol. 2, 2nd ed.). (pp. 1–62). Consulting Psychologist Press.

Meindl, J. R. (1995). The romance of leadership as a follower-centric theory: A social constructionist approach. *The Leadership Quarterly, 6,* 329–341.

Meindl, J. R., Ehrlich, S. B., & Dukerich, J. M. (1985). Romance of leadership. *Administrative Science Quarterly, 30*(1), 78–102.

Morrison, E. W., & Phelps, C. C. (1999). Taking charge at work: Extrarole efforts to initiate workplace change. *Academy of Management Journal, 42*, 403–419.

Organ, D. W. (1988). *Organizational citizenship behavior: The good soldier syndrome.* Lexington Books.

Parker, S. K., & Collins, C. G. (2010). Taking stock: Integrating and differentiating multiple proactive behaviors. *Journal of Management, 36*, 633–662.

Pearce, C. L., & Conger, J. A. (Eds.). (2002). *Shared leadership: Reframing the hows and whys of leadership*. SAGE.

Podsakoff, P. M., MacKenzie, S. B., Moorman, R. H., & Fetter, R. (1990). Transformational leader behaviors and their effects on followers' trust in leader, satisfaction, and organizational citizenship behaviors. *The Leadership Quarterly, 1*(2), 107–142.

Reichard, R. J., Riggio, R. E., Guerin, D. W., Oliver, P. H., Gottfried, A. W., & Gottfried, A. E. (2011). A prospective, longitudinal study of the relationship between adolescent personality and intelligence and adult leader emergence and transformational leadership. *The Leadership Quarterly, 22(3),* 471–481.

Reitan, T., & Stenberg, S. (2019). From classroom to conscription. Leadership emergence in childhood and early adulthood. *The Leadership Quarterly, 30*(3), 298–319.

Richards, S. A., & Jaffee, C. L. (1972). Blacks supervising Whites: A study of interracial difficulties in working together in a simulated organization. *Journal of Applied Psychology, 56,* 234–240.

Riggio, R. E. (Ed.). (2019). Introduction: What's wrong with leadership? Improving leadership theory, research, and practice. In *What's wrong with leadership* (pp. 1–6). Taylor & Francis/Routledge.

Schmitz, P. (2011). *Everyone leads: Building leadership from the community up*. Wile.

Scott, C. P. R., Jiang, H., Wildman, J. L., & Griffith, R. (2018). The impact of implicit collective leadership theories on the emergence and effectiveness of leadership networks in team. *Human Resource Management Review, 28*(4), 464–481.

Scott, S. G., & Bruce, R. A. (1994). Determinants of innovative behavior: A path model of individual innovation in the workplace. *Academy of Management Journal, 37*, 580–607.

Sherrod, L. R., & Lauckhardt, J. (2009). The development of citizenship. In R. M. Lerner & L. Steinberg (Eds.), *Handbook of adolescent psychology: Contextual influences on adolescent development* (Vol. 2, 3rd ed., pp. 372–407). Wiley.

Shondrick, S.J. & Lord, R.L. (2010). Implicit leadership and followership theories: Dynamic structure for leadership perceptions, memory, and leader-follower processes. In G.P. Hodgkinson, & K.J. Ford (Eds.), *International review of industrial and organizational psychology*. (pp. 1–33). Wiley-Blackwell.

Spychalski, A. C., Quiñones, M. A., Gaugler, B. B., & Pohley, K. (1997). A survey of assessment center practices in organizations in the United States. *Personnel Psychology, 50*, 71–90.

Streufert, S., Pogash, R., & Piasecki, M. (1988). Simulation-based assessment of managerial competence: Reliability and validity. *Personnel Psychology, 41*, 537–557.

Taysum, A. (2003). In search of the holistic leader. *Management in Education, 17*(5), 9–12.

Uhl-Bien, M., & Carsten, M. (2018). Reversing the lens in leadership: Positioning followership in the leadership construct. In I. Katz, G. Eilam-Shamir, R. Kark, & Y. Berson (Eds.) *Monographs in leadership and management, Vol. 9: Leadership now: Reflections on the legacy of Boas Shamir* (pp. 195–222) Emerald.

Uhl-Bien, M., Riggio, R. E., Lowe, K. B., & Carsten, M. K. (2014). Followership theory: A review and research agenda. *Leadership Quarterly, 25*, 83–104.

van Dierendonck, D. (2011). Servant leadership: A review and synthesis. *Journal of Management, 37*(4), 1228–1261.

Van Dyne, L., & LePine, J. A. (1998). Helping and voice extra-role behaviors: Evidence of construct and predictive validity. *Academy of Management Journal, 41*, 108–119.

Wollowick, H. B., & McNamara, W. J. (1969). Relationship of the components of an assessment center to management success. *Journal of Applied Psychology*, 53, 348–352.

Yukl, G. (2012). Effective leadership behavior: What we know and what questions need more attention. *The Academy of Management Perspectives, 26*(4), 66–85.

Zaff, J., Boyd, M., Li, Y., Lerner, J. V., & Lerner, R. M. (2010). Active and engaged citizenship: Multi-group and longitudinal factor analysis of an integrated construct of civic engagement. *Journal of Youth and Adolescence, 39*(7), 736–750.

APPENDIX APPEARS ON NEXT PAGE

APPENDIX A: EXAMPLE BEHAVIORALLY ANCHORED RATING SCALES FOR ROLE PLAY SIMULATION

Relational Transparency

Shares information with others in an open and honest manner.

Key behaviors:

- Is truthful with the resident and encourages the same from the resident.
- Does not hesitate to accept responsibility for mistakes.
- Maintains consistency in what he/she says.

Consistency

<table>
<tr><td colspan="5">Flip flops back and forth between what his/her statements refer to; argues against what he/she already stated previously as fact.</td><td colspan="5">Is somewhat consistent in saying what he/she means, but may have to clarify later.</td><td colspan="5">Says exactly what he/she means and does not later argue against what he/she already stated as fact.</td></tr>
<tr><td colspan="3">1</td><td colspan="3">2</td><td colspan="3">3</td><td colspan="3">4</td><td colspan="3">5</td></tr>
</table>

Mistakes

<table>
<tr><td colspan="5">Adamantly denies any mistakes or wrong-doing on the part of oneself or the HOA.</td><td colspan="5">Somewhat acknowledges mistakes after being prompted, but does not offer to correct the problem.</td><td colspan="5">Readily and openly admits any mistakes when they are made by himself/herself or the HOA, apologizes, and takes responsibility for correcting the problem.</td></tr>
<tr><td colspan="3">1</td><td colspan="3">2</td><td colspan="3">3</td><td colspan="3">4</td><td colspan="3">5</td></tr>
</table>

Candid

<table>
<tr><td colspan="5">Misleads or deceives the resident.</td><td colspan="5">Skirts some issues, but generally seems honest with the resident.</td><td colspan="5">Speaks honestly and candidly with the resident.</td></tr>
<tr><td colspan="3">1</td><td colspan="3">2</td><td colspan="3">3</td><td colspan="3">4</td><td colspan="3">5</td></tr>
</table>

Honesty

<table>
<tr><td colspan="5">Does not encourage the resident to speak their mind.</td><td colspan="5">Generally encourages the resident to speak their mind.</td><td colspan="5">Consistently encourages the resident to speak their mind.</td></tr>
<tr><td colspan="3">1</td><td colspan="3">2</td><td colspan="3">3</td><td colspan="3">4</td><td colspan="3">5</td></tr>
</table>

Truth

Avoids telling the resident hard truths about the situation, to the point that little progress is made in fixing the situation.		Occasionally tells the resident the hard truth.		Does not hesitate to tell the resident the hard truth, so that everyone can fully understand the situation and determine how to work past it.
1	2	3	4	5

Comments:

Printed and bound by CPI Group (UK) Ltd, Croydon, CR0 4YY

15/09/2026

14962340-0002